IMPACT EVALUATION OF DEVELOPMENT INTERVENTIONS

A Practical Guide

Howard White
David A. Raitzer

ASIAN DEVELOPMENT BANK

© 2017 Asian Development Bank
6 ADB Avenue, Mandaluyong City, 1550 Metro Manila, Philippines
Tel +63 2 632 4444; Fax +63 2 636 2444
www.adb.org

Some rights reserved. Published in 2017.
Printed in the Philippines.

ISBN 978-92-9261-058-6 (print), 978-92-9261-059-3 (electronic)
Publication Stock No. TCS179188-2
DOI: http://dx.doi.org/10.22617/TCS179188-2

The views expressed in this publication are those of the authors and do not necessarily reflect the views and policies of the Asian Development Bank (ADB) or its Board of Governors or the governments they represent.

ADB does not guarantee the accuracy of the data included in this publication and accepts no responsibility for any consequence of their use. The mention of specific companies or products of manufacturers does not imply that they are endorsed or recommended by ADB in preference to others of a similar nature that are not mentioned.

By making any designation of or reference to a particular territory or geographic area, or by using the term "country" in this document, ADB does not intend to make any judgments as to the legal or other status of any territory or area.

Please contact pubsmarketing@adb.org if you have questions or comments with respect to content, or if you wish to obtain copyright permission for your intended use that does not fall within these terms, or for permission to use the ADB logo.

Photos in this publication are the property of ADB.

Notes:
In this publication, "$" refers to US dollars.
Corrigenda to ADB publications may be found at http://www.adb.org/publications/corrigenda.

Contents

Tables, Figures, and Boxes

Tables

Figures

Figures, continued

Boxes

Foreword

Two important trends are shaping the future of development assistance, particularly in Asia. First, developing countries are ever more able to access finance from a wider variety of sources including private ones. Second, policy makers are increasingly attuned to evidence that can make programs more effective. This means that the value proposition of development agencies, such as the Asian Development Bank (ADB), increasingly depends on the ability to offer knowledge, rather than finance alone. A critical element of this knowledge is derived from evidence on the intended and unintended effects of interventions. Impact evaluation is the main means for empirically testing what actually happens when interventions are implemented.

In parallel to these trends, behavioral economics has increasingly attracted interest within the field of development economics. Prior to the past 2 decades in the field, human behavior was often largely assumed to mechanistically follow neoclassical assumptions. In the period since, economists have increasingly recognized the need to go back and test whether those assumptions hold, by using experimental and quasi-experimental impact evaluation techniques that have been largely pioneered in medicine and other science fields.

This convergence of rising need for impact evaluation evidence among development practitioners and increased interest among academics presents a unique opportunity for intersecting research and practice. Impact evaluation can attract some of the world's leading economic talent to engage with specific development projects. Such engagement not only leads to rigorous new evidence on "what works" in development, but also directly enhances project implementation. Leading researchers who have worked across many countries and programs often have insights that can contribute to better intervention design during impact evaluation conceptualization. Impact evaluation also necessitates that project results logics and underpinning assumptions are clarified before they are tested, making projects better designed.

Impact evaluation can help bring the types of positive feedback that have been routinely used in product development in the private sector. Evidence can offer a rationale for continuing or expanding effective projects and programs, regardless of political environment. Impact evaluation can test different ways of tackling a problem, identify what factors condition intended effects, and provide insights on how interventions should be rolled out and combined. Impact evaluation also offers a platform for generating proof of concept for innovations. Ultimately, it can also help build fundamental theories about human behavior and development, shift conventional wisdom, and reorient development toward more effective approaches.

For this to happen, impact evaluation needs to be mainstreamed, so that development practitioners regularly consider what prior impact evidence implies for their activities, as well as how impact evaluation of their interventions can help contribute to that evidence. This book is intended to help in this mainstreaming by serving as an accessible reference for a range of audiences, backed by years of experience in implementing impact evaluation studies. For non-economist audiences, it offers lay descriptions of core concepts, introductions to key methods, and "rules of thumb" for understanding technical topics, such as power calculation. For more academic audiences, it offers more detailed descriptions of techniques and introductions to STATA commands in technical appendixes. Compared with previous texts, this book introduces a greater range of methodologies, as well as more description of practical considerations.

ADB is currently expanding its impact evaluation coverage, and is devoting increased attention and resources to new impact evaluation studies. To backstop this process, this book is a valuable resource that can help to increase awareness of what impact evaluation offers and how it can be applied. I recommend it as a practical resource for those who have interest in generating or using rigorous evidence on "what works" in development.

Yasuyuki Sawada
Chief Economist and Director General
Economic Research and Regional Cooperation Department

Acknowledgments

This book reflects the contributions of many individuals within and outside of the Asian Development Bank (ADB). It has been produced under the overall guidance of Edimon Ginting, Director of the Economic Analysis and Operations Support Division and Rana Hasan, Director of the Development Economics and Indicators Division. The volume has also benefited from overall orientation by ADB's interdepartmental Impact Evaluation Committee. Howard White, independent consultant, and David Raitzer, Economist, Economic Analysis and Operations Support Division, have authored the contents.

Sakiko Tanaka provided valuable insights and contributions to early versions of this book. Background materials were also provided by Scott Rozelle of Stanford University, and some sections drew on materials prepared by independent consultant Nina Blöndal. Additional inputs and contributions were provided by Jasmin Sibal and Marie Anne Cagas. Administrative support has been provided by Lilibeth Poot, Amanda Mamon, Gee Ann Burac, Ricasol Calaluan, Roslyn Perez, and Glennie Castillo. Valuable peer reviews have been provided by Impact Evaluation Committee Members Ari Perdana, Artur Andrysiak, Arturo Martinez, Bernard Woods, Christopher Edmonds, Elisabetta Gentile, Joao Fahrina, K. E. Seetharam, Kiyoshi Taniguchi, Lakshman Nagraj Rao, Lars Johannes, and Maya Vijayaraghavan. Initial conceptualization was under the overall guidance of Cyn-Young Park, former Director of the Economic Analysis and Operations Support Division.

Tuesday Soriano copyedited the manuscript, and Joe Mark Ganaban prepared the layout. This book is produced under Technical Assistance 0012-REG: Developing Impact Evaluation Methodologies, Approaches, and Capacities in Selected Developing Member Countries.

Abbreviations

3ie	–	International Initiative for Impact Evaluation
ADB	–	Asian Development Bank
ATE	–	average treatment effect
ATT	–	average treatment effect on the treated
ATU	–	average treatment effect on the untreated
CCT	–	conditional cash transfer
DiD	–	difference-in-differences
DMF	–	design and monitoring framework
ICC	–	intracluster correlation coefficient
IE	–	impact evaluation
IPW	–	inverse probability weighting
ITS	–	interrupted time series
ITT	–	intention to treat
IV	–	instrumental variable
LATE	–	local average treatment effect
MDE	–	minimum detectable effect
MES	–	minimum effect size
OLS	–	ordinary least squares
PMT	–	proxy means test
PSM	–	propensity score matching
RCT	–	randomized controlled trial
RDD	–	regression discontinuity design
ToC	–	theory of change

Chapter 1
Introduction: Impact Evaluation for Evidence-Based Development

Key Messages

- Impact evaluation empirically estimates the effects attributable to a specific intervention and the statistical significance of those effects.

- Deriving reliable knowledge and evidence from development operations depends on impact evaluation.

- Impact evaluation can serve a number of roles. It can determine not only whether an intervention is effective, but it can also compare options for making interventions more effective.

- Evidence from impact evaluation can inform assumptions underpinning economic analysis of specific investments, as well as broader strategies for sectors, regions, and countries.

1.1   Why Does Impact Evaluation Matter?

Development organizations have an ultimate mandate to contribute to development goals. For example, Strategy 2020 of the Asian Development Bank (ADB) reaffirms ADB's vision of an Asia and Pacific region free of poverty. ADB's mission is to help developing member countries improve living conditions and the quality of life of their citizens. To this end, billions of dollars of funding are mobilized each year. What have been the impacts of the funded programs?

The answer to this question requires evidence that is produced by "counterfactual" impact evaluations (IEs). Without IE, it is not possible to ascertain the causal effects of development interventions. In the absence of understanding what effects have occurred as a result of development efforts, it is neither possible to keep accountability about development expenditures, nor to derive meaningful knowledge from development operations to improve development policies.

Impact evaluations are empirical studies that quantify the causal effects of interventions on outcomes of interest. This is far different from traditional process evaluations that are concerned with characterizing how projects were implemented. IEs are based on analysis of what happened with an intervention, compared with an empirically estimated counterfactual scenario of what would have happened in the absence of the intervention. This difference between the observed outcomes and the counterfactual outcomes is the measure of impact, i.e., the difference that can be attributed to the intervention. Effects can be quantified at any level and, contrary to popular perception, do not need to concern only long-term goals or "impacts" in the jargon of logical frameworks. At the same time, IE is the only method that can provide evidence as to those long-term effects.

IE is unique in that it is data driven and attempts to minimize unverifiable assumptions when attributing effects. A core concept is that identified impacts are assessed not only in magnitude, but also in terms of statistical significance. This approach is not to be confused with "impact assessment," which often includes modeling rooted in taking structural and often neoclassical assumptions about behavior as given, and which cannot ascertain statistically significant effects.

Development assistance's drive toward evidence-based policy and project design and results-based management depends on mainstreaming IE. IE allows for assumptions underpinning the results logic of interventions to be tested and for previously unknown consequences to be revealed.

At the heart of evidence-based policy is the use of research results to inform and supplant assumptions as programs and policies are designed (Sanderson 2002). In turn, this depends on the generation of new evidence on effectiveness, and the incorporation of evidence into program conceptualization. One linkage by which this can be achieved is by informing economic analysis of investments. IE validates and quantifies the magnitude of the effects of an intervention, and these effect magnitudes are critical to understanding project benefits. The impact findings for one intervention can inform the economic analysis for a follow-on project to scale up the investment, or for similar investments elsewhere.

One of the best known examples of evidence-based policy in international development has been the growth of conditional cash transfers (CCTs) in Latin America (Box 1.1). Similarly, an ADB-supported IE of the Food Stamps Program in Mongolia played a part in persuading the government to scale up the program (ADB 2014).

> **Box 1.1: The Use of Evidence from Impact Evaluations to Inform the Spread of Conditional Cash Transfers in Latin America**
>
> The conditional cash transfer (CCT) program, PROGRESSA, was started by the Mexican government in the mid-1990s. The government decided to build a rigorous, randomized evaluation into the program design. The study showed the positive impact of CCT on poverty and access to health and education. These findings meant that the program survived a change in government with just a change in name. A similar story can be told about Colombia's CCT, Familias en Acion. In Brazil, the President commissioned an impact evaluation of the Bolsa Familia program to be able to address critics of the program, especially those who argued that it discouraged the poor from entering the labor market. The study showed it did not, and Bolsa Familia continued to expand, reaching over 12 million families by 2012.
>
> Source: Behrman (2010).

The IE movement has spread across the world and across sectors (Figure 1.1). A database of over 4,000 development IEs shows this rapid growth, with 500 new studies a year by 2015. Most of these studies are in the social sectors, but there are growing numbers for many other topics, such as rural electrification, water supply, and transportation.

Figure 1.1: Annual Publication of Impact Evaluations

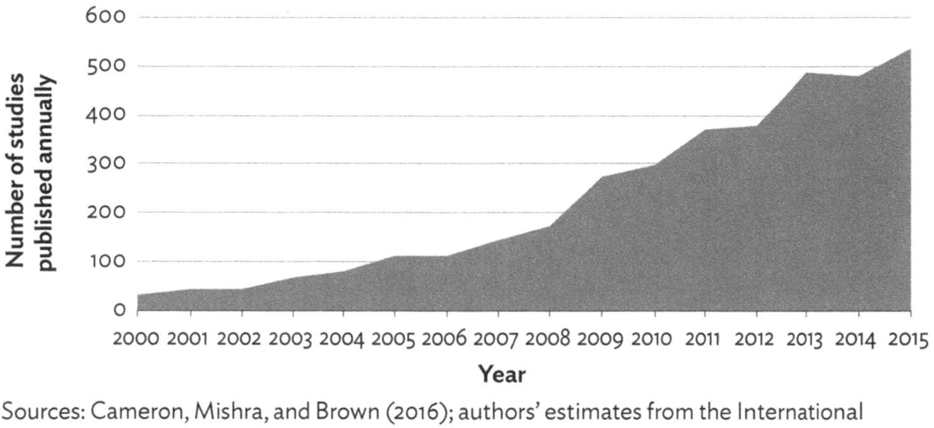

Sources: Cameron, Mishra, and Brown (2016); authors' estimates from the International Initiative for Impact Evaluation (3ie) impact evaluation repository.

1.2 The Purposes of Impact Evaluation

IE, like other forms of evaluation, has two principal purposes. The first is *accountability*, so as to ensure that development actions actually lead to development outcomes. The second is *learning*, so as to offer an evidence base for selecting and designing development interventions that are likely to be effective in fostering outcomes of interest.

Both purposes are manifest in important trends, to which development agencies must respond. A range of policy makers and stakeholders have been stepping up requirements for rigorous demonstration of results from development finance (OECD 2011). This is starting to drive resource allocation toward agencies and programs that make an effort to credibly estimate whether expected outcomes and effects actually occur as a result of their interventions.

There is also increasing demand from a range of stakeholders that policy and investment proposals reflect insights based on systematic use of evidence (Parkhurst 2017). Development agencies can be responsive to these requirements, by both (i) presenting earlier IE results in their project/sector experience, and (ii) promoting new pilot initiatives that include IE as a systematic means of testing innovations. By doing so, agencies position themselves as "knowledge" institutions of reference in their respective sectors.

Multilateral development banks, notably the World Bank and the Inter-American Development Bank, have been important players in the rise of IE. The World Bank has various programs to provide technical and financial support to IE, including a Strategic Impact Evaluation Fund. By 2013, all new loan approvals at the Inter-American Development Bank included an IE in their design. In 2014, the African Development Bank has developed a new policy that requires more IEs.

ADB has joined this movement through various activities. Recently, ADB established substantial technical assistance funds to resource additional IEs. This book is to serve as a tool for project staff, government partners, and other development practitioners who may be interested to include IEs in their projects, generate evidence from other related interventions, or understand how to use IE findings.

1.3   What Questions Can Impact Evaluation Answer?

IE answers questions, such as (i) what difference does a policy or program make?, or (ii) which program designs are more effective for one or more specific quantifiable outcomes? It can also offer understanding of how those outcomes differ among different populations and what factors condition those outcomes.

The central role of counterfactual analysis

IEs are designed to address the causal or attribution question of effectiveness: did the intervention make a statistically significant difference to specific outcomes? Answering this question requires a counterfactual analysis of an alternative scenario in which the intervention did not occur, where that alternative may be no intervention, or an alternative intervention (a so-called A/B design as it compares intervention A with intervention B). Establishing the counterfactual is the core challenge of IE. This is because, while the actual scenario is directly observed, the counterfactual is usually not. Despite this challenge, counterfactual analysis is necessary to establish which programs are most effective, or indeed whether a program makes any difference at all.

Impact evaluation questions

IE is the only way to test, empirically, the extent to which project and policy initiatives produced measurable differences in outcomes compared with counterfactual estimates (i.e., in the no intervention scenario). Rigorous IE usually requires the implementation of baseline and endline surveys that are carefully designed to enable the most credible estimation of a counterfactual. Monitoring systems or process data can track welfare outcomes that indicate what happened in project areas. These are factual data. These do not answer the causal questions: "what difference did the project make?" and "to what extent are observed changes attributable to the intervention?." Only IE can answer these questions.

The central "what works" question of whether intended development outcomes are attributable to a project has been the focus of most IEs, and can be termed a "first generation question." Box 1.2 gives examples of first generation questions from an ADB-supported IE.

Box 1.2: Example of First Generation Questions: The Tbilisi Metro Extension Project

The evaluation will address questions on the welfare impact of the project:

1.   To what extent will the metro extension lead to local economic development, including increased business activity, revenue, and employment generation?

2.   To what extent will the metro station affect university students commuting to and from Tbilisi State University? In particular, how will it affect their time use, expenditure patterns, attendance rates, and test scores?

3.   To what extent will the metro extension contribute to improved air quality/ reduction in pollution?

Source: ADB (2012).

IEs can reveal a great deal of evidence about a wide range of effects, some of which may not have been considered by project implementers. Evidence from IE about how a particular intervention fits into a broader process of development, the role of complementary interventions, and the contexts under which development effectiveness is greatest can help to improve how projects are designed and implemented (Boxes 1.3 and 1.4 offer sample insights for energy and transport).

Box 1.3: Impact Evaluation Findings on Electricity Infrastructure

Although the number of impact evaluations on energy interventions has grown more slowly than in other sectors, studies conducted to date offer exciting evidence as to the effects of electricity access. The findings from these studies show effects on a range of outcomes from education, to health, income, and gender equality. At the same time, most of these results are from specific situations and interventions, so that additional studies are needed to verify the generalizability of findings.

1. Electricity connection can lead to *changes in time use*, particularly to increased study time for children, longer working hours, and increased time spent on nonagricultural income-generating activities for adults (Barron and Torero 2015, Grimm et al. 2013, Dasso and Fernandez 2015, Arraiz and Calero 2015).

2. Increased study time due to electricity access can lead to *improved educational outcomes* for children (Arraiz and Calero 2015, Khandker et al. 2013). However, it may also lead to increased childhood employment at the expense of education (Squires 2015).

3. Time use changes from electrification can lead to *microbusiness generation* (Dinkelman 2011, Khandker et al. 2013, Rao 2013, Dasso and Fernandez 2015).

4. Increased employment due to electricity can lead to *increased income, consumption, and expenditure* (Dinkelman 2011, Khandker et al. 2013, Rao 2013, Dasso and Fernandez 2015).

5. Electricity access may lead to *improved health* measured as a decline in reported respiratory infections and other smoke-related illnesses. This appears to follow improvement in indoor air quality as households substitute kerosene for electricity (ADB 2010, Barron and Torero 2015).

6. Some results have suggested that electricity access can *enhance family planning*. Increased TV viewing due to electrification has been observed to reduce fertility rates, partly as a result of higher exposure to family planning information that helps increase utilization of contraception (Grimm et al. 2015).

7. Other findings suggest that electrification can lead to *improved gender equality*. Effects on education have been found to be more positive for girls than for boys (van de Walle et al. 2013), as have effects on employment (Barron and Torero 2015, Grogan and Sadanand 2012).

Source: Authors.

Box 1.4: Impact Evaluation Findings on Transport Infrastructure

There is a small but rapidly growing body of rigorous evidence on the impacts of transportation investments. These studies show a range of effects on a wide range of development outcomes, although more studies are needed to explore how and whether these effects occur beyond specific studied contexts.

1. Transport interventions can affect *property markets*. A randomized controlled trial of urban street paving found substantial effects on property and land values (Gonzalez-Navarro and Quintana-Domeque 2016).

2. Transport infrastructure can *reduce migration*. Improvement of rural roads has been found to reduce outmigration from less favored rural areas, due to better economic development (Akee 2006, Gachassin 2013).

3. Improved road infrastructure may lead to *better school attendance*, particularly at the secondary level, as a result of reduced travel cost (Khandker et al. 2009, Sengupta et al. 2007). In some cases, this effect is more pronounced for girls than for boys (Iimi et al. 2015).

4. Transport interventions have important *effects on health*. Better roads were found to facilitate improved access to and use of health facilities (Lokshin and Yemtsov 2003). Simple road safety interventions were also found to significantly reduce accidents and injuries (Habyarimana and Jack 2009, Habyarimana and Jack 2012, Banerjee et al. 2014).

5. Better transport can *spur market development*. Improved road networks were found to lower input costs, allow more flexibility in firm input supplies, increase local trade, and allow new output markets to be pursued (Mu and van de Walle 2011, Lokshin and Yemtsov 2003). Corollary effects were found on enterprise development, as well as improved firm productivity (Datta 2011, Ghani et al. 2016).

6. *Economic activity increases* due to transportation improvements. Increases in gross domestic product in areas with transport interventions can be significant (Banerjee et al. 2012, Faber 2014, Wang and Wu 2015, Yoshino and Abidhadjaev 2015).

7. Improved transport can lead to greater *demand for labor and increased wages*. This, along with improved mobility to access labor market opportunities, can drive substantial effects on employment and incomes (Akee 2006, Gertler et al. 2015, Rand 2011).

8. The *poverty reduction effects* of transport interventions can be significant (Dercon et al. 2009, Sengupta et al. 2007). Moreover, road development has been found to have the greatest effects on firm performance and employment in areas that are poorest (Gibson and Rozelle 2002, Mu and van de Walle 2011).

Source: Authors.

IEs can also answer questions that are more directly about project implementation. Often, those preparing projects are not sure of the best program design. If a program can be delivered with two or more competing designs in different areas, then IE methods can be used to test which program design is most effective in delivering a desired change in outcomes.

These design questions can be called "second generation" questions. Both first and second generation questions are important. Evidence of effectiveness is especially important for accountability and for higher level policy makers who make resource allocation decisions. Project managers are often more interested in the "how to" questions answered by second generation studies. There is a natural progression in IEs on a given topic from first ascertaining that the type of intervention can be effective (first generation question), and once this is established, subsequently refining understanding on how effectiveness can be further advanced (second generation question).

An example of evidence on program design comes from the many IEs of the impact of conditional cash transfers on educational outcomes. By synthesizing the evidence from these studies, several important lessons for effective design of conditional cash transfers (CCTs) to incentivize school attendance have been identified (Baird et al. 2014):

- CCTs are more effective at secondary school level than primary school level.

- CCTs are more effective with fewer, larger payments, than more frequent smaller ones.

- Money matters: the larger the payment, the larger the effect.

- Programs with more monitoring and enforcement of conditions have a larger impact than those with weak monitoring and enforcement. Children living in communities with a CCT with strong monitoring and enforcement are 60% more likely to attend school than children living in areas with a transfer program with no monitoring or enforcement mechanism.

Combining contextual and counterfactual analysis

Although the counterfactual is at the heart of IE, there is an important role for contextual analysis in IE to help understand why an intervention works or does not in different contexts and for different groups. IE and process evaluation are complementary approaches, not alternatives.

An important area of contextual analysis is targeting. Quantitative data can be used to assess targeting errors, such as when members of the target group are missed, or when there are beneficiaries who are not in the target group. Qualitative data can generally be useful in identifying barriers to adoption.

If contextual analysis suggests possible reasons for nonparticipation, then quantitative analysis may be used to test these. For example, the ADB-supported study of the use of compact fluorescent light bulbs in Pakistan found that the vast majority of those targeted underestimated the energy savings of these bulbs compared with traditional incandescent bulbs (Box 1.5).

> ### Box 1.5: Learning about Project Design from Impact Evaluation: Energy-Efficient Light Bulbs in Pakistan
>
> The Government of Pakistan launched a national program costing $60 million to replace 30 million incandescent light bulbs with compact fluorescent light bulbs (CFLs) in the residential sector. ADB supported this program with a $40 million loan. An impact evaluation undertaken during the preparation of the loan found the following results:
>
> - A significant minority (11%) of households are unaware of CFLs.
> - The substantial majority of households have incorrect knowledge of CFLs' greater efficiency. CFLs last at least 10 times as long as incandescent bulbs. However, one-third of respondents replied they did not know the difference, and a quarter said that CFLs last just twice as long. Fewer than 10% replied that CFLs last 10 times as long.
> - Benefits are overestimated if based on adoption alone since there is a "rebound effect" as households consume more light when using CFLs rather than incandescent bulbs.
>
> The first two findings show the importance of including a demand (consumer education) component in the program, and the third informs the economic analysis.
>
> Source: Chun and Jiang (2013).

Impact evaluations for pilot testing of innovative interventions

IEs can be built into innovative projects to inform other project designs through IE for pilot testing. For example, different methods of promoting adoption of a technology or service, or encouraging efficient use of water or energy, may be assessed against each other in an A/B design, i.e., a study with two treatment arms. Incorporating these approaches into interventions that can be piloted replicates, in the public sector, the sort of "learning" processes that are "second nature" to many private sector activities (Box 1.6). These pilot studies will be rapid IEs (Box 1.7), with explicit feedback loops to inform project design and rollout.

Box 1.6: Pilot Testing in the Private Sector

Randomized controlled trials (RCTs) have been widely adopted in the private sector to inform management approach and product design. Leading tech firms, such as Microsoft, Google, Amazon and retail sites, such as Booking.com routinely undertake over 10,000 RCTs annually. These studies are usually rapid impact evaluations with A/B designs to compare, for example, different product presentation or marketing.

More specifically, the search engine company, Yahoo, trials redesigns of its home page to increase clicks to other sites (from which it earns money) by randomly assigning 100,000 of its visitors in 1 hour to the redesigned site (treatment arm A). The other millions of visitors are directed to the existing site (treatment arm B, the existing treatment). After as little as 1 hour the study is completed by comparing click-through rates from A and B.

Source: Kohavi and Thomke (2017).

Box 1.7: Rapid Impact Evaluations

Rapid impact evaluation (IE) refers to randomized controlled trials (RCTs) with shorter time frames and lower budgets than traditional IEs.

An RCT can be rapid (meaning 12–18 months) under the following conditions:

- It is a simple RCT, meaning that random assignment is at the level of the individual, firm, or household.
- The outcomes being measured are ones on which a sufficiently large impact can reasonably be expected within a sufficiently large group during the time of the evaluation. Rapid IEs often focus on adoption rather than final welfare outcomes, which take longer to be realized and require a larger sample to be measured.

Pilot testing IEs can be well suited to the rapid impact evaluation approach.

Source: Cody and Ascher (2014).

Pilot testing can often be part of formative evaluation (or evaluation to inform program formation), in which the program is evaluated on a small scale prior to more widespread application. Formative evaluations usually focus on proximate effects, such as adoption rates.

There remain many important contextual issues that are not addressed by IE, such as the fidelity of implementation. Thus, it can be useful to embed the causal analysis of the IE in a broader evaluation framework, so the analysis can better address "what works and why?" (discussed in Chapter 2).

1.4 Impact Evaluation in the Project Cycle

Figure 1.2 shows where IE fits in the project cycle of development organizations, such as ADB. From this overlay, some of the (political economy) challenges that need to be overcome in many IE efforts become apparent. In addition to efforts to promote awareness of IE methodologies, issues of timing and stakeholder motivation need attention.

Figure 1.2: Impact Evaluation and the Project Cycle

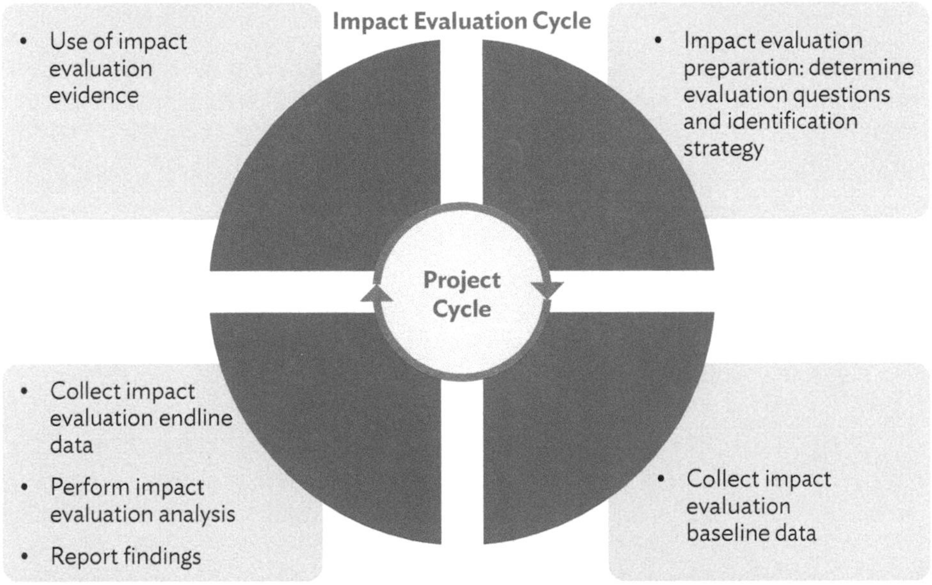

Impact Evaluation Cycle

- Use of impact evaluation evidence

- Impact evaluation preparation: determine evaluation questions and identification strategy

Project Cycle

- Collect impact evaluation endline data
- Perform impact evaluation analysis
- Report findings

- Collect impact evaluation baseline data

Source: Authors.

Motivation and timing

IE considerations can be complex and are best initially considered early on in the project cycle, preferably during project design and processing (so that IE implementation activities, such as baseline surveys, are inserted in the project's scope). Many project staff can be unfamiliar with IE methodologies, and may for that reason prefer to avoid additional activity during project preparation, in particular if the IE design requires efforts that are not perceived to meet immediate requirements. Moreover, if operational staff frequently change, they may not still be in the same role to either benefit from IE findings or receive any possible recognition for IE conduct.

What may not be appreciated in the context of project preparation deadlines is that IE efforts directly lead to better projects that have smoother implementation, and more timely disbursement, as critical assumptions become better considered (Legovini et al. 2015). In addition, data from the baseline can offer valuable inputs for project implementation, if project staff are engaged to ensure that their information demands are satisfied. Operational staff may need to be made aware of these benefits.

Initiation

IE initiation usually occurs in the early stages of project implementation. After project approval, there is often a substantial lag period as project agreements are signed, procurement contracts are awarded, and the groundwork is laid for making project outputs a reality. During this period, how rollout will occur often becomes more predictable, but outputs are not yet effective or available, so that baseline surveys can still be conducted.

- If the IE includes random assignment, there are implications for project design, and the random assignment mechanism needs to be built into the project design.

- IE estimates are always strengthened by the availability of baseline data, which can be better assured through early planning.

- At project preparation, it may be possible to integrate IE with the collection of project monitoring and evaluation data to avoid duplicative surveys, improve project monitoring and evaluation, and leverage scant survey resources more effectively.

Implementation

Pilot testing IEs will take place in the initial years of project implementation. A midterm survey may be included in an IE, which may be more oriented toward process issues to inform midterm corrections. However, depending on the timing of the endline, it may also be necessary to orient the midterm to decisions regarding any follow-on project.

Completion

At or near completion, the endline survey is conducted to allow the impact to be evaluated. Two key considerations may affect timing:

- Project funds may be used to finance data collection and possibly analysis, so that the study has to be completed while the project is still open. In this setting, care may need to be taken to share costs with the government or other funding sources, so that analysis can be conducted after financial closing.

- IE findings can help to inform decisions regarding the funding and design of follow-on interventions. Yet, the design of individual follow-on projects may happen before the timing of an IE based on a survey at project completion. For this reason, IEs may create influence indirectly by providing evidence to inform larger country or sector strategies.

1.5 Impact Evaluation, Evaluation, and Economic Analysis

Non-economists and non-evaluators, at times, may be confused by the differences between IE, evaluation, and economic analysis. Evaluation at ADB and many other agencies is most frequently *process evaluation* about how projects and programs are implemented. This is mostly concerned with how inputs were used in activities to generate outputs, and the focus of any original data collection is mostly qualitative and descriptive. Often, the objective is to give a normative rating to project/program implementation. This is fundamentally different from IE, which is a positive form of applied research, and focused on the causal effects of interventions, so as to draw broader policy-relevant conclusions.

Organizational units tasked with evaluation at ADB and other international financial institutions are also usually independent of project implementation, and often can only conduct activities *ex post*. However, more rigorous IE methods require close engagement during project implementation, so as to ensure appropriate data collection, and possibly randomized assignment of the intervention prior to widespread implementation. This also places IE often in the domain of research and implementation entities, rather than evaluation departments.

Confusion may also arise because both economic analysis and IE involve economists analyzing effects of development interventions. Yet, economic analysis at ADB and many other agencies is mostly focused on *ex ante* analysis during project preparation, when effects of projects must be forecasted or assumed. IE focuses on providing rigorous evidence-based estimates of those effects (Table 1.1). IE, in a strict sense, is only possible once some degree of intervention implementation has occurred, although this may be at an early stage (Box 1.2). At project preparation, it is possible to draw on evidence from existing IEs of similar projects to help justify the investment and inform project design. Systematic reviews also synthesize all relevant rigorous evidence on a topic and can be key to help inform *ex ante* assessment.

Table 1.1: Impact Evaluation and Economic Analysis of Investments

Areas of Economic Analysis	Specific Analyses	Contribution of Evidence from Impact Evaluation and Systematic Reviews
Validating economic rationale	Macro context and sector analysis	Evidence as to the most important investments for sector outcomes
	Economic rationale	Evidence as to effects of alleviating constraints in previous interventions
	Demand analysis	Revealed willingness to pay from experiments elsewhere
	Design and monitoring framework	Evidence on critical assumptions and steps in the causal chain to be monitored
Conduct of *ex ante* economic analysis	Alternative and least-cost analysis	Evidence as to comparative effectiveness of alternative intervention approaches elsewhere
	Ex ante cost–benefit analysis	Quantification of effect magnitudes from previous interventions
	Sustainability of project investment	Evidence on factors affecting (i) adoption, and (ii) sustainability at scale
	Risk and sensitivity analyses	Evidence on why similar interventions fail to have expected impacts
	Distribution analysis	Evidence on uptake/participation and how behavior conditions distributional impacts in similar interventions
Conduct of *ex post* economic analysis	*Ex post* cost–benefit analysis	Estimates of effects attributable to interventions

Note: Topics and areas from ADB (2013), except *ex post* economic analysis which is not covered in that document.
Source: Authors.

1.6 About This Book

The primary audience for this book consists of evidence-oriented development practitioners and researchers in developing countries and in development agencies, such as ADB. Compared with other guidance books, this volume offers a broader range of practical and methodological options, presented in an accessible, nontechnical manner.

Theories of change can help to inform IE designs and are covered in Chapter 2. The basics of IE are laid out in Chapter 3, with more details on different IE designs in Chapters 4 and 5. Chapters 6 and 7 deal with data collection and sampling issues. Chapter 8 addresses key issues in managing IEs and lists the main research agencies involved in producing IEs.

The book is written at an introductory level with no prior knowledge required, although it also includes content for more advanced audiences. It is written as a *practical guide*. It focuses on lessons from experience and key tips which will be of use to those considering and planning IE studies.

Appendixes 1 and 2 provide more technical presentations of estimation methods and data collection for those who will conduct IEs. Appendix 1 also includes introduction of commands and packages for implementing the methods in STATA, software that is frequently used for econometric analysis.

References*

Asian Development Bank (ADB). 2010. *Impact Evaluation Study: ADB's Assistance for Rural Electrification in Bhutan – Does Electrification Improve Quality of Rural Life?*. Manila.

ADB. 2012. *Impact Evaluation Study: Tbilisi Metro Extension Project in Georgia – Evaluation Design and Baseline Survey Report*. Manila.

ADB. 2013. *Key Areas of Economic Analysis of Investment Projects: An Overview*. Manila.

ADB. 2014. *Food Stamps and Medicard – Impact Evaluation Report: Final Report*. Manila.

Akee, R. 2006. The Babeldaob Road: The Impact of Road Construction on Rural Labor Force Outcomes in the Republic of Palau. *The Institute for the Study of Labor (IZA) Discussion Paper*. No. 2452. Bonn.

Arraiz, I. and C. Calero. 2015. From Candles to Light: The Impact of Rural Electrification. *IDB Working Paper Series*. No. IDB-WP-599.

Baird, S., F. H. G. Ferreira, B. Özler, and M. Woolcock. 2014. Conditional, Unconditional and Everything in Between: A Systematic Review of the Effects of Cash Transfer Programmes on Schooling Outcomes. *Journal of Development Effectiveness*. 6 (1). pp. 1–43.

Banerjee, B., E. Duflo, and N. Qian. 2012. On the Road: Access to Transportation Infrastructure and Economic Growth in China. *NBER Working Paper Series*. No. 17897.

Banerjee, A., E. Duflo, D. Keniston, and N. Singh. 2014. The Efficient Deployment of Police Resources: Theory and New Evidence from a Randomized Drunk Driving Crackdown in India. Massachusetts Institute of Technology Working Paper.

Barron, M. and M. Torero. 2015. Household Electrification and Indoor Air Pollution. *Munich Personal RePEc Archive*. MPRA Paper No. 61424.

Behrman, J. R. 2010. The International Food Policy Research Institute (IFPRI) and the Mexican PROGRESA Anti-Poverty and Human Resource Investment Conditional Cash Transfer Program. *World Development*. 38 (10). pp. 1473–1485.

Cameron, D. B., A. Mishra, and A. N. Brown. 2016. The Growth of Impact Evaluation for International Development: How Much Have We Learned? *Journal of Development Effectiveness*. 8 (1). pp. 1–21.

CAREC Institute Research Program. 2010. Final Report: Retrospective Impact Evaluation of the Korday–Almaty Road Project (Zhambyl Oblast). http://www.carecprogram.org/uploads/docs/Research/Impact-Evaluation/2010/IE-Report-Korday-Almaty-Road-Project-Final.pdf.

---

* ADB recognizes "China" as the People's Republic of China, and "Vietnam" as Viet Nam.

Chun, N. and Y. Jang. 2013. How Households in Pakistan Take on Energy Efficiency Lighting Technology. *Energy Economics*. 40. pp. 277–284.

Cody, S. and A. Asher. 2014. Proposal 14: Smarter, Better, Faster: The Potential for Predictive Analytics and Rapid-Cycle Evaluation to Improve Program Development and Outcomes. In Section 4: Improving Safety Net and Work Support. The Hamilton Project. Washington, DC: The Brookings Institution. https://www.brookings.edu/wp-content/uploads/2016/06/predictive_analytics_rapid_cycle_evaluation_cody_asher.pdf.

Dasso, R. and F. Fernandez. 2015. The Effects of Electrification on Employment in Rural Peru. *IZA Journal of Labor & Development*. 4 (6).

Datta, S. 2011. The Impact of Improved Highways on Indian firms. *Journal of Development Economics*. 99 (1). pp. 46–57.

Dercon, S., D. Gilligan, J. Hoddinott, and T. Woldehanna. 2009. The Impact of Agricultural Extension and Roads on Poverty and Consumption Growth in Fifteen Ethiopian Villages. *American Journal of Agricultural Economics*. 91 (4). pp. 1007–1021.

Dinkelman, T. 2011. The Effects of Rural Electrification on Employment: New Evidence from South Africa. *American Economic Review*. 10. pp. 3078–3108.

Faber, B. 2014. Trade Integration, Market Size and Industrialization: Evidence from China's National Trunk Highway System. *Review of Economic Studies*. 81. pp. 1046–1070.

Gachassin, M. 2013. Should I Stay or Should I Go? The Role of Roads in Migration Decisions. *Journal of African Economies*. 22 (5). pp. 796–826.

Gertler, P., M. Gonzalez-Navarro, T. Gracner, and A. Rothenberg. 2015. Road Quality, Local Economic Activity, and Welfare: Evidence from Indonesia's Highways. Preliminary Draft October 2015.

Ghani, E., A. Goswami, and W. Kerr. 2016. Highway to Success: The Impact of the Golden Quadrilateral Project for the Location and Performance of Indian Manufacturing. *The Economic Journal*. 126 (591). pp. 317–357.

Gibson, J. and S. Rozelle. 2002. Poverty and Access to Infrastructure in Papua New Guinea. Department of Agricultural and Resource Economics, University of California Davis Working Paper No. 02-008.

Gonzalez-Navarro, M. and C. Quintana-Domeque. 2016. Paving Streets for the Poor: Experimental Analysis of Infrastructure Effects. *Review of Economics and Statistics*. 98 (2). pp. 254–267.

Grimm, M., J. Peters, and M. Sievert. 2013. Impacts of Pico-PV Systems Usage using a Randomized Controlled Trial and Qualitative Methods. Evaluation report commissioned by the Operations Evaluation Department (IOB) of The Netherlands Ministry of Foreign Affairs.

Grimm, M., R. Sparrow, and L. Tasciotti. 2015. Does Electrification Spur the Fertility Transition? Evidence from Indonesia. *Demography.* 52 (5). pp. 1773–1796.

Grogan, L. and A. Sadanand. 2012. Rural Electrification and Employment in Poor Countries: Evidence from Nicaragua. *World Development.* 43. pp. 252–265.

Habyarimana, J. and W. Jack. 2009. Heckle and Chide: Results of a Randomized Road Safety Intervention in Kenya. *Center for Global Development.* Working Paper No. 169.

Habyarimana, J. and W. Jack. 2012. State vs. Consumer Regulation: An Evaluation of Two Road Safety Interventions in Kenya. *NBER Working Paper Series.* No. 18378.

Iimi, A., E. Lancelot, I. Manelici, and S. Ogita. 2015. Social and Economic Impacts of Rural Road Improvements in the State of Tocantins, Brazil. *World Bank Policy Research Working Paper.* No. 7249.

Khandker, S., Z. Bakht, and G. Koolwal. 2009. The Poverty Impact of Rural Roads: Evidence from Bangladesh. *Economic Development and Cultural Change.* 57 (4). pp. 685–722.

Khandker, S., D. Barnes, and H. Samad. 2013. Welfare Impacts of Rural Electrification: A Panel Data Analysis from Viet Nam. *Economic Development and Cultural Change.* 61 (3). pp. 659–692.

Kohavi, R. and S. Thomke. 2017. The Surprising Power of Online Experiments. *Harvard Business Review.* September–October 2017 issue. pp. 74–82. https://hbr.org/2017/09/the-surprising-power-of-online-experiments

Legovini, A., V. Di Maro, and C. Piza. 2015. Impact Evaluation Helps Deliver Development Projects. *World Bank Policy Research Working Paper.* No. WPS 7157. http://documents.worldbank.org/curated/en/676351468320935363/Impact-evaluation-helps-deliver-development-projects.

Lokshin, M. and R. Yemtsov. 2003. Evaluating the Impact of Infrastructure Rehabilitation Projects on Household Welfare in Rural Georgia. *World Bank Policy Research Working Paper.* No. 3155.

Mu, R. and D. van de Walle. 2011. Rural Roads and Local Market Development in Vietnam. *The Journal of Development Studies.* 47 (5). pp. 709–734.

Organisation for Economic Co-operation and Development (OECD). 2011. *Aid Effectiveness 2005–10: Progress in Implementing the Paris Declaration.* Paris: OECD Publishing.

Parkhurst, J. 2017. *The Politics of Evidence.* London: Routledge.

Rand, J. 2011. Evaluating the Employment-Generating Impact of Rural Roads in Nicaragua. *Journal of Development Effectiveness.* 3 (1). pp. 28–43.

Rao, N. 2013. Does (Better) Electricity Supply Increase Household Enterprise Income in India?. *Energy Policy.* 57. pp. 532–541.

Sanderson, I. 2002. Evaluation, Policy Learning and Evidence-Based Policy Making. *Public Administration.* 80 (1). pp. 1–22. doi:10.1111/1467-9299.00292.

Sengupta, R., D. Coondoo, and B. Rout. 2007. Impact of a Highway on the Socio-Economic Well-Being of Rural Households Living in Proximity. *Contemporary Issues and Ideas in Social Sciences*. 3 (3).

Squires, T. 2015. The Impact of Access to Electricity on Education: Evidence from Honduras. Job Market Paper.

Van de Walle, D., M. Ravallion, V. Mendiratta, and G. Koolwal. 2013. Long-Term Impacts of Household Electrification in Rural India. *World Bank Policy Research Working Paper*. No. 6257.

Wang, Y. and B. Wu. 2015. Railways and the Local Economy: Evidence from Qingzang Railway. *Economic Development and Cultural Change*. 63 (3). pp. 551–588.

Yoshino, N. and U. Abidhadjaev. 2015. An Impact Evaluation of Investment in Infrastructure: The Case of the Railway Connection in Uzbekistan. *ADBI Working Paper Series*. No. 548. Tokyo: Asian Development Bank Institute.

Other Resources

Gertler, P., S. Martinez, L. B. Rawlings, P. Premand, and C. M. J. Vermeersch. 2016. *Impact Evaluation in Practice: Second Edition*. Washington, DC: World Bank and Inter-American Development Bank. https://openknowledge.worldbank.org/handle/10986/25030.

Khandker, S., G. Koolwal, and H. Samad. 2009. *Handbook on Impact Evaluation: Quantitative Methods and Practices*. Washington, DC: World Bank. https://openknowledge.worldbank.org/bitstream/handle/10986/2693/520990PUB0EPI101Official0Use0Only1.pdf.

World Bank. Impact Evaluation Toolkit. http://web.worldbank.org/WBSITE/EXTERNAL/TOPICS/EXTHEALTHNUTRITIONANDPOPULATION/EXTHSD/EXTIMPEVALTK/0,,contentMDK:23262154~pagePK:64168427~piPK:64168435~theSitePK:8811876,00.html.

Chapter 2
Using Theories of Change to Identify Impact Evaluation Questions

Key Messages

- A theory of change is a heuristic tool that can be used for identifying possible outcomes and relationships to test and quantify via impact evaluation.

- The intent of a theory of change is to express linkages in a results chain connecting activities, outputs, outcomes, and longer-term goals, along with conditioning assumptions.

- The theory of change can offer a menu of options for impact evaluation of an intervention. It can help to identify attrition considerations that inform sampling and data collection, as well as behavioral assumptions, which impact evaluation can help to investigate.

2.1   Introduction

The intent of an impact evaluation (IE) is to quantify the causal effects of an intervention for a defined population. However, any intervention can have many possible consequences. Describing what consequences can be expected for whom, via what mechanism, and under which time frames allows the impact evaluator to understand which options exist for IE. These options can be considered against current understanding of the sector to narrow down to hypotheses of interest for testing through IE approaches.

Most development agencies employ logical frameworks that show relationships between project activities, outputs, outcomes, and longer-term goals, or a "results chain." At ADB, this takes the form of a Design and Monitoring Framework (DMF) (ADB 2006). The results chain is an articulation of a theory as to how the intervention is meant to generate intended effects. When those assumptions are articulated more explicitly, they become a "theory of change" (ToC), which describes how causal relationships among activities, outputs, outcomes, and impacts are intended to function. Explicitly articulating the theory will help to identify the current situation, the planned or intended situation, and what needs to be done to move from one to the other.

Basing the IE design on an explicit ToC helps to identify the data to be collected and how those data should be analyzed and reported. It can also allow the study to move beyond answering the question "what works?" to answering "what works and why?." This Chapter provides an overview of what a ToC is and how to prepare it.

2.2 What Is a Theory of Change?

The ToC is a statement of how the inputs being provided (funds, people, and changes in regulatory or policy environment) lead to intended outcomes and impacts. The theory identifies the steps in the causal chain (the DMF in ADB terminology) and the underlying assumptions which need to hold in order for the theory to operate as expected. The ToC also helps to identify the indicators or variables on which data should be collected, and it may identify "counter-theories" in which the intervention works in ways other than those which were planned, resulting in unintended outcomes (Carvalho and White 2004). Problem trees used at ADB and elsewhere for intervention design can serve as useful inputs for defining ToCs.

What a theory of change looks like

ToCs can take many forms, but they all intend to make causal connections and assumptions explicit (Vogel 2012). It may be useful to represent a ToC pictorially, as is done for a water supply and sanitation program in Figure 2.1. A ToC may also be presented in text or table form, but the pictorial representation is generally clearest for identifying causal relationships.

To make the ToC linkages as clear as possible, each area of activity should be distinguished. To do so, the ToC should go beyond "silos" that lump all inputs, all outputs, and all outcomes together. Specific activities should instead be linked to specific outputs, and specific outputs should link to specific outcomes. This presentation differs from that of traditional log frames, such as the ADB DMF, since there is not a single causal chain but many. This more detailed specification of causal relationships is helpful for evaluation design.

Typically, there is a progression from either left to right or from top to bottom, starting from inputs and ending at outcomes or impacts. Feedback loops can be readily incorporated into a pictorial representation of the ToC. Both unintended consequences and spillovers to non-intervention groups can be included.

All ToCs are contingent upon assumptions, and they need to make those assumptions clear. For example, in Figure 2.1, assumptions are written below the diagram, so that the behavioral characteristics and necessary conditions at each step are articulated.

Figure 2.1: Theory of Change for a Water and Sanitation Project

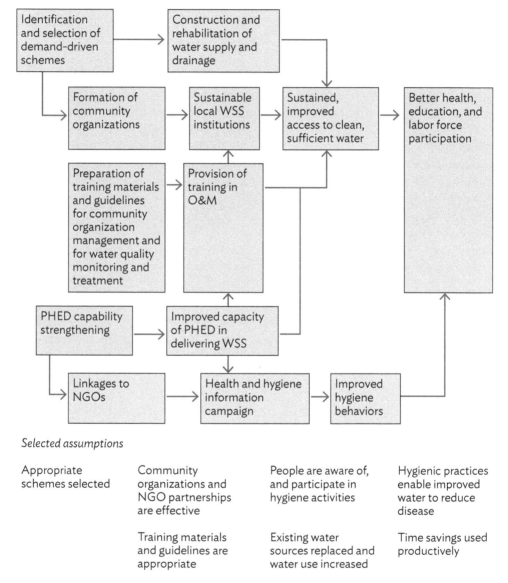

Selected assumptions

Appropriate schemes selected	Community organizations and NGO partnerships are effective	People are aware of, and participate in hygiene activities	Hygienic practices enable improved water to reduce disease
	Training materials and guidelines are appropriate	Existing water sources replaced and water use increased	Time savings used productively

NGO = nongovernment organization, O&M = operation and maintenance, PHED = Public Health Engineering Department, WSS = water supply and sanitation.
Source: Adapted from Evaluation Analysis Plan for Impact Evaluation of Punjab Rural/Community Water Supply and Sanitation Sector Projects in Pakistan.

A temporal dimension can be added to the ToC based on the intervention timeline and the time needed for outcomes to occur. This analysis can inform the timing of data collection (discussed further in Chapter 8).

2.3 Issues Raised by the Theory of Change

Barriers and facilitators along the causal chain: the funnel of attrition

The funnel of attrition (Figure 2.2) is a heuristic device for presenting and conceptualizing underlying assumptions of the causal chain (White 2013). The motivation behind the funnel is that participation rates and effect sizes diminish along the causal chain, so that final effects are not as large as project designers often envision. This matters for IE, as overestimating expected participation rates and effect sizes can result in studies with sample sizes that are too small for significant findings.

One use of the funnel of attrition, illustrated in Figure 2.2, is to answer the question, "of 100 intended beneficiaries, how many actually benefit from the program?". There may be substantial attrition because exposure is not universal, participation may be partial, behavior change may not always occur, and conditions for full effects may not always be present.

Figure 2.2: Example Funnel of Attrition

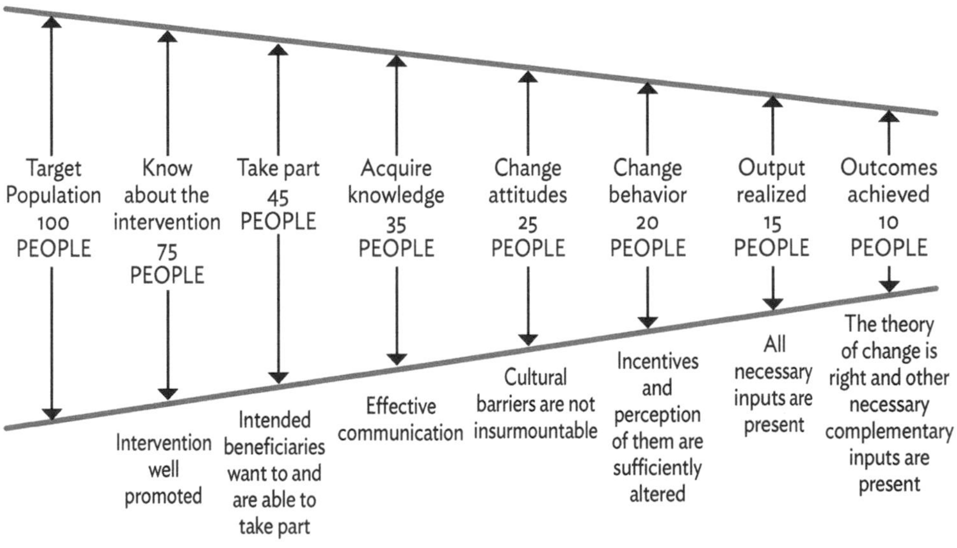

Target Population 100 PEOPLE	Know about the intervention 75 PEOPLE	Take part 45 PEOPLE	Acquire knowledge 35 PEOPLE	Change attitudes 25 PEOPLE	Change behavior 20 PEOPLE	Output realized 15 PEOPLE	Outcomes achieved 10 PEOPLE
	Intervention well promoted	Intended beneficiaries want to and are able to take part	Effective communication	Cultural barriers are not insurmountable	Incentives and perception of them are sufficiently altered	All necessary inputs are present	The theory of change is right and other necessary complementary inputs are present

Source: White (2013).

Common attrition considerations include the following:

- **Are intended beneficiaries aware of the program?** Is dissemination in appropriate media (via mechanisms that reach those with limited literacy, via TV in remote locations where few own or watch) or the local language? If intended beneficiaries are not aware, they are unlikely to participate.

- **Do intended beneficiaries want to take part in the program?** There are many reasons why this may not be so. Two often important reasons include that (i) their own assessment of the private costs and benefits lead them to conclude it is not worthwhile, and (ii) they are suspicious of the intervention.

- **Are beneficiaries able to take part?** Are project activities at a time, place, and cost (including opportunity cost) which make it possible for them to do so? Will intended beneficiaries feel socially excluded and unwelcome, or intimidated by the setting for project activities?

- **Is knowledge transfer effective?** Most development projects include knowledge transfer of some sort, to project or agency staff, to intermediaries, and to intended beneficiaries. A common weak link in the causal chain is to assume that knowledge transfer is effective, or that participants learn what they are meant to.

- **Does behavior change take place as expected?** Most development interventions require a change in behavior, among government officials, intermediaries, or intended beneficiaries. Often, actual behavior change for those who participate may differ substantially from what project managers expect.

- **Do other constraints to effectiveness remain unaddressed?** One constraint on being able to change behavior may be complementary inputs. For example, even after transport costs are reduced from a road project, firms may still face credit constraints for expanding capacity.

- **Does the intervention have a frequent effect?** Impact is often infrequent, even if all conditions for effectiveness are in place. For example, if improved residential water supply reduces the average frequency of waterborne illness, such illness may still be transmitted outside of the home or via other channels and an effect on health status may only be infrequently observed. Similarly, the direct effect of an insurance intervention on coping mechanisms may only be observed in years when a loss event occurs.

Evolution of effects

IE takes place at a particular point of time, most usually at the end of a project or program. It is assumed that the effects measured will be sustained at a similar level thereafter. The ToC can play an important part in articulating this sustainability assumption.

The sustainability of benefits depends on proper use and maintenance of the outputs, such as infrastructure. Attrition may occur when maintenance has not been adequate. Complementary inputs necessary for impact may also become more or less frequent, as a result of contextual changes.

The time dimension of attrition depends on the diffusion curve for any change being promoted by an intervention. Classic diffusion theory predicts an S-shaped diffusion pattern, with an initial slow take-up by early participants (Rogers 2003). Once the change is proven, there is rapid take-up, which then levels off for a slower rate of adoption among late participants. At the same time, changes may be disadopted and alter expected diffusion over time. Initial adopters may also have important differences from later adopters, such as younger age, better connectedness, and higher education, which will mean that they have different effects from an intervention.

Identifying the behavioral elements of intended change

IE is an approach that is particularly relevant when the effects of interventions depend upon human behavior and responses, which cannot be mechanically forecasted. For this reason, an important element of IE can be to test whether behavioral change occurs as expected from an intervention. An important heuristic to this end can be a behavioral change model (Table 2.1). This type of model allows the behavioral assumptions of an intervention to be made very explicit and translated into variables that an IE can help measure. These variables may serve as outcomes to estimate or as mediating variables that explain when and whether longer-term impacts occur.

Table 2.1: A Tabular Means of Depicting a Behavioral Change Model

Intended outcome	Actor (or group of actors who are expected to change in the same way) who must change behavior	Change in behavior required to achieve intended outcome	Indicators of change in behavior expected

Source: Authors.

Identifying externalities and unintended consequences

Interventions can have both benefits and adverse consequences. For example, new roads can increase accident rates, displace local businesses, and introduce unwanted social influences. Stakeholder engagement in preparing the ToC (discussed below) can help identify possible unintended consequences.

The ToC can also inform analysis of spillovers, or effects beyond the treated population, and help identify unintended consequences. Diffusion through word of mouth or observation effects is an example of a positive spillover, which may be an explicit part of the ToC, as in the case of farmer field schools. Other examples of positive externalities are reducing pollution, congestion, or cases of communicable diseases. Negative spillovers could include the inverse of these, or reductions in unskilled labor demand.

2.4 Constructing the Theory of Change

Steps in constructing the theory of change

The following seven steps are a useful way to approach identifying the ToC.

(i) **Undertake contextual analysis.** The ToC should start by identifying the root problem that the intervention should address, consequences of the problem, and causes that make the problem arise. Opportunities for addressing the problem, in light of other existing and planned initiatives should be considered.

(ii) **Define intervention, objectives, and outcomes.** The ToC requires clear identification of what the interventions are, the outputs they provide, and their related activities. These should be made as specific as possible. The selected outcomes should often be aligned with the intervention objectives.

(iii)   **Lay out main steps in causal chain.** The ToC links the inputs to the intended outcomes through activities, outputs, and intermediate outcomes. How the different causal chains are linked through these should be identified.

(iv)   **Conceptualize indicators along the causal chain.** These indicators can be used to trace causal connections and identify obstacles to impact. For example, the ADB-supported IE of the Tbilisi metro extension examines the impact on university students by collecting data on time use, transport modes, travel costs, and related impacts on consumption patterns, attendance rates, and test scores (Box 1.2).

(v)   **Identify underlying assumptions.** In addition to the links in the causal chain, there will be underlying assumptions which need to hold for the causal chain to operate. No assumptions should be taken for granted.

(vi)   **Distinguish among outcome channels.** It can be useful for the ToC to use one presentation axis to distinguish among pathways to specific outcomes for specific beneficiary groups or different classes of outcomes.

(vii)   **Validate and revise.** The ToC should be validated through discussions with key stakeholders such as program staff and managers, intended beneficiaries, and agencies with similar programs. These consultations may lead to revisions in the ToC and evaluation questions (Box 2.1).

Box 2.1: Revising the Theory of Change Based on Stakeholder Input: School Vouchers in the Philippines

The common theory of change for school vouchers is that children who receive the vouchers access better education in the private sector and so have improved learning outcomes. When this theory of change was presented to staff of the Department of Education in the Philippines, they objected that this was not how school vouchers were meant to work in the Philippines. Vouchers were one of the programs to address overcrowding in government schools. Removing the students who receive vouchers lowers the pupil–teacher ratio, improving learning outcomes for those remaining in the government school. Without this consultation, which resulted in the identification of a new causal chain, the impact evaluation would not have considered the impact of the program on non-recipients of vouchers.

Source: Authors.

The process for constructing the theory of change

The ToC is initially conceptualized when projects, policies, and programs (hereafter termed "interventions") are initially designed, but IE often is planned after this point, when there is more certainty about whether an intervention will occur. This means that the first step becomes reviewing the existing expressions of the ToC, such as logical frameworks (DMFs), and consulting relevant stakeholders about updates and revisions. In most cases, a higher level of detail than was previously developed for project preparation will need to be generated to inform IE design.

Preparing the ToC is a consultative process best informed by regularly involving key stakeholders, whose views may be sought as the ToC is developed. One way to do so is to hold preparatory workshops with program staff and management during the IE design phase. Having obtained the program staff buy-in to identifying the ToC that underpins evaluation questions will help with their support for proposed evaluation designs.

The causal links in the ToC may be backed by existing research to provide a framework as the basis for specific links. Many projects rely on traditional microeconomic assumptions for the ToC. When it comes to behavior change, many models can be adopted from behavioral psychology and other disciplines. Issues, such as asymmetric information and the role of transaction costs often are relevant to consider, as well.

2.5 Applying the Theory of Change

The ToC informs the selection of evaluation questions and variables to capture in survey instruments. A primary role of the ToC is as a heuristic tool that helps to spur discussion of which outcomes are expected and how they should be captured in the IE design. Rarely can all outcomes be captured in a single IE. However, illustrating the causal relationships that can be potentially investigated allows those relationships to be compared with available evidence, so as to identify hypotheses where new understanding can be generated. These relationships can also be screened against the funnel of attrition to assess whether sample and effect sizes are likely to be sufficient for analysis at particular points in time. Consideration of adoption curves and characteristics of initial adopters can also help to understand the population for which effects can be measured at different time periods.

The initial branches of the ToC can be used to establish indicators that reveal how implementation or conditional factors affect outcomes. This can further enrich hypotheses related to second generation IE questions. Indicators associated with the results chains chosen for investigation should serve to orient variables captured in the data collection design and identification strategy of the IE. The behavioral change model developed can provide a menu of possible outcome and mediating variables for use in the IE analysis.

References

ADB. 2006. *Guidelines for Preparing a Design and Monitoring Framework*. Manila.

Carvalho, S. and H. White. 2004. Theory-Based Evaluation: The Case of Social Funds. *American Journal of Evaluation*. 25 (2). pp. 141–60.

Rogers, E. 2003. *The Diffusion of Innovations*. Fifth Edition. New York: The Free Press.

Vogel, I. 2012. Review of the Use of "Theory of Change" in International Development. Review Report for the Department for International Development of the United Kingdom. http://www.dfid.gov.uk/r4d/pdf/outputs/mis_spc/DFID_ToC_Review_VogelV7.pdf.

White, H. 2013. Using the Causal Chain to Make Sense of the Numbers. Evidence Matters. Blog. 12 February. http://blogs.3ieimpact.org/using-the-causal-chain-to-make-sense-of-the-numbers/.

Further Reading

Taplin, D. and H. Clark. 2012. *Theory of Change Basics: A Primer on Theory of Change*. New York: Actknowledge. http://www.theoryofchange.org/wp-content/uploads/toco_library/pdf/ToCBasics.pdf.

Rogers, P. 2014. *Theory of Change: Methodological Briefs – Impact Evaluation No. 2*. Florence: UNICEF Office of Research. https://www.unicef-irc.org/publications/747/.

Stein, D. and C. Valters. 2012. Understanding Theory of Change in International Development. JSRP Paper 1. London: Justice and Security Research Programme, London School of Economics. http://www.theoryofchange.org/wp-content/uploads/toco_library/pdf/UNDERSTANDINGTHEORYOFChangeSteinValtersPN.pdf.

Chapter 3
The Core Concepts
of Impact Evaluation

Key Messages

- Impact evaluations use empirical techniques to identify or model a counterfactual scenario without the intervention of interest for comparison with the actual situation.

- Techniques for impact evaluation include experimental designs, quasi-experimental methods, and regression-based approaches.

- All impact evaluation methods depend on having observations of both populations that are affected by and are not affected by an intervention.

- A key issue for impact evaluation to tackle is selection bias, which is that those populations who have interventions are not the same as those who do not.

- It is important to understand the unit of assignment, unit of treatment, and unit of analysis for an intervention.

- Different impact evaluation techniques produce effect estimates that are valid for different populations.

3.1 What Is Impact Evaluation?

Impact evaluations measure *treatment effects*, for which treatment means being exposed to an intervention, such as a new policy or project, and effects are the difference that exposure makes to outcomes, such as income, productivity, poverty, health, and many other aspects.

An impact evaluation is based on *counterfactual analysis* that compares what would have happened in the absence of an intervention to actual outcomes occurring with the intervention.[1] Impact evaluation can also compare the results of a particular intervention with those of a different intervention.

Figure 3.1 portrays impact evaluation visually. An intervention occurs in time *t*, when the level of our outcome of interest is Y_t. After the intervention, the outcome of interest becomes Y^1_{t+1}, while it would have been only Y^0_{t+1} without the intervention. The latter is the counterfactual value of Y.

Figure 3.1: Illustration of an Impact Evaluation

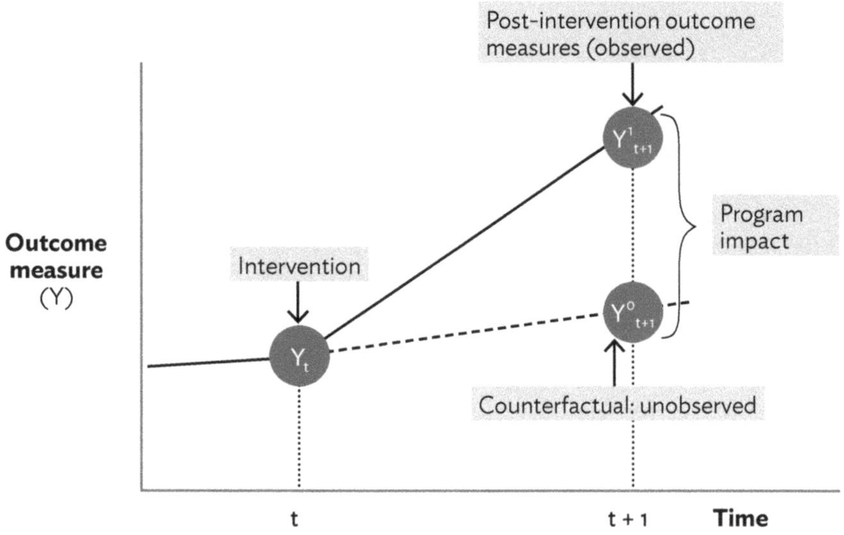

Source: Authors.

Impact evaluation, as illustrated in Figure 3.1, can be stated algebraically as in equation 3.1:

$$Impact = Y^1_{t+1} - Y^0_{t+1} \tag{3.1}$$

Where Y is the outcome of interest such as the poverty headcount, time use, or disease incidence. The subscript *t*+1 refers to a point of time after the intervention, or sufficiently far into the intervention to reasonably expect that there has been an effect on the outcome. The superscript 1 indicates the outcome when taking part in the intervention, i.e., the factual. The 0 superscript indicates the same outcome, for the same

---

[1]   Intervention ranges from specific activities, such as providing cash grants to poor families or nutritious meals to schoolchildren, provision of infrastructure such as rural roads or urban sewage treatment, to more general policies, such as education reform.

group of people, at the same point in time had they not taken part in the intervention, i.e., the counterfactual.

The key challenge for an impact evaluation is identifying and measuring valid counterfactual estimates of the outcomes of interest. While one can observe what happens to those who receive, say, a microfinance program (Y^1), one cannot observe the outcomes for the same group had they not participated (Y^0).

Outside of rigorous impact evaluation, simple comparisons are often used to draw conclusions about the effects of interventions. However, these comparisons have critical flaws.

Reflexive comparison. One possibility is to compare the outcomes before and after the intervention, which is termed as reflexive comparison. For example, an income survey will be conducted among microfinance recipients. A year after, another income survey will be conducted, and then the average incomes before and after the program are compared. This is very rarely valid because change in income, positive or negative, can be due to many other factors apart from the program.

Outcomes usually change over time regardless of the intervention, so that monitoring how outcomes have changed over time provides information about the effects of all factors changing over time, rather than the intervention of interest. This means that this simple technique has problems of confounded causality.

Cross-sectional comparison. Another possibility is to compare outcomes for the recipients of the microfinance program to other people in the village who did not participate. Yet, those who participated in microfinance programs may have different characteristics from those who did not, so the increase in income may be due to the other characteristics and not the program itself. Again, most simple cross-sectional techniques confound the intervention with other factors.

3.2 Identifying Control and Comparison Groups

To obtain a valid measure of impact from an intervention, techniques are needed to make the comparison unconfounded with other factors. One key approach is to use a control or comparison group, which is a group of subjects that closely resemble the characteristics of the group that received the intervention, but that did not receive the intervention.[2] The comparison group is a sample of individuals,

---

[2] Sometimes "comparison group" and "control group" are used interchangeably. This text follows the convention that "comparison group" is the term used in the nonexperimental designs, whereas the term "control group" is used in the experimental designs. The differences between each design are discussed in the following section.

households, firms, or some other unit drawn from the same broad geographic area as the intervention. The comparison group should have, on average, the same characteristics as the treatment group at baseline, which is called balance (Box 3.1 provides an example). In order to identify a comparison group, the analyst needs to understand the *assignment mechanism*, which is the process by which those who receive the intervention are selected for it and can self-select into participation.

Box 3.1: Demonstrating Balance in a Study of Handwashing Promotion in Pakistan

Bowen et al. (2013) report a 5-year follow-up study of a handwashing promotion project in Karachi. At follow-up, 84% of the households who had taken part in the original study were reenrolled for the survey. The table shows the average characteristics of treatment and control households for a number of variables. As can be seen, the numbers are very similar. The last column in the table reports the probability that the averages come from populations which are different from one another, this being the case if the p-value is less than 0.1. In all cases, the p-value is substantially higher, showing that the treatment and control groups are the same.

Variable	Treatment	Control	p-value
Household size	8.4	8.5	0.8
Mother literate	33%	31%	0.6
Father literate	64%	55%	0.6
Speak Urdu within home	96%	96%	0.9
Own radio	14%	13%	1.0
Own television	91%	92%	0.9
Own refrigerator	56%	56%	1.0
House receives municipal water supply	31%	35%	0.9
n	301	160	

Source: Bowen et al. (2013).

In a laboratory experiment, where researchers control the intervention of interest, full understanding of assignment is possible. However, in the context of development programming, this is more difficult. The problem that often exists when trying to identify a comparison group is that the intervention is put in specific places or targets specific people for a reason. In addition, those people who choose to participate in the program are usually not the same as those who do not. They may be better informed or educated, more willing to take risk, more proactive, or have other behavioral differences from those who do not participate. Replicating placement and selection choices to obtain a valid comparison group is often far from simple.

To define a control or comparison group, there are both experimental and nonexperimental designs for impact evaluations.

1. *Experimental design* is the term used when the treated and non-treated groups are randomly assigned by an exogenous factor that is not related to the intervention.

    ☐ *Randomized controlled trials (RCTs).* Sometimes these are also called *randomized experiments* or *randomized evaluations*. The approach involves random assignment of who or where gets the treatment. This means that groups that are in the intervention group and those that are in the control group are chosen at random from a list of groups eligible for the program. This is not the same as taking random samples of those already in the treatment and nontreatment groups. RCTs are discussed in greater detail in Chapter 4.

2. *Nonexperimental designs* are used when an experimental design is not possible due to costs or other considerations that prevented random assignment. Non-experiments are often considered if the decision to do an impact evaluation is taken after the intervention has taken place.

    ☐ *Natural experiments.* When a natural condition, geographic locations, or a government policy separates a population which is homogenous by nature into two or more groups only differentiated by exposure to an intervention, it may be considered a natural experiment. Some examples are as follows: (i) a river (or a newly built highway) splits a village into two, while a health clinic is located in one half, making it easier for the villagers in that side to get access to the health facility than the other; and (ii) two residential areas in which residents from the same socioeconomic group are located across each other but belong to two different provinces, so a change in the tax policy of one province affects one-half of the residents. Natural experiments, although uniquely suited for impact evaluation, are, in practice, addressed through quasi-experimental designs or regression-based approaches.

    ☐ *Quasi-experimental designs.* The designs employ statistical methods to establish a comparison group, which has the same characteristics as the treatment group, apart from treatment. The main quasi-experimental approaches are double difference or difference-in-differences, propensity score matching, and regression discontinuity design, which are discussed in Chapter 5. These approaches have been the most common in ADB-supported studies to date. A regression continuity design can be used when there is a threshold eligibility rule.

☐ *Regression–based approaches.* These estimate regression models in which participation is usually captured through a dummy variable. Less commonly, the treatment is a continuous variable such as loan size or duration of training. These approaches include endogenous treatment models, instrumental variables, switching regressions, and double robust regression. These approaches are discussed in Chapter 5.

If only one round of observations is used to show that the comparison group is valid—that is, that the analysis really is comparing like with like—quasi-experimental studies should report a balance table showing this check that the treatment and comparison/control groups were the same before the intervention (as demonstrated in Box 3.1). However, balance tables can only check balance on observable characteristics, so there may still be bias from lack of balance on characteristics that have not been observed.

3.3 Biases and Challenges for Causal Inference

There are several challenges in defining a valid comparison group for causal inference:

1. *Selection bias.* Those who do not participate in the program are likely to be different in important ways from those who do take part. Selection bias arises both from program placement (*placement bias*) and self-selection into programs. If the determinants of selection into the program are correlated with the outcomes of interest, then a "naïve impact estimate," which compares outcomes between random samples of participants and nonparticipants, will yield a biased estimate of program impact (Box 3.2 provides an example). For example, a project may target the poor: so project beneficiaries are poorer than non-beneficiaries, not because the project failed but because it succeeded in its targeting. To know if the project had effects, it is necessary to compare what happened to the outcomes of a similar set of poor households who did not take part in the project. The approach adopted to dealing with selection bias and other conflating factors is called the

identification strategy. Having a strong identification strategy is the main theme of the methods discussed in this book. Selection may be on *observables* or variables that are observed, in which case there are many options to control for selection bias. Selection may also be on *unobservables*, which are characteristics (often behavioral) for which data are not available. If the latter is the case then it can be more difficult to implement a valid identification strategy.

2. *Contamination or contagion.* The comparison group is meant to be the same as the treatment group, except that the former is not exposed to the program. However, in the real world, evaluators do not have full control over what happens in the comparison group. It may be that another agency implements another program in the comparison area, which affects the outcomes of interest. *Contamination* of the comparison group must be understood to be addressed. To help mitigate this risk, it is useful to include data collection on other past and ongoing interventions in the area of study. In addition, some interventions, such as information provision, may autonomously spread beyond the intervention location. Sampling needs to consider if such contagion within a location is likely.

3. *Spillover effects.* The Stable Unit Treatment Value Assumption, often known as SUTVA, is critical to impact evaluation (Rubin 1980). This assumption basically means that treatment and control populations are distinguishable and do not have unrecognized interaction effects from the intervention. This cannot be taken as granted, as a program may indirectly affect people beyond the intended target group with positive or negative spillover effects. For example, an intervention might change market demand and prices for a broader location, or it may lead to other social externalities. If such spillovers are expected to be important, then they should be explicitly accommodated. To do so, the evaluation design may include a treated population, untreated but exposed to spillovers, and untreated and not exposed to spillovers. How these groups are identified depends on the geographic scope of the spillovers, specifically whether they are within or between clusters or both. If spillovers affect the no-spillover comparison group, this is *self-contamination*, which biases the impact estimate. To avoid self-contamination, it is best to have a geographic separation between treatment and control areas, rather than them being geographically contiguous. At the same time, they should not be so distant so as not to be comparable.

Box 3.2: Selection Bias in Access to Improved Water in Nepal

The first two columns of the table show the average characteristics of households with and without access to improved water supply. The two groups of households are very different. Those with improved water are wealthier, better educated, and more likely to be urban. So any difference observed in outcomes, such as child diarrhea, may not result from the clean water, but from the other characteristics which affect both access to water and the outcome.

The final two columns show the average characteristics after matching using propensity score matching (a method explained in Chapter 5). It can be seen that the two groups are now broadly similar, so the difference in outcome can now be attributed to the intervention.

| | Simple Comparison | | After Matching | |
| | With improved sanitation | Without improved sanitation | With improved sanitation | Without improved sanitation |
Variable				
Piped water in house	23%	5%	23%	15%
Rural	52%	84%	53%	58%
Household head has at least secondary education	56%	30%	45%	41%
Cement house floor	29%	3%	30%	33%
Richest quintile	54%	4%	52%	52%

Source: Bose (2009).

Impact evaluation methods in the context of biases and challenges

If assignment and participation in the program is "randomized," so that it is analogous to a laboratory experiment, bias due to participant self-selection and where the program is placed can be completely eliminated. Careful randomized assignment also can ensure the control of contamination and appropriate accommodation of spillover effects. For these reasons, many academics consider RCTs as the "gold standard" in impact evaluation (Athey and Imbens 2015). Natural experiments, when assignment is exogenous, contamination is controlled, and spillover effects are addressed, are widely considered nearly as ideal as experiments.

Selection bias can also be avoided by nonexperimental designs. Nearly all nonexperimental designs depend upon understanding how the intervention was assigned and on modeling determinants of selection. Based on the model of selection, differences correlated with selection and existing prior to or independent of treatment can be controlled or eliminated. A key aspect conditioning validity is thus whether the model of selection is valid. Some nonexperimental designs, under certain assumptions, control for both selection on observables and selection on unobservables. However, for others, it is not always possible to establish whether selection on unobservables is present and adequately taken into account.

Almost no technique is possible without having observations with different levels of exposure to (e.g. with and without) the intervention during the same time period, under the SUTVA. More rigorous methodologies generally depend on having observations of individuals with the intervention and without the intervention during the period before and after the intervention. These observations should be for the same individuals in both periods, as panel data.

Large-n versus small-n impact evaluations

The major impact evaluation approaches are all "large-n" statistical designs. This means that there is a large number of observations on which to do tests of statistical significance on the difference in outcomes between the treatment and comparison groups. Whether the sample size is sufficiently large for this purpose is determined by power calculations, which are discussed in Chapter 7. As discussed in that Chapter, the number of units of assignment matters most for statistical power rather than the total number of observations. If the sample size is not large enough, then the impact evaluation will be underpowered, meaning that there is a high risk of not finding a statistically significant effect even though the program actually does have an impact.

ADB and other donors support various activities that are likely to require "small- to middle-n" designs, where there are not many similar communities with and without the intervention at the same time. The most obvious project components in this category are support to policy reform at the national level or within a single agency. Large-scale infrastructure, such as ports and highways, may also be such a case, though as is shown below, large-n designs may still be possible.

When there are sufficient observations over time, the "small-n" problem can be circumvented by a couple of techniques.

- *Synthetic controls* offer potential to generate counterfactual impact estimates when there are larger numbers of observation periods than treated units (discussed in Chapter 5).

- *Interrupted time series* approaches may allow for breaks in trends over time at the point of interventions to identify program impacts (also discussed Chapter 5).

When neither of these techniques nor a large-n design is possible, a choice has to be made whether to forgo an impact evaluation or proceed with a small- or middle-n approach. These approaches are not covered in this book. Further information may be found in the following sources:

- Middle-n interventions, such as support to a dozen financial intermediaries, can use *qualitative comparative analysis*, a relatively untested quantitative approach to causal analysis which looks for patterns in the data to identify necessary and sufficient conditions for causality without tests of statistical significance (Ragin 2000).

- Small-n qualitative approaches to causal inference rely on systematic analyses of the theory of change, which are sometimes called *context-mechanism outcomes* (White and Phillips 2012).

- Impact evaluation is empirical and usually strives to minimize structural assumptions. A theoretical rather than empirical, alternative to impact evaluation is simulation modeling. For example, the effects of macroeconomic reform and large-scale infrastructure may be modeled using computable general equilibrium analysis. New programs may be introduced as changes in exogenous variables ("shocks"), whereas policies may require changes in parameters or even model specification (Bourguignon and de Silva 2003).

3.4 Time Dimension of Impacts

The effects of an intervention often take a long time to occur, and this poses quandaries for when to attempt to evaluate impacts. In addition, effects change over time. This may be because of gestation periods for learning about how to apply an intervention, or it may be because initial participants are different from those who join programs later. For example, Figure 3.2 shows paddy yields in an area benefiting from an irrigation project. The red line shows the actual yields. During the first 7 years, while construction is under way, yields average 2.6 tons per hectare. Over the following 5 years, secondary and tertiary canals are completed so average yields in the catchment area increase as more farmers connect to the system, reaching 4.3 tons per hectare by year 12.[3]

The gray line shows the counterfactual of what would have happened in the absence of the intervention. Note this is the true counterfactual. If the

---

[3] Paddy yields are just one outcome to be considered since irrigation has a large part of its impact through its effect on cropping patterns. Net farm income and household income should also be included as outcomes.

counterfactual yields were to be estimated using a comparison group, the yield should be similar but not identical in the pre-project period.

Timing of data collection requires careful consideration, as it can determine the scope and results of an IE. The irrigation project in Figure 3.2 closed in year 8, with locally funded work continuing to expand connections in the catchment area. Measuring impact in year 8 would underestimate impact since many farmers were yet to connect; hence, an impact evaluation in the year of project closure would be premature. Designing an impact evaluation means understanding the temporal aspects of the theory of change and when effects on outcomes of interest can realistically be expected. A diarrhea intervention program may yield a quick impact on incidence rates, but a governance reform may take several election cycles before the impact is measurable at all.[4]

Figure 3.2: Factual and Counterfactual Yields from an Irrigation Project

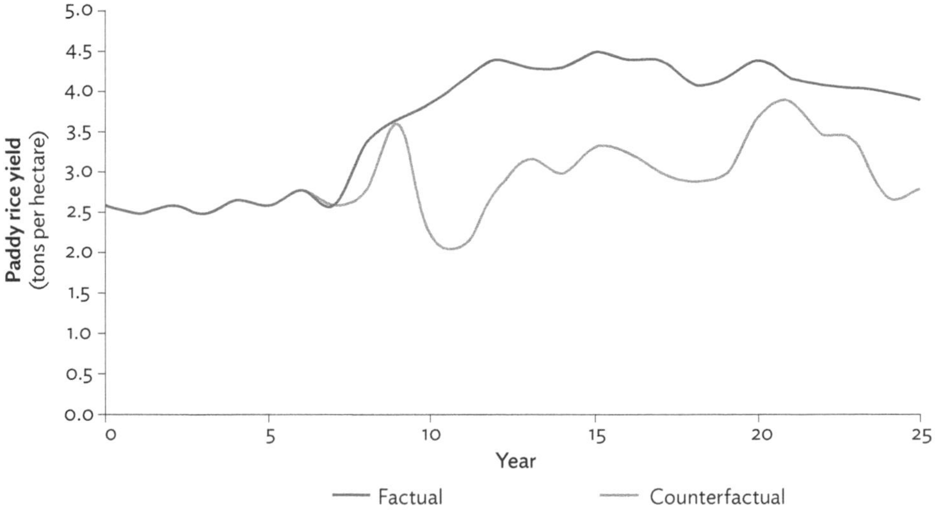

Source: Author's simulation.

In the real world, however, knowledge of actual impact is not available prior to the surveys conducted for impact evaluation; hence, it requires a combination of judgments based on theories and professional experience. The critical issue to consider is whether sufficient time has passed from the intervention for effects of interest to become manifest. Attempting to measure impact prematurely

---

4   Asked about the impact of the 1789 French Revolution, Premier Zhou Enlai of the People's Republic of China replied, "It is too early to say."

may either lead to false conclusions of limited impact, or may limit whether meaningful effects can be evaluated. Even when sufficient time has passed for effects to be measurable, there may be differences in the effects for initial participants and the overall targeted population.

When to plan impact evaluation

Impact evaluations are usually conducted at or toward the end of a project. This does not mean that all thought of the impact evaluation can be postponed until these closing years. *Ex ante* impact evaluation plans, undertaken before intervention effectiveness in the field, are stronger because (i) they allow for the collection of appropriate baseline data from both project/intervention (treatment) and comparison areas; and (ii) random assignment can be considered. Randomization is necessarily an *ex ante* approach since random assignment has implications for how the project will be implemented and so cannot be undertaken *ex post*.

The reality is that the demand for an impact evaluation may come only once the project or program is under way, and possibly no baseline data have been collected. Although these circumstances are far from ideal, *ex post* impact evaluation designs are possible, so the best possible design should be chosen under the circumstances.

3.5 Unit of Assignment, Treatment, and Analysis

Planning impact evaluation design requires a clear understanding of the unit of assignment, treatment, and analysis:

- The *unit of assignment* is the lowest (usually geographic) unit at which an intervention decision is made, which will typically be a municipality, district, subdistrict, agency, community, group, or firm. The types of intervention supported by ADB or other donors will very rarely be assigned at the household level.

- The *unit of treatment* is the unit to which the treatment is delivered, which may be a lower level than the unit of assignment. For example, a microfinance program will provide support through microfinance institutions (the unit of assignment), but the unit of treatment are firms receiving loans.

- The *unit of analysis* is the unit in which outcomes are measured. Again, this may be a lower level than the unit of assignment or treatment.

In the example of the microfinance project, an outcome might be the wages paid to employees of the enterprise, so enterprise workers are the unit of analysis.

It is not usually the case that the unit of assignment, treatment, and analysis are the same. If they are not the same, a cluster design is necessary, with cluster sampling used for data collection. This fact has implications for data collection. Table 3.1 lists some examples of how the units of assignment, treatment, and analysis may differ.

Table 3.1: Examples of the Unit of Assignment, Treatment, and Analysis

Intervention	Assignment	Treatment	Analysis
Improved sanitation	Village	Village, schools, and households	Households and children
Arterial highway upgrading	City	City	Firm
Vocational training	School	School	Student

Source: Authors.

Large infrastructure projects appear to present a particular difficulty for large-n statistical designs, since in some cases, such as port rehabilitation or building a national highway, the treated n equals to 1. However, it is possible to construct treatment and comparison groups by considering those communities (villages, subdistricts, towns, etc.) as the unit of assignment. In the example in Table 3.1 of highway improvements, cities along the four highways are taken as the treatment group, with 18 cities not on the highways as a comparison group. In contrast, education interventions are often very amenable to large-n impact evaluation designs, as the school is a common unit of assignment, as in the case of vocational training in Table 3.1.

In short, (i) the unit of treatment is usually at the same, or a lower level, than the unit of assignment, and the unit of analysis is usually at the same, or a lower, level, than the unit of treatment; and (ii) there may be multiple units at each level, such as different treatments for village, schools, and households as in the example of sanitation in Table 3.1.

3.6 Different Impact Measures – Impacts for Whom?

Impact evaluation can give different measures of intervention effects, depending on the population for which the estimate is generated. This is important to understand, as not all methodologies can estimate all measures.

- *Average treatment effect* (ATE): the average impact of participation in the program on the entire eligible population.

- *Intention to treat effect* (ITT): the average impact of exposure to the program, e.g., on all those living in a program area eligible to take part in the program.

- *Average treatment effect on the treated* (ATT): the average impact on those who actually take part in (choose to comply or adopt) the intervention.

- *Average treatment effect on the untreated* (ATU): the average potential impact on those not taking part in the treatment were they treated. This is a relevant measure for understanding the potential effects of program expansion.

- *Local average treatment effect* (LATE): the average impact on a subgroup of the beneficiary population, usually those at the threshold for eligibility. Some impact evaluation designs yield a LATE rather than an ATE.

The ITT and ATT are linked by the participation rate:

$$ITT = \frac{Total\ effect}{No.\ of\ intended\ beneficiaries} \qquad (3.2)$$

$$= \frac{Total\ effect}{No.\ participating} \ x \ \frac{No.\ participating}{No.\ of\ intended\ beneficiaries}$$

$$= Average\ treatment\ effect\ on\ treated\ (ATT)\ x\ Participation\ rate\ (PR)$$

Hence, it is clear that

$$ITT \le ATT \qquad (3.3)$$

That is, the average effect on the target population will necessarily be no greater than the average effect on those who actually take part. Low participation rates drive a wedge between the two. An intervention may have a very large impact on those actually taking part, but only few actually do take part so that the ITT effect is very low.

The average impact achieved by program exposure to date is measured by ITT, while LATE often provides a marginal impact from expansion of the intervention. ATT provides a measure of impact for those who actually participate, and is often the metric of choice for researchers concerned with impact to date. On the other hand, ATU may be more relevant for informing policy decisions on program expansion.

Assuming that people are logical, purposive program placement is for locations and populations that better respond to interventions, and those who self-select into interventions gain more than those who do not, the following relationship should be observed among impact indexes:

$$ATT > ATE > ATU \tag{3.4}$$

If this pattern does not emerge, it may indicate that either the identification strategy for the impact evaluation is flawed or that the program has large defects in targeting or placement.

3.7 Internal and External Validity

A study has *internal validity* if the study estimates are valid for the assessed sample. Internal validity is a function of the rigor of the evaluation design. For an impact evaluation, a crucial aspect of internal validity is the strength of the identification strategy, that is, the approach used to address the problem of causality, including selection bias. Other factors also affect internal validity, such as the sampling strategy used to collect data in the treatment and control areas and the quality of the data collected.

While internal validity deals with how the evaluation can eliminate potential biases, *external validity* is the extent to which study findings can be generalized. A single study is insufficient to make a broad statement that, for example, "index-linked weather insurance does not work" or "PPPs are the most cost-effective means of delivering large-scale infrastructure." To make such statements, one would need to draw on a broader body of evidence including many studies. However, this does not mean that no general lessons may be drawn from a single study. Often, lessons can reasonably be transferred to a similar context.

External validity is enhanced (i) by having a strong theory of change with analysis along the causal chain; (ii) when the study sample is representative of the project/program population (and generalizations made to similar populations); (iii) when the intervention assessed either is currently widely implemented or has wide potential for application; and (iv) when the analysis is relevant to economic logic that applies more broadly than in the intervention context. In general, establishing external validity is often more of a challenge for RCT-type approaches, where experimental application leads to interventions that may have limited real world relevance, while internal validity is more of a challenge for nonexperimental approaches, where controls for confounding factors are incomplete.

References

Athey, S. and G. W. Imbens. 2017. Chapter 3: The Econometrics of Randomized Experiments. In E. Duflo and A. Banerjee, eds. *Handbook of Field Experiments*. Volume 1, 1st Edition. Amsterdam: North Holland.

Bourguignon, F. and L. A. Pereira da Silva, eds. 2003. *The Impact of Economic Policies on Poverty and Income Distribution: Economic Techniques and Tools*. Washington, DC: World Bank and Oxford University Press.

Bose, R. 2009. The Impact of Water Supply and Sanitation Interventions on Child Health: Evidence from DHS Surveys. Paper prepared for the Bi-Annual Conference on Impact Evaluation. Colombo, Sri Lanka. 22–23 April 2009.

Bowen et al. 2013. Sustained Improvements in Handwashing Indicators More than 5 Years after a Cluster-Randomised, Community-Based Trial of Handwashing Promotion in Karachi, Pakistan. *Tropical Medicine and International Health*. 18 (3). pp. 259–267.

Ragin, C. C. 2000. *Fuzzy-Set Social Science*. Chicago: University of Chicago Press.

Rubin, D. B. 1980. Comment on: Randomization Analysis of Experimental Data in the Fisher Randomization Test by D. Basu. *Journal of the American Statistical Association*. 75. pp. 591–593.

White, H. and D. Phillips. 2012. Addressing Attribution of Cause and Effect in Small-n Impact Evaluations: Towards an Integrated Framework. 3ie Working Paper 15. Delhi.

Further Reading

ADB. 2011. *A Review of Recent Developments in Impact Evaluation*. Manila. https://www.adb.org/sites/default/files/publication/28622/developments-impact-evaluation.pdf.

Caliendo, M. and R. Hujer. 2005. The Microeconometric Estimation of Treatment Effects – An Overview. Discussion Paper No. 1653. IZA. Bonn, Germany. http://citeseerx.ist.psu.edu/viewdoc/download?doi=10.1.1.421.6476&rep=rep1&type=pdf.

Ravallion, M. 2001. The Mystery of the Vanishing Benefits: An Introduction to Impact Evaluation. *The World Bank Economic Review*. 15 (1). pp. 115–140. http://documents.worldbank.org/curated/en/410881468180273314/The-mystery-of-the-vanishing-benefits-an-introduction-to-impact-evaluation.

Chapter 4
Randomized Controlled Trials

Key Messages

- Properly conducted randomized controlled trials ensure balanced characteristics between those with and without interventions, so that differences are only due to the intervention.

- Most randomized controlled trials are cluster designs, where the unit of assignment contains multiple treated units.

- Random assignment can be done in several ways, some of which only alter the sequencing, eligibility threshold, or incentives to use an intervention, rather than overall project rollout.

- Randomized controlled trials can contain different permutations of interventions to test interaction effects and make comparisons.

- Careful oversight is needed to ensure the fidelity of randomized controlled trials in the field.

4.1 Introduction

A randomized controlled trial (RCT), sometimes called a randomized evaluation or experimental design, involves the random assignment of members of the eligible population to one or more "treatment groups" that receive the intervention, and to the "control group" that receives no intervention, a comparator reference intervention or, in some cases, a placebo.[1]

With sufficient sample size, random assignment ensures balance. That is, the average characteristics of the treatment and control groups are on average the same at baseline. This statement will be true for both observable

---

[1] In clinical trials the treatment group may receive a placebo. For ethical and practical reasons, this may not be an option in many social and economic interventions.

and unobservable characteristics. There will be no selection bias since the assignment has not been purposively selected, but made at random. Impact can be calculated as the difference in outcomes between treatment and control at endline. A difference-in-differences estimate (described in Chapter 5) comparing the difference in changes over time between treatment and control groups is preferable, as it reduces differences resulting from sampling error.

Random assignment should not be confused with random sampling. Random sampling refers to how a sample is drawn from one or more populations. Random assignment refers to how individuals or groups are assigned to either a treatment group or a control group. RCTs typically use both random assignment and random sampling, since the whole treatment population is not required for the impact evaluation analysis.

4.2 Why Randomize?

The logic of random assignment is straightforward. If a representative sample is drawn from a population, then the expected value of the mean of any characteristic for the sample is the true population mean. The larger the sample drawn, the more likely it is that the sample mean is close to the population mean.

It follows that if two or more samples are drawn from the same population, then the average characteristics of each sample should be basically the same, as both are expected to have the average characteristics of the population as a whole. This is shown in Table 4.1, which shows the average characteristics of households in two samples, one called treatment and the other control. The similarity of the two samples increases as the sample size increases, with no statistically significant differences once samples become sufficiently large. That is, the samples are balanced.

Table 4.1: Similarity of Samples Drawn from the Same Population

Sample Size	Rural (%)			Years of Education			Household Size		
	Treatment	Control		Treatment	Control		Treatment	Control	
1	100	0	*	12.0	9.0	*	9.0	5.0	*
10	70	80	*	6.4	5.8	*	6.4	6.7	
25	72	60	*	5.8	5.3		6.4	6.5	
100	64	61		6.0	5.5		6.7	6.5	
1,000	66	64		5.2	5.4		6.5	6.5	

Notes: Sample size per sample. * Indicates difference is significant at 5% level.
Source: Authors.

Table 4.1 shows that the samples are balanced on observable characteristics. Proper randomization should also result in balance on unobservable characteristics as well, although this cannot be directly tested. Once balance is established by random assignment into treatment and control, it follows that, since the two samples have the same characteristics, any difference in outcomes after the intervention must be attributable to the intervention.

There are two important implications of this discussion:

(i)   Treatment and control must be drawn from the same population; that population is not the population as a whole, but the one defined by the intervention's eligibility criteria or the population in the intervention catchment area.

(ii)   The sample size has to be large enough to be reasonably confident that the two samples will have the same average characteristics.

Random assignment ensures that all eligible potential beneficiaries have an equal chance of being included in the intervention. Where scarce resources mean that the whole population cannot be served, randomization is a transparent and equitable means of allocating these resources.

Randomization has a secondary benefit that may often be nearly as important as its theoretical superiority. In order to effectively randomize intervention rollout, impact evaluators must become closely involved in intervention implementation, since they are involved in the assignment of the treatment. This involvement has benefits both for program staff and the evaluators. It enhances the relevance of the evaluation and it also provides opportunities for the impact evaluation process to help improve project design and administration (Glennerster et al. 2017).

4.3 Types of Randomized Controlled Trial Designs

There are many different RCT designs. The differences relate to (i) the level of assignment, (ii) different approaches to random assignment, and (iii) the type of treatment combinations assessed. The choices that are made between these different designs depend on the intervention design, in particular its operational rules for determining who is eligible for the program or how the catchment area is defined.

For all approaches, it is important to ensure that an appropriate assignment concealment or timing mechanism is in place. In other words, those involved in treatment implementation should not have advanced notice of assignment, which could allow introduction of bias or manipulation of assignment (Kim and Shin 2014).

The level of assignment: simple versus cluster randomized controlled trials

The unit of assignment in an RCT is the unit used for selecting who gets treated. In a *simple RCT*, the unit of assignment is the same as the unit of treatment and measurement. An example could be a business development program for small and medium-sized enterprises in which eligible enterprises are randomly assigned to treatment and control groups. The outcomes could include firm-level sales, profitability, and employment.

For both practical and ethical reasons, a *cluster RCT* design is often used, in which the unit of assignment contains multiple treatment units. In practical terms, it is more feasible to randomly assign a service with shared community infrastructure, such as electrification or water supply at community or block level, rather than at a household level. For example, rural electrification and roads treat communities, although benefits may be measured at firm or household level. Logistical and ethical questions from creation of visible inequity may arise if assignment is at the household or individual level, such as to some members of a school class but not to others.

Cluster RCT designs also help to contain spillover effects and contamination. Knowledge of treatment often spreads within a community. If assignment is at the household or individual level, this knowledge creates a spillover effect that may alter the behavior of the untreated, which biases the experiment if the control group is drawn from untreated neighbors. Cluster RCTs can help to create large and distinct enough units of assignment so that these spillovers are minimized.

In a cluster RCT, the unit of assignment is higher than the unit of treatment or measurement. For example, a business development program may work in certain towns, with all firms in that town eligible for the program. The towns would be randomly chosen from a list of eligible towns, with those not chosen (or a random sample of those not chosen) forming the control group.

The statistical power of the design is largely determined by the number of clusters in the study rather than the number of treated units. This means that the example program will have to cover a reasonably large number of treatment towns to obtain a sufficiently powered study (Chapter 7 provides more details on power calculations for determining sample sizes).

Different approaches to random assignment

There are several approaches to random assignment. The appropriate approach needs to be determined based on the program's operational rules.

- When there is excess demand (oversubscription) for a program or the eligible population exceeds that which can be served with available resources, then *random selection*, such as a lottery, can be used to determine which of the eligible applicants are included and which are in the control group. Since the program will not be made available to all of those who are eligible, random selection into the program can be the fairest and most transparent means of deciding who gets in. A random number generator can be used, but increasingly public randomization ceremonies are held to increase transparency.

- *Altered threshold randomization* enables random assignment by slightly altering the eligibility threshold. By relaxing the threshold, it is possible to identify a larger eligible population than can be treated, within which treatment is assigned randomly. For example, if the eligibility criterion for a nutrition program is households with children aged up to 24 months, this threshold could be raised to 30 months. An analogous approach can be used geographically. A program planning to work in 50 communities can first identify 100 communities and then randomly select 50 communities from this total to enter the program. In this latter case, the technique of matched pair randomization (discussed below) would increase the power of the design.

- *Pipeline* or *step-wedged designs* randomize the order of treatment, rather than the treatment itself. Pipeline randomization means that all units of assignment will receive the program over time. It is the time of entry to the program that is randomly assigned. Implementing agencies often roll out a program in stages, making it possible to randomly select the order in which the participants receive the program. For example, if budgetary and logistical constraints prevent the immediate nationwide rollout of a program, it may be possible to randomly select units that will receive the program during the first stage. One example of this approach is the Pantawid Pamilya conditional cash transfer program in the Philippines. In its initial phase, the program was a pilot for 140 communities, half of which received the program first and half of which acted as a control group for 2 years (World Bank 2014). Hence, the communities were randomly allocated into the two groups to receive the program in either year 1 or year 3 (i.e., those receiving the program in year 3 served as a control group for 2 years).

- *Encouragement designs* can be used for programs and policies that are universally available but not universally adopted. The treatment group is provided with an encouragement to take up the intervention, but this encouragement should not be something that affects the outcomes of interest. An example of a suitable encouragement is an information campaign for an ongoing program. The villages where the campaigns will be conducted are selected at random from among all of the villages where the program has been implemented (which may be all villages in the country for a national program). The impact of the program on outcomes of interest is measured by comparing the outcome between the control and treatment villages—in this case, villages exposed to the information campaign. This approach allows a local average treatment effect impact estimate to be made because of the differential take-up rates between those villages exposed to the information campaign and those that are not.

- *Stratification* or *prior matching* can be used to ensure balance with a smaller sample size. Matched pair randomization matches units (e.g., communities) into pairs based on observed characteristics, randomly assigning one community of each pair into the treatment group and the other to control. So if there are, for example, two communities which are particularly remote, or large, or with minority ethnic populations, prior matching ensures that one of these goes in the treatment group and the other in control. Without prior matching both may end up in one of these two groups, unbalancing the sample. When possible to conduct, matched pair randomization has the potential to improve sample power, efficiency, robustness, and increase power (Imai et al. 2009). With stratification, participants are divided into groups (strata)—such as low, medium, and high income—and then randomization is conducted for each group. Stratification ensures that both treatment and control have the same proportion of units for variables used for the stratification (e.g., low/medium/high income, rural/urban, poor/nonpoor), and can also help to increase power and facilitate subgroup analysis (Imai et al. 2008).

Multiple treatment arms and treated control groups

The control group need not be untreated (termed a *passive control*). An untreated control group (or *study arm*) provides a counterfactual of no intervention, and so answers the question, "how does this intervention compare with doing nothing?" However, this is rarely the only policy question of interest.

Policy makers are often interested in knowing how doing A compares with doing B. *A/B designs* compare two treatment arms, treatment A and treatment B. In the medical field, treatment B is often what is called "existing standard of care." That is, the counterfactual is the current policy, and so the evaluation question is "how does this intervention compare with what is currently done?" In this case, A is called an "active control." Alternatively, A and B may be two different approaches to implementing a project. A/B designs are appropriate for adaptive learning to improve project design. More treatment arms may be added (e.g., A/B/C designs), but each arm drives up the sample size requirements.

The drawback of not having a no-treatment control arm is that it is not possible to calculate absolute effectiveness. The two interventions being tested may be shown to work equally well. But neither may in fact have any impact. If the existing treatment has been shown to work by previous rigorous studies, that problem does not occur. Yet, often it is still useful to have an absolute effectiveness estimate for the purposes of cost-effectiveness or cost–benefit analysis.

Factorial designs are a special type of a multiple arm study in which one arm receives multiple interventions. For example, one arm gets intervention A, another gets intervention B, the third gets both A and B, and the fourth is untreated. Factorial designs allow testing of whether different interventions are complements or substitutes. It is often claimed that there is complementarity between different interventions (e.g., microfinance and business development, input subsidies and extension services, and improved water and hygiene education). Factorial designs allow that claim to be tested.

Crossover designs are related to factorial designs, but treatments are sequential, rather than simultaneous. This means that the third arm gets B followed by A, and an additional arm might get A followed by B, rather than a factorial design where A and B are given together. This can test if intervention sequencing matters, but requires more treatment arms than a factorial design.

Different approaches can be combined in a single study, as in the case of ADB's impact evaluation of rural electrification in Madhya Pradesh (Box 4.1).

Box 4.1: A Multi-Treatment Arm, Pipeline Encouragement Design

The ADB-supported Impact Evaluation of Rural Electrification on Women's Quality of Life and Empowerment in Madhya Pradesh (India) combines three designs: multiple treatment arms with an encouragement which is rolled out over time (pipeline).

The multiple treatments are subsidized connection costs and training on electricity use. Treatment arm one just receives the subsidized connection, and treatment arm two the subsidized connection and the training. There is an untreated control arm which does not receive electricity at all.

The selection of villages to be connected was not randomized. However, the selection into the two treatment arms was randomly assigned across 240 villages. The connection subsidy is an encouragement, which should result in higher adoption in treatment villages in the control, making analysis of the impact of electrification. In the 160 treatment villages, the connection subsidy is available from 2015 to 2017, and is subsequently rolled out to the control villages thereafter.

Note: Design simplified for purposes of exposition.
Source: Impact Evaluation Study Proposal, 21 November 2014.

4.4 Steps in Implementing a Randomized Controlled Trial

An RCT needs to be planned before wide field implementation of an intervention. RCTs cannot be undertaken retrospectively.[2] Pilot testing impact evaluations may be built into the early stages of a project so that project designs can be improved through the evidence gathered from these studies. Designing an RCT involves the following steps (White 2013):

(i) *Identify questions of interest.*

The overall evaluation design involves selecting evaluation questions derived from the theory of change. Staff of the implementing agency, from top management to field staff, have to buy into the randomized design in order for randomization to be feasible in the first place and to preserve the integrity of the design in practice.

(ii) *Isolate treatment(s) of interest.*

The treatments of interest will be manifestations of the questions that the study should help answer. For an RCT, the treatment being evaluated has to be

---

[2] The possible exception to this statement is an "encouragement design," which does not randomly assign participants to an intervention but to receive an incentive to participate.

clearly defined so that it can be applied in a uniform manner. This also matters for external validity: what has been evaluated needs to be clear. In general, the intervention should be as unbundled as possible, with intervention combinations only assessed in factorial or crossover designs. Otherwise, it will not be possible to determine which components of interventions led to identified effects, and external validity will be limited.

In addition, the evaluator should determine whether a placebo should be used for any control arm of the experiment. Placebos can eliminate bias imparted by knowledge of treatment and improve rigor. However, placebos often are not feasible for many real world interventions, and raise ethical issues about study representation and informed consent. This means that placebos are rare in practice for impact evaluation of development interventions.

    (iii)   Consider spillover effects.

If the theory of change suggests that there will be spillover effects, these spillovers need to be considered in the study design. The unit of assignment should be aggregated enough so that there are no spillovers between treated and untreated units. When spillover effects are expected to be substantial, random assignment may apply to three groups: treated, untreated but subject to spillover, and untreated but not subject to spillovers.

    (iv)   Determine levels of assignment, treatment, and analysis.

The randomization design depends on clearly identifying the unit of assignment, treatment, and analysis. Randomization is primarily at the level of assignment. Random assignment must occur over a universe from which there is a sufficient listing to randomly draw equivalent treatment and control units. Sample power calculations (discussed in Chapter 7) should be conducted at this point to ascertain that enough units can be included to have a high likelihood of detecting effects.

The study team should also decide upon the potential subgroups of interest at the beginning of the study, to ensure that the study is sufficiently powerful to conduct the subgroup analyses.

    (v)   Decide on the type of randomized controlled trial (discussed in section 4.3).

The choice of the type of RCT depends on the intervention design, the evaluation questions, and what is feasible. The nature of development interventions will usually require a cluster RCT since projects are assigned by geographic unit, and spillovers often occur within communities.

First generation questions (does the intervention work?) will require an untreated control group and a large sample, as effect sizes for final outcomes are typically relatively small. Second generation questions (which intervention approaches are most effective?) are more likely to use A/B designs. In some cases, these require shorter time frames and smaller samples, as the outcome of interest is more proximate (typically adoption), where effect sizes are larger and take place more quickly than final outcomes.

RCTs are usually designed *ex ante*. But if an intervention is ongoing, it may be possible to (i) use random assignment in the rollout of the program, (ii) introduce variations into program implementation for adaptive learning purposes, or (iii) use an encouragement design.

(vi)   Identify eligible population (the universe for random assignment).

In order for the participation rate to be sufficient for treated sample sizes to offer sample power, an RCT should focus on a targeted population that is likely to participate and/or be targeted by the evaluated intervention. Randomization is thus done within this population, not the population as a whole. To do so, the eligibility criteria or planned catchment areas for the units of assignment have to be clearly defined. Criteria may be geographic, such as all subdistricts in 10 preselected districts, or characteristic-based, such as small enterprises headed by women. Several criteria may be combined, e.g., female-headed small enterprises in subdistricts from 10 preselected districts where the subdistrict poverty index is below some threshold.

Definition of the eligible population can happen in one or both of two ways: identification or self-selection. For identification, a list of the eligible population is made. The "population" may not be individuals, households, or firms, but could be villages, towns, subdistricts, or districts. Such lists are often available from administrative sources or are drawn up as part of project design.

As a form of self-selection, the program can be announced and those interested can apply. Applicants are screened for eligibility. Assuming there is oversubscription, then random assignment takes place among eligible applicants.

(vii)   Draw sample for analysis.

From the eligible or targeted population, a representative sample is drawn, unless the entire population is used for analysis. In the case of a cluster RCT, the sampling will be a two-stage design, first sampling clusters, if there are more project clusters than needed for the study. It will nearly always be the case with a cluster RCT that within-cluster sampling needs to be carried out.

> *(viii) Assign to treatment and control.*

Eligible units need to be assigned to treatment and control before implementing the intervention in treated locations. The maximum possible size of the treatment group is given by the intended coverage of the project. It is not necessarily the case that the whole treatment population will be in the sample for the impact evaluation, which depends on the sample size requirements as given by the power calculation.

Random assignment can be restricted to a subset of a project or program, if that gives sufficient sample size. For example, suppose a slum upgrading project plans to upgrade 200 settlements over a 5-year period, taking on 40 new settlements each year. Power calculations show that 40 settlements should be included in the sample, consisting of 20 treatment and 20 control, with 15 households sampled per settlement. A possible design would be to randomly assign the 20 settlements for year 1 and year 5, the latter acting as the control for years 1 to 5. Program staff are free to assign the remaining 160 settlements across the other years as they wish.[3]

> *(ix)   Collect baseline data and check for balance.*

While baseline data are not required in theory for an RCT, in practice they are usually collected to ensure balance between treatment and control. Baseline data usually need to be collected before the intervention can have any effect at field level They may be collected before treatment assignment to avoid any bias in data collection, where possible.

Once the data have been collected and cleaned (Chapter 6 discusses data collection), and assignment into treatment has been performed, a balance check should be conducted. If balance is not found, field implementation of the randomization protocol may be compromised, and further investigation should be performed on how randomization was implemented.

> *(x)   Ensure integrity of the design and monitor for contamination and attrition.*

---

[3]   A case may be made for doing the random assignment in years 2 and 5. It is likely that there will be learning in year 1 resulting in project adaptation, so it makes sense to evaluate the project as implemented in year 2 when the design has "settled down."

The study team needs to stay closely involved as implementation progresses to ensure the integrity of the design, with randomization protocols strictly followed so that treatment groups get treated and that control groups do not. Randomization often means more work for field teams to reach more inaccessible communities, deal with less receptive potential beneficiaries, or do things in an inefficient order. Field teams may thus have incentives to shortcut randomization if there is not very close control to ensure that the randomization protocol is followed.

Even if the integrity of the design is ensured at start-up, it may be compromised later by contamination (discussed in Chapter 3). It is important to check that those in the control group do not suffer from contamination, either through a similar intervention being carried out in the control areas or through self-contamination, where participants of the study cross over from one arm of the study to the other, thereby contaminating the initial randomization process.

As an example of lack of compliance leading to contamination, an RCT in the People's Republic of China studied a project which provided eyeglasses to high school students and found that glasses usage had also risen in some of the control group (Glewwe et al. 2009). Further inquiry revealed that the doctors performing the eye tests had glasses left over from the treatment group and had given them to students in the control areas—an example of self-contamination. The study used a matched-pair design and so was able to drop the pairs in which the control had been contaminated.

It is also important to check attrition—when participants of the study drop out from the sample between one data collection round and another—between the groups, as this can produce misleading results. For example, if fewer people in the control group provide outcome data than in the treatment group, this would skew the results as those participants who drop out are therefore excluded from the analysis.

In addition, it is critical to establish field monitoring and verification protocols when implementing an RCT, so as to understand potential misreporting incentivized by the presence of the intervention. There can be differential expectations among those treated and those untreated about the potential implications of responses when there is a perception that impact evaluators can offer or influence interventions. For example, untreated populations may believe that they can exaggerate problems so as to receive future treatment, or those treated may believe that they can get compensation if they report an intervention does not perform as stated. Triangulation of responses with direct observations and monitoring can help to mitigate these types of biases.

4.5 Reporting Randomized Controlled Trials

An RCT requires assurance of both the appropriateness of the assignment mechanism and the fidelity of randomization in order to guarantee the quality of the study. For this reason, it is important to provide sufficient detail when presenting the methodology and findings. It is also important to sufficiently describe the intervention being evaluated and the sampling strategy. In this description, it is essential to describe both the number of clusters and the number of households and/or individuals in the treatment group and the control group over time. The report should also include tables on balance checks (described above) and discuss whether there are any likely biases in the collected data.

When baseline data are available, the impact estimates can be reported using difference-in-differences analysis. Although it should not be necessary with random assignment, economists often estimate the impact with a regression model, which controls for remaining variation in observed covariates. The findings from the analysis can be reported for the entire sample, as well as for subgroups, to analyze heterogeneous effects.

As with all impact evaluation, attention should be paid to the effect size, not just its significance. The effect size could be used for further economic analysis, such as cost-effectiveness or cost–benefit analysis.

4.6 Working with Randomized Controlled Trials in Practice

Overcoming resistance to randomization

Randomization often meets with initial opposition from implementation teams. However, there are many reasons that randomization is both a good idea and not as onerous to projects as may be perceived.

1. The biggest selling point is that a **well-designed RCT tells the clearest causal story possible**. There is, by design, no link between beneficiary characteristics and intervention assignment. Any difference in outcomes must be because of the intervention, and not any underlying difference in treatment and control groups.

2. **RCTs are easy to analyze,** as results are driven by the difference in mean outcomes between treatment and control. That is easy to calculate and easy to present. There is no need for complex statistical

analysis. (Economists usually calculate the mean difference using a regression with control variables added, but it can readily be presented as a simple mean difference.)

3. **RCTs are a fair and transparent means of program assignment.** In a typical development program, intended beneficiaries and even agency staff may have little idea about how or why communities get chosen to benefit from the program. Random selection can improve fairness, compared with program placement that may be affected by political considerations or based on patronage networks. Transparent processes, such as public lotteries, may also be appreciated by beneficiaries as an improved means of participant selection.

4. **It is not necessary to have an untreated control group.** An RCT may have multiple treatment arms, at its simplest, comparing intervention A with intervention B, and where treatment B may be— as with many clinical trials—what is being done already. A factorial design adds an additional treatment arm that receives both A and B. This helps to answer the question of whether the two interventions work better together or separately.

5. **RCTs can lead to better targeting.** Randomization occurs across the eligible population, so the intervention is still targeted as planned. Since an RCT requires project staff to clearly identify and list the eligible population, it may result in better targeting than would have been achieved without this discipline.

6. **Randomization does not have to affect an entire project or program.** Once power calculations are performed, there will be an estimate of the size of the sample required for randomization. For a large program, it is likely that only a subset of the intended beneficiary population is required. The program managers can do what they like with the rest, which may well be the majority.

7. **Randomization does not necessarily mean large changes in program rollout:**

    (i)   Minor adjustments can be made to the eligibility criteria (a "raised threshold design") to yield a valid control group in a nonintrusive way. Oversubscription can be generated by adjusting the threshold. Participants are then selected at random, that is, by a lottery.

(ii) An encouragement design randomly assigns an encouragement to participate in the program, not the program itself. This will have no effect on how the program is run, and will in fact additionally yield useful information on increasing take-up of the program.

(iii) Finally, a pipeline RCT exploits the fact that the program is being rolled out over time and that there are almost certainly untreated members of the eligible population who can form a valid control group. The RCT therefore simply randomizes the order of the treatment.

8. **Well-designed RCTs can open the black box of how impact happens.** RCTs need not just focus on the "does it work question." They can also look at variations in intervention design to determine how to make it work better. Even when the causal chain of a program is too complex to unravel, RCTs can still offer insights on the conditions under which impacts occur.

Ten things that can go wrong with randomized controlled trials

Although using random assignment can provide valid impact estimates, it is necessary to guard against running expensive, unnecessary experiments. Here are 10 important things that may go wrong with RCTs. Many of these points apply to impact evaluations in general:

1. **Evaluating interventions where adoption/participation is far lower than expected.** Many impact evaluations fail because there is little or no take-up of the intervention. If only a small share of intended beneficiaries is interested in an intervention, impact evaluation may not be necessary. The funnel of attrition (discussed in Chapter 2) is a tool that can help to identify low take-up and assess whether it can be fixed. A diagnostic study before the impact evaluation can give information on facilitators of and barriers to participation.

2. **Researcher capture.** Researchers may be more interested in carrying out a study that produces an academic publication, rather than answering the evaluation questions of interest to program implementers. Typically, verification of behavioral economic theory offers the most prestigious publication possibilities for researchers. However, such a focus can take evaluation further from external validity or practical information demands of policy makers. If designed

by academics without knowledge of the field context, such studies may also contain critical design flaws. Chapter 8 has more discussion of researcher capture.

3. **Carrying out underpowered evaluations.** Studies are generally designed to have power of 80%, which means that one-fifth (20%) of the time that the intervention works, the study will fail to find that it does so. In reality, the actual power of many RCTs is only around 50%. In these cases, an RCT is no better than tossing a coin for correctly finding out if an intervention works. Even when power calculations are properly done, studies can be underpowered. Most often, this is because it is assumed that the project will have a much larger impact than it actually does, or that participation rates will be higher than actually occur. Power calculations are discussed in Chapter 7 and Technical Appendix 2.

4. **Getting the standard errors wrong.** Most RCTs are cluster RCTs in which random assignment is at a higher level than the unit at which outcomes are measured. For example, an intervention is randomly assigned to schools, but the outcome of interest is child learning. Or the intervention is randomly assigned to districts, but village-level outcomes are evaluated. The standard errors in these cases have to be adjusted for this clustering, which makes them larger and statistical significance more difficult to attain. Studies that do not adjust standard errors for clustering may incorrectly conclude that an impact is significant. If clustering is not taken into account in the sample size calculations, an underpowered study with too few clusters may be the result (discussed in Chapter 7).

5. **Not getting buy-in or sufficient oversight for randomization.** The idea of random allocation of a program remains anathema to many program implementers, as it can come at the expense of short-term efficiency. Random assignment may fail if the researchers miss getting the buy-in of a key agency for field implementation. In addition, for field staff, random assignment may appear counterintuitive and may create substantial additional work. For example, random assignment may imply that an easily accessed location needs to be bypassed in favor of a remote area, or that an interested, easy-to-engage population needs to be ignored in favor of a disinterested, difficult one. Without sufficient oversight or accountability, field staff will face strong incentives to deviate or manipulate the randomization protocol.

6. **Self-contamination.** Contamination occurs when the control group is exposed to the same intervention or another intervention that affects the same outcomes. Self-contamination occurs when the intervention or project itself causes the contamination. Such contamination may occur through spillovers, such as word of mouth in the case of information interventions. It could happen if the people in the control group use services in the treatment area. In addition, it can occur when staff from the implementing agency are left with unutilized resources from the project area, which they use for additional dissemination in control areas.

7. **Measuring the wrong outcomes.** The study may be well conducted but fail to influence intended audiences if it does not measure the impact on the outcomes they are interested in, or those which matter most to beneficiaries. A common reason that important outcomes are not measured is that unintended consequences, which should have ideally been captured in the theory of change, were ignored. Prior qualitative work at the evaluation design stage and engagement with policy makers, intended beneficiaries, and other key stakeholders can reduce the risks of this situation.

8. **Mistaking expectations for true intervention effects.** The expectation of an intervention may have effects, rather than the intervention itself, e.g., investments or changes in property prices in anticipation of new infrastructure. In the absence of a placebo, these expectation effects often cannot be fully separated out.

9. **Looking at the stars.** The "cult of significance" has a strong grip on the economics profession, with too much attention paid at times to statistical significance, and too little to the size and importance of the treatment effect coefficient. Hence, researchers can miss the fact that a very significant impact is actually really rather small in absolute terms and too little to be of interest to policy makers. Where there is a clear single outcome of the intervention, then cost-effectiveness is a good way of reporting impact, preferably in a table of comparisons with other interventions affecting the same outcome. Where researchers do examine cost-effectiveness, it may change the policy conclusion derived from focusing on statistical significance alone.

10. **Reporting biased findings.** Studies should report and discuss all estimated outcomes. Preferably, these outcomes should have been identified in the evaluation design stage. The design should also be

registered, for example in the International Initiative for Impact Evaluation's (3ie) Registry for International Development Impact Evaluations (http://www.3ieimpact.org/en/evaluation/ridie/). Many studies focus unduly on significant coefficients, often the positive ones, discounting "perverse" (negative) and insignificant results. There is an implicit bias, in that a failure to identify impact is not a determinate finding that there is no impact, and thus is inconclusive. Inconclusive results are difficult to publish in peer-reviewed literature and may meet substantial skepticism. Differential attrition between treated and control populations can also lead to unintentional bias.

4.7 Summary

RCTs provide a platform for development action to become integrated with research and for innovations to be systematically tested. There is no other approach that drives such a close integration of research and development, and this integration serves to improve both the evaluated intervention and the impact evaluation.

A key advantage of RCTs is the strength of the identification strategy, which ensures balance on observables and unobservables. This makes them easy to explain to policy makers. A key difficulty may be the opposition to randomization which may be encountered, despite the fact that objections are readily countered, which may compromise the integrity of design. Ensuring fidelity of implementation is also a key challenge, so that implementation of the project in areas with random assignment may require additional oversight.

There are many possible RCT designs, so it will often be possible to find one to suit at least some component of an intervention. For infrastructure interventions many of these possibilities will involve second generation questions, for example, around maintenance or inspection, rather than the first generation "does it work" question.

References*

Glennerster, R. 2017. The Practicalities of Running Randomized Evaluations: Partnerships, Measurement, Ethics, and Transparency. In E. Duflo and A. Banerjee, eds. *Handbook of Field Experiments*. Volume 1, 1st Edition. Amsterdam: North Holland.

Glewwe, P., A. Park, and M. Zhao. 2009. Visualizing Development: Eyeglasses and Academic Performance in Rural Primary Schools in China. Working Paper No. 12–2. Center for International Food and Agricultural Policy, University of Minnesota. http://purl.umn.edu/120032.

Imai, K., G. King, and C. Nall. 2009. The Essential Role of Pair Matching in Cluster-Randomized Experiments, with Application to the Mexican Universal Health Insurance Evaluation. *Statistical Science*. 24. pp. 29–53.

Imai, K., G. King, and E. Stuart. 2008. Misunderstandings among Experimentalists and Observationalists about Causal Inference. *Journal of the Royal Statistical Society: Series* A. 171. pp. 481–502.

Kim, J. and W. Shin. 2014. How to Do Random Allocation (Randomization). *Clinics in Orthopedic Surgery*. 6 (1). pp. 103–109. https://doi.org/10.4055/cios.2014.6.1.103.

White, H. 2013. An Introduction to the Use of Randomised Control Trials to Evaluate Development Interventions. *Journal of Development Effectiveness*. 5 (1). pp. 30–49.

World Bank. 2014. Philippines Conditional Cash Transfer Program: Impact Evaluation 2012. Report Number 75533-PH. Washington, DC.

Further Reading

Bloom, H. S. 2006. The Core Analytics of Randomized Experiments for Social Research. MDRC Working Papers on Research Methodology. New York. http://www.mdrc.org/sites/default/files/full_533.pdf.

Duflo, E., R. Glennerster, and M. Kremer. 2006. Using Randomization in Development Economics Research: A Toolkit. NBER Technical Working Paper Series. No. 333. http://www.nber.org/papers/t0333.pdf.

King, G., R. Nielsen, C. Coberley, J. E. Pope, and A. Wells. 2011. Avoiding Randomization Failure in Program Evaluation. *Population Health Management*. 14 (1). pp. S11–S22. http://j.mp/2oTEZI6.

Riecken, H. W., R. F. Boruch, D. T. Campbell, N. Caplan, T. K. Glennan, Jr., J. W. Pratt, A. Rees, and W. Williams. 1974. The Purposes of Social Experimentation. *Educational Researcher*. 3 (11). pp. 5–9. https://www.jstor.org/stable/1175978.

---

* ADB recognizes "China" as the People's Republic of China.

Chapter 5
Nonexperimental Designs

Key Messages

- Rigorous impact evaluation can often still be conducted even when randomized controlled trials are not possible.

- It substantially strengthens impact evaluation designs to have data from before and after an intervention for populations that are treated and those that are not treated.

- Nonexperimental methods rely on conceptualizing how interventions have been assigned and understanding what variables serve as predictors of treatment.

- In addition, most nonexperimental methods require data on other determinants of outcomes than the intervention of interest.

- All nonexperimental designs rely on conditioning assumptions. Those assumptions can be minimized in cases where there is a clear rule or factor conditioning eligibility at a sharp cutoff, and baseline data are present.

- As different methods give estimates valid for different populations, care is needed in interpretation of nonexperimental findings.

5.1 Introduction

Random assignment is often not an option for practical reasons. For example, implementing agencies may not be willing to accept randomization. Networked infrastructure may not be possible to effectively roll out in a random sequence. Large investment projects may not be able to be altered in location or sequencing. Or interest in the impact evaluation may have arisen only after the program is already under way or even completed. When randomization is not possible, impact often can still be estimated through a range of nonexperimental designs.

Nonexperimental methods may be broadly divided into two categories:

- *Quasi-experimental methods* form a comparison group by statistical methods, rather than by random assignment. These approaches include propensity score matching, difference-in-differences (DiD), synthetic controls, and regression discontinuity designs. All these approaches seek to establish a comparison group that is as similar to the treatment groups as possible. That is, treatment and comparison groups are balanced, meaning that the average values of observable characteristics are approximately the same. Impact is then calculated as either the difference in outcomes after the intervention (*ex post* single difference), or the difference in the differences in outcomes between baseline and endline (DiD). To improve control of selection bias, differencing may be combined with some form of matching.

- *Regression-based approaches* do not establish an explicit comparison group, though the data have to include observations on untreated or less treated units. These approaches include instrumental variables (often estimated as two-stage least squares), endogenous treatment models, endogenous switching regressions, and fixed effects models, which combine differences in differences with a structural model. Regression-based approaches are based on specifying the underlying structural model, that is, the set of behavioral relationships which lead to program impact. This structural model embodies the theory of change. Hence, estimation of the parameters of the model can be a useful part of causal chain analysis. Regression-based approaches are usually the only option if treatment is continuous (changes in quantity/level), rather than binary (treated versus untreated).[1]

Selection and design of these approaches require a good understanding of intervention design, in particular program placement. Key program placement questions include the following:

1. What procedures and criteria were used to select project/intervention areas?

2. If there is self-selection into the program, what are the likely characteristics that determine participation?

---

[1] Many interventions that initially appear to be dichotomous may actually be continuous, because the degree of treatment varies within the treated population. For example, road infrastructure will have different effects on travel times and cost, depending on a household's distance down the road.

3. Is either program placement or self-selection likely to be a function of variables which are both unobservable and correlated with the outcomes of interest?

Nonexperimental approaches require data from both treated and untreated populations. Data from the latter are used to form comparisons. Since not all untreated observations will be suitable for comparison, larger sample sizes are generally required than in the case of randomized controlled trials (RCTs). Stronger designs that lead to more reliable impact estimates, are usually possible if baseline data are available, since baseline data (i) allow calculation of DiD estimates rather than *ex post* single difference; and (ii) variables used for matching must be unaffected by the intervention, which is by definition the case for data collected before the intervention.[2] The subsequent sections introduce major techniques, which are described more technically and introduced in STATA in Appendix 1.

5.2 Difference-in-Differences Estimates

The method in brief

DiD estimates are based on the difference in the changes in the outcome between treatment and comparison groups over time. Fixed effects models combine differencing with multivariate models that can account for differences in observed variables over time.

Description of the method

The method takes the trajectory of the comparison group as the counterfactual trajectory for the treatment group. That is, the change in the outcome that takes place in the comparison group is taken as what would have happened to the treatment group in the absence of the intervention. Therefore, subtracting the change in the outcome observed in the comparison group from that observed in the treatment group gives the measure of impact. The effects of all factors that do not change over time or that do not affect changes over time are thereby eliminated from the impact estimate. Many determinants of program placement or participation can be expected to be rather time invariant, hence the attractiveness of this approach.

---

[2] A caveat is that if there are expectation effects created by the intervention, then these may affect baseline values. For example, people may adjust savings or investment behavior if they know they will be receiving access to microfinance in the near future.

Ex post single difference (SD) impact estimators are the difference between the indicator (Y) (usually an outcome) after the intervention (i.e., at endline = time E) for a group with the intervention (Y^1), compared with the indicator for a comparison group without the intervention (Y^0), which is the formula given as equation (5.1). That is as follows.

$$SD = Y_E^1 - Y_E^0 \qquad (5.1)$$

The DiD, or double difference, impact estimate is the difference between the changes over time for the two groups (Figure 5.1). In other words, it is based on subtracting the changes from baseline (before intervention) to endline (after intervention) for the comparison group from the changes from baseline to endline for the treated group:

$$DiD = (Y_E^1 - Y_B^1) - (Y_E^0 - Y_B^0) \qquad (5.2)$$

Figure 5.1: Illustration of Difference-in-Differences

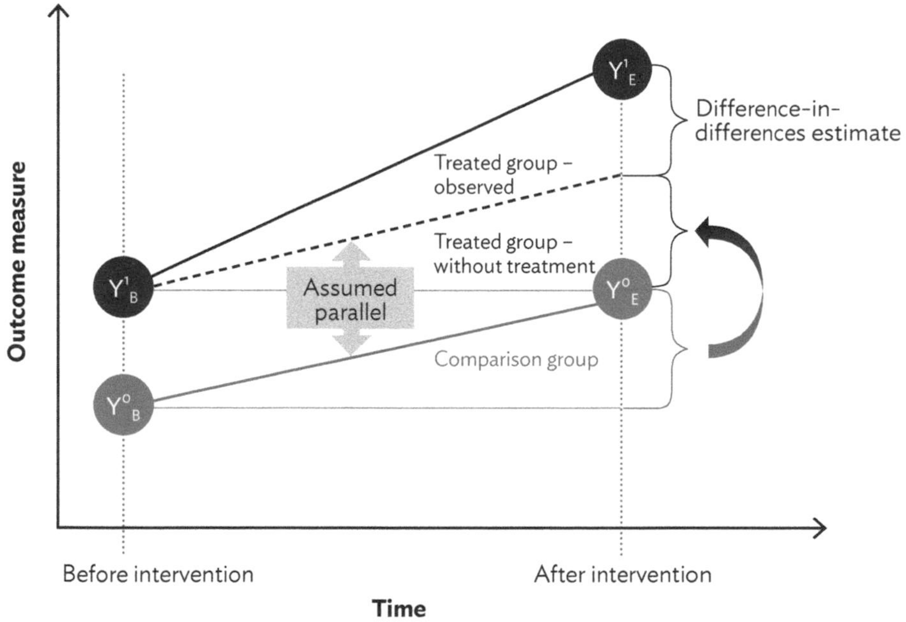

Source: Authors.

DiD removes any difference in the indicator between treatment and comparison groups which was present at baseline, and this is useful because these differences are obviously not a result of the intervention. It also removes the effects of general trends affecting both treated and comparison observations.

It is readily apparent that if the treated and comparison group values of the indicator are the same at baseline ($Y_B^1 = Y_B^0$) then the single and double difference estimates are equivalent, as the Y_B^1 and Y_B^0 terms cancel out in equation (5.2). However, even if the treated and comparison group estimates of the baseline value are sample estimates from the same underlying population, it may not be fully the case that $Y_B^1 = Y_B^0$ due to sampling error.

DiD estimates require baseline data. Baseline data should be collected immediately before the intervention. However, if project funding is being used for the baseline then this is often not possible. In practice, that often does not matter, as what is needed are baseline data before the program affects the intended beneficiary population, and there is often a 6–12 month project start-up period before there are any activities at field level, so the baseline can be conducted in this period.

Calculating impact: an example

Table 5.1 shows data from an impact evaluation of the Viet Nam Rural Transport Project which constructed and rehabilitated 5,000 kilometers of rural roads between 1997 and 2001 in communes in 18 provinces across Viet Nam. The table shows measures of market development in Viet Nam, as measured by commune-level averages, for treatment and comparison communes before and after the road construction or rehabilitation.

Table 5.1: Impact of Rural Roads on Market Development in Viet Nam
(commune level averages)

| | 1997 | | 2003 | | |
	Project	Non-Project	Project	Non-Project	Difference-in-Differences
Market	0.51	0.44	0.62	0.46	0.09
Market frequency	1.13	1.05	1.43	1.16	0.19
Shop	0.63	0.59	0.84	0.77	0.03
Pharmacy	0.62	0.58	0.69	0.52	0.13

Source: Mu and Van de Walle (2011).

The single difference estimate is the difference in commune-level averages of market development variables between communes with improved rural roads and those without them. For example, the proportion of communes by a rural road with their own market rose from 11% (from 0.51 to 0.62) compared with a 2% rise in villages without an improved road (0.44 to 0.46). This means that the DiD impact estimate is (0.62-0.51)–(0.46-0.44) = 0.11-0.02 = 0.09 (9%). DiD removes the initial difference in market development between treatment and comparison group. The *ex post* single difference does not do this, and so would overestimate program impact (0.62–0.46 = 0.16 or 16%).

DiD provides an unbiased estimate of program impact if the "parallel trends" assumption holds, which is the assumption that the outcome variable follows the same trajectory over time in treatment and comparison groups without the intervention. The parallel trends assumption can be tested with pre-intervention data if they are available, though this test only lends support to the assumption rather than demonstrates that it is valid. The assumption is more likely to hold if a matching method, such as propensity score matching (described in section 5.4), has been used to control for observable causes of differences in trajectory.

Fixed effects models combine DiD approaches with multivariate regression. This allows for control of other factors which may be influencing the outcome, to give a stronger estimate than the simple DiD of mean outcomes. By including observable changes in covariates over time in the regression, the parallel trends assumption is reduced to only unobservable factors.

What is needed for difference-in-differences?

Implementation of the method requires data on outcomes from the treatment and comparison groups at baseline and endline. Data are preferably available on the outcome pre-intervention to test the parallel trends assumption. If matching is to be used, then data for matching are also required, and if a fixed effects model is applied, other determinants of outcomes should be characterized by data as well. Simple DiD models may be specified in STATA using "regress" with appropriate dummy variables for time, treatment, and treatment by time interaction terms, as discussed in Appendix 1, section 3.2. Fixed effects models may be specified in STATA using "xtreg", as described in Appendix 1, section 3.3.

Advantages and disadvantages of difference-in-differences

DiD is easy to implement and easy to understand. Yet, data are usually not available to test model validity. Hence, it is more rigorous to use with a matching technique or to apply a fixed effects model, which can control better for observable confounders. The model generates an average treatment effect on the treated (ATT), which is useful for understanding effects on those already participating, but is not a measure of the effects of the intervention on the overall population.

5.3 Synthetic Controls

The method in brief

Synthetic controls build on the concepts of difference-in-differences approaches, in that the difference in trends between the outcome and comparison group observations provides the estimate of impact (Abadie et al. 2010). However, synthetic controls relax the parallel trends assumption and build the control by weighting the comparison group observations such that trends in covariates and outcomes of the synthetic control match those of treatment prior to the intervention.

Description of the method

Under this method, a panel regression of outcomes on covariates (excluding treatment) is conducted, and a binary variable indicating the treatment status of individual observations is specified. An optimization procedure is conducted to identify weights for individual comparison group observations, such that the weighted synthetic control trends in covariates and outcomes match those of the treated units prior to treatment as closely as possible. Application of these weights to the comparison group observations during the treatment period allows for a synthetic control, or counterfactual that can be compared with the actual trend of treated groups.

Statistical significance is not tested under this method in the conventional manner. Instead, placebo-test simulations are conducted based on the distribution of observations for variables in the synthetic control, and the probability distribution of modeled outcomes is used to infer a p-value.

What is needed for synthetic controls?

Synthetic controls are only applicable to panel data, in which treatment is binary and treatment applies only to the latter time periods of observations. The STATA package "synth_runner" enables automated application (Quistorff and Galiani 2017), as discussed in Appendix 1, section 4.1. Current techniques only apply to completely balanced panels, but methods for unbalanced panels are under development. Like DiD, there must be untreated units still in the final observation periods. Unlike conventional approaches, synthetic controls do not need many treated observations, so they can be applicable to small-n interventions, such as large infrastructure. However, it does need a sequence of observations prior to treatment, so as to make the weighting match the time dynamics of the synthetic control to the treated units.

Advantages and disadvantages of synthetic controls

The main advantages of synthetic controls are as follows: (i) they allow for treatment effect estimation even when the number of treated units is small; and (ii) bias is reduced when the "parallel trends" assumption underpinning DiD do not hold. The disadvantages are that the technique is less efficient than DiD when the parallel trend assumption is valid, and that the technique is only applicable in existing statistical packages when relatively specific data requirements are met (balanced panels with long periods of pre-treatment observations and treatment that is binary). Care is also needed to ensure that the comparison units considered do not include observations with confounding developments over time. The lack of traditional statistical significance tests may also make interpretation of results confusing for policy audiences. Like DiD, this method generates an ATT.

5.4 Propensity Score Matching

The method in brief

The propensity score is the estimated probability of being in the treatment group given the observable characteristics from a regression model of participation (Rosenbaum and Rubin 1983). Estimated propensity scores can be used to underpin a range of impact evaluation methods, including propensity score matching (PSM), the most common technique; weighting estimators; and weighted regressions. PSM creates a comparison group from untreated observations by matching treatment observations to one or more observations from the untreated sample, based on observable characteristics. Treated units are matched to untreated units with a similar propensity score. Propensity score approaches cannot incorporate selection on unobservables, so they may give biased estimates if these are important.

Description of the method

Perfect matching would require matching each individual or unit in the treatment group with a person or unit in the comparison group that is identical on all relevant observable characteristics, such as age, education, religion, occupation, wealth, attitudes to risk, and so on. Clearly, this is not possible. But nor is it necessary. Balance requires that the average characteristics of the treatment and comparison groups are the same prior to the intervention. Although individual one-on-one matching would achieve that, it is not practical. However, there are other matching methods that are practical and do ensure balance, of which one of the most common approaches is propensity score matching. In propensity score matching, matching is not on every single characteristic but on a single number: the propensity score.

The propensity score is a conditional probability. More specifically, it is the likelihood of a person or unit taking part in the intervention given their observable characteristics. This probability is obtained from the "participation equation": a probit or logit regression in which the dependent variable is dichotomous, taking the value of 1 for those who took part in the intervention, and 0 if they did not. The explanatory variables include all observed variables (individual, household or firm, and community or market) that may affect participation, but that are not affected by the intervention. Baseline values of all variables, including outcomes, cannot be affected by the intervention, so having baseline data helps to obtain a stronger match. A recent innovation is the *covariate balancing propensity score*, which applies weighting to propensity score estimates to ensure that covariates are more fully balanced before the propensity scores are applied in matching (Imai and Ratkovic 2014).

As the analysis does not concern the significance of the individual coefficients, all variables for which there are data can be included in the participation equation, provided they meet the criterion of not being affected by the intervention. That is, multicollinearity is not a concern in the participation equation, if it is estimated using a conventional propensity score. For example, in Jalan and Ravallion (2001) the analysis of piped water in India has 90 independent variables in the participation equation: 15 state-level dummies, 20 village-level variables, and 55 household-level variables (Table 5.2). However, covariate balancing propensity scores will need to be more selective in variables used, so that balancing can be achieved.

An individual's propensity score is the fitted value from the participation equation. Having calculated the propensity scores for all observations, the region of common support is identified. Observations in the untreated observations with a propensity score lower than the lowest observed value in the treatment group are outside of common support, and are unused. Similarly, observations in the treatment group with a propensity score higher than the highest observed value in the untreated group are not used. Those observations that are retained from the untreated group form the comparison group.

Table 5.2: Example of Independent Variables in the Participation Equation for Propensity Score Matching

Level	Variables
State	State-level dummy
Village	Village size (log), Proportion of gross cropped area which is irrigated, Whether village has a day care center, Whether village has a primary school, Whether village has a middle school, Whether village has a high school, Female-to-male students in the village, Female-to-male students for minority groups, Main approachable road to village, Whether bus stop is within the village, Whether railway station is within the village, Whether there is a post office within the village, Whether the village has a telephone facility, Whether there is a community TV center in the village, Whether there is a library in the village, Whether there is a bank in the village, Whether there is a market in the village, Student–teacher ratio in the village
Household	Whether household belongs to the Scheduled Tribe, Whether household belongs to the Scheduled Caste, Whether it is a Hindu household, Whether it is a Muslim household, Whether it is a Christian household, Whether it is a Sikh household, Household size. Utilization of landholdings used for cultivation, Whether the house belongs to the household, Whether the household owns other property, Whether the household has a bicycle, Whether the household has a sewing machine, Whether the household owns a thresher, Whether the household owns a winnower, Whether the household owns a bullock cart, Whether the household owns a radio, Whether the household owns a TV, Whether the household owns a fan, Whether the household owns any livestock, Nature of house, Condition of house, Rooms in house, Whether household has a separate kitchen, Whether the kitchen is ventilated, Whether the household has electricity, Occupation of the head, Whether male members listen to radio, Whether female members listen to radio, Whether male members watch TV, Whether female members watch TV, Whether male members read newspapers, Whether female members read newspapers, Proportion of household members who are 60+, Proportion of females among adults, Proportion of males among children, Proportion of females among children, Sex of household head, Household head marital status, Household head education, Whether household head is higher secondary, Gross cropped area, Gross irrigated area, Landholding size

Source: Jalan and Ravallion (2001).

Figure 5.2 shows a typical distribution of propensity scores. The distribution for the treatment group is "to the right" of that of the untreated group, that is, treatment group individuals tend to have higher propensity scores than those in the untreated group. No member of the treatment group has a propensity score of less than 0.3, and no member of the untreated group has a propensity score of more than 0.8. So, in establishing the region of common support, the 39% of untreated group observations with a propensity score from 0 to 0.3, and the 19% of the treatment observations with a propensity score of 0.8–1.0 are not used. (In practice, this would use a more precise cutoff, rather than that shown by the categorical classification of the data.)

Figure 5.2: Example of Distribution of Propensity Scores

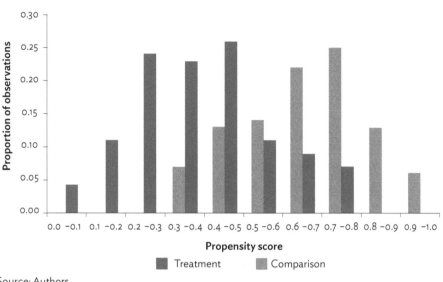

Source: Authors.

Each member of the treatment group is matched to one or more members of the comparison group. Nearest neighbor matching matches the treatment individual to the comparison group individual with the nearest propensity score. It is more usual to match to more than one neighbor, such as the nearest five. Caliper matching matches to all comparison group observations within a certain "distance" (i.e., up to a maximum difference in propensity scores) and kernel matching matches to all comparison observations in the region of common support with a weight inversely proportional to distance. A single observation in the comparison group may be matched to several different observations in the treatment group. Those members of the comparison group that do not match those treated are discarded.

Once the matching is done, a test is performed for balance by comparing the mean characteristics of treatment and comparison groups. There should be no significant differences in average characteristics between the two groups.

After matching, the differences between the two groups are reduced. This convergence of characteristics is also captured in the propensity score, as this figure is a weighted average of these characteristics. In the propensity score matching analysis of piped water in India in Jalan and Ravallion (2001), the average propensity score in the treatment and comparison groups was 0.5495 and 0.1933, respectively, before matching; and 0.3743 and 0.3742 after matching.

Finally, the impact estimate—either single or double difference—is calculated by first calculating the difference in between the indicator for the treatment individual and the average value for the matched comparison individuals; and second, by averaging over all these differences. For example, if matching to the nearest five neighbors (the equation is for single difference):

$$IMPACT = \frac{1}{n} \sum_{i=1}^{n} \left(Y_{1,t+1,i} - \frac{1}{5} \sum_{j=1}^{5} Y_{0,t+1,i,j} \right) \qquad (5.3)$$

Table 5.3 shows a numerical example, using data on learning outcomes for grade-6 students on a standardized test. Column 1 shows the test score for individual i from the treatment group, and columns 4–8 those for the nearest five neighbors. The average score for the five neighbors is shown in column 2, and the difference in test scores for the treatment individual and their nearest neighbors is shown in column 3.

Table 5.3: Calculation of the Propensity Score Impact Estimate: Example Using Test Score Data

Obs (i)	Y_{1i} (1)	$Y_{0i(ave)}$ (2)	$Y_{1i}-Y_{0i(ave)}$ (3)	$Y_{0i(1)}$ (4)	$Y_{0i(2)}$ (5)	$Y_{0i(3)}$ (6)	$Y_{0i(4)}$ (7)	$Y_{0i(5)}$ (8)
1	48.2	42.4	5.8	44.1	45.1	43.8	43.2	35.8
2	50.2	42.6	7.6	42.1	45.2	48.1	38.4	39.3
3	50.6	43.1	7.5	40.8	43.7	45.3	44.1	41.8
4	48.1	38.9	9.1	43.6	35.6	36.9	41.4	37.2
5	69.0	59.7	9.3	55.6	57.6	57.1	62.4	65.8
...	...	...	...	...	...	...	...	...
199	58.6	52.2	6.4	55.5	48.2	54.7	53.4	49.1
200	45.4	39.3	6.1	41.2	39.1	38.7	40.1	37.5
Ave.	52.9	45.5	7.4					

... = intermediate rows omitted for presentation purposes.
Source: Authors.

What is needed to conduct propensity score matching?

Propensity score matching requires data from both a treatment group and an untreated group, from which the comparison group is drawn. The data should include community, household, and individual characteristics that determine program participation from both program placement and self-selection. Both samples need to be larger than the sample size suggested by simple power calculations, since observations outside the region of common support are discarded. In practice, the researcher does not need to perform the above steps manually. Statistical packages have a single command to conduct the analysis, such as the "teffects" followed by "psm" command in STATA, which is discussed in Appendix 1, section 5.2.

Advantages and disadvantages of propensity score matching

The two main advantages of propensity score matching are that it is always possible for a binary treatment if sufficient data are available (and so can be seen as a "method of last resort"), and that it can be done *ex post*, including in the absence of baseline data. If baseline data are not available, matching can be done on time invariant characteristics, such as sex and religion, and recall on pre-intervention characteristics that can be reliably recalled, such as education of household head and ownership of major assets. PSM can also generate an ATT and an average treatment effect (ATE) that is valid for the overall population.

The drawback is that PSM relies upon matching on observables. If selection (participation) is affected by unobservables, PSM will yield biased impact estimates for *ex post* single difference estimates. Some empiricists argue that the application of PSM may actually exacerbate the effects of unobservables, as the comparison observations utilized have participation behavior that more defies what observables suggest (King and Nielsen 2016).

5.5 Propensity Score Weighting and Double Robust Techniques

The method in brief

Matching is only one form of application of the propensity score. The propensity score can also be applied in weighting of observations, so as to achieve covariate balance between treated and untreated observations (Lunceford and Davidian 2004). The simplest approach, termed "inverse probability weighting" (IPW), calculates the difference in the weighted average of individual values of the dependent variable for treated and untreated observations. More details on this method are presented in Appendix 1, section 5.3.

Weighting can be combined with regression techniques when there is a known relationship between covariates and outcomes. Moreover, that combination of weighting and outcome regression can be done in a manner that is "double robust," so that an unbiased ATE is estimated if either the propensity score regression or outcome regression is correctly specified. The technical term for a leading form of double robust techniques is *augmented inverse probability weighted regression*.

Description of the method

Double robust regression consists of a propensity score model and a switching outcome regression of the dependent variable against independent variables conditioning it. The outcome regression is switching, in that it is separately estimated for treated and untreated observations. Inverse probability weights are calculated from the propensity score and are used in combination with predicted values from the two outcome equations to generate a weighted average that represents the ATE.

What is needed to conduct double robust regression?

The double robust technique has the same general requirements as PSM, and can be used with the same types of data. It can be called by "teffects" in STATA, with the option "aipw" as described in Appendix 1, section 5.4. However, this technique requires that those variables that condition outcomes be identified in a structural relationship. Generally, all variables in the outcome equation should appear in the propensity score model, but the propensity score model can (although it need not) include additional determinants of participation that do not directly affect outcomes.

Advantages and disadvantages of double robust regression

Double robust regression is less prone to specification error or bias than PSM, as it provides two opportunities for specifying relationships appropriately. The disadvantage is that the method can only estimate an ATE. IPW can estimate an ATT but does not gain the double robust property of less sensitivity to specification. Both techniques, like PSM, cannot account for selection on unobservables. Yet, where an ATE is of interest and variables conditioning outcomes can be identified in a structural model, double robust regression offers advantages of allowing multiple possibilities to avoid bias.

5.6 Regression Discontinuity Design and Interrupted Time Series

The method in brief

Regression discontinuity design (RDD) is used when there is a threshold rule for program eligibility, such as the poverty line; villages either side of an administrative boundary; or a score used to rank potential subprojects (Thistlewaite and Campbell 1960). The assumption, which is tested as part of the procedure, is that units in proximity to either side of the boundary are sufficiently similar for those excluded from the program to be a valid comparison group.

The difference in outcomes between those near either side of the boundary, as measured by the discontinuity in the regression line at that point, is attributable to the program, and so is the measure of impact.

Interrupted time series (ITS) is a specific application of RDD in which the threshold is the point in time at which the program came into effect (Sween and Campbell 1965). This can be a particularly relevant method where intervention effectiveness is sudden, rather than gradual, such as the completion of a bridge or major power transmission connection.

Description of the method

RDD can be used when there is a threshold rule which determines eligibility for the program and where the threshold is based on a continuous *assignment variable* assessed for all potentially eligible units of assignment (individuals, households, firms, etc.)—for example, households above or below the poverty line, firms above or below a certain credit rating, students above a certain test score who are awarded a scholarship, or women above or below a certain age for a health program. If the threshold is imperfectly applied, a variation on the approach, called *fuzzy RDD*, can be used. The assignment variable must not be one which can be manipulated to become eligible for the program, as that would open the door to selection bias.

In the case of ITS, the threshold is the point in time at which the policy or program was introduced. In the case of a policy, e.g., telecoms deregulation, this point in time is common to all households. But other interventions, e.g., electrification or connection to a sewage disposal system, may affect different communities at different points in time.

The threshold should be unique to the program. In India, for example, official "Below Poverty Line" status is used as an eligibility criterion for many programs. In such a case, RDD cannot disentangle the effect of a specific program using the "Below Poverty Line" threshold in areas where other programs use the same threshold. Similarly, people become eligible for a pension once they reach retirement age. However, they also stop working, so it is not possible for RDD to separate the effects of the pension and retirement on many outcomes such as health outcomes, which are plausibly affected by both events.

This situation arose in the ADB-supported evaluation of the Mongolia Food Stamps Program (ADB 2014). The same proxy means test (PMT), with the same threshold, was used as the eligibility criterion for both Food Stamps Program and the Medicard program. Hence, as stated in the report, "as both programs were administered according to this identical eligibility criterion (PMT assessment), and there is therefore perfect overlap in the treatment selection, it is not technically possible for an impact evaluation to disentangle the effects of the two programs. As a consequence, any impact found must be considered as the 'combined impact' of both programs."

Clearly, those above and below the threshold have some differences. In addition, the threshold criterion may be correlated with the outcome, so that there is selection bias if simple comparisons are made. For example, scholarships are awarded to improve learning outcomes, but those with better learning outcomes are picked to be in the program. Older women are more likely to get breast cancer, and it is older women who are selected for screening.

However, those very near either side of the threshold are much more similar. For example, students with a test score of 58.0–59.9, who are not selected for a scholarship with an eligibility threshold of 60.0, are not very different to those getting 60.0–60.9 who were accepted. In many cases, the differences between these two groups may be more attributable to measurement error than other factors. Regression discontinuity is based on a comparison of the difference in average outcomes for these two groups.

In the case of ITS, it is accepted that other factors are affecting outcomes of interest. Even so, those other factors will not be playing so much of a role over time periods immediately on each side of the time an intervention is introduced, as they will not change much in such a short period.

An iterative approach is used to determine the margin around the eligibility threshold. Initially, one sets a small margin and checks for balance of the resulting treatment and comparison groups. If the match is close, the margin may be widened a little and balance checked again. This can be repeated until the samples start to become dissimilar. Although balancing is done on observables, if the eligibility criterion is enforced and participation for the eligible population is widespread, there is no reason to expect imbalance on unobservables.

Once the sample is established, a regression line is fitted to the sample around the threshold (Figure 5.3).[3] The sample for the regression is restricted to observations just either side of the threshold, via one or more bandwidths (Table 5.4 provides an example). Specifically, the outcome indicator is

---

[3]   To keep this exposition simple, it is assumed that there is a linear relationship. In practice a nonlinear form is tested, since assuming linearity may give the impression of a discontinuity which is not in fact there. However, testing more complex functional forms may require using the whole sample, thus giving weight to observations away from the cutoff.

Figure 5.3: Example of Regression Discontinuity Around Eligibility Threshold of Assignment Variable

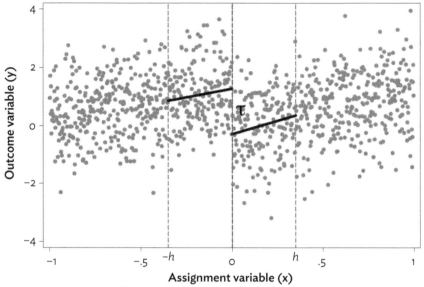

τ = local average treatment effect.
Source: Orbeta et al. 2014.

Table 5.4: Regression Discontinuity Annual Per Capita Expenditure Impact Estimates from the Impact Evaluation of the Philippines' Conditional Cash Transfer Program Pantawid Pamilya,
(2013 Philippine Pesos)

Outcomes		CCT	Bandwidth IK	Sampling
Education (per school-aged children 3–20 years old)	Impact	206.61**	200.56**	77.67
	Standard error	70.51	55.32	50.50
	Non-Pantawid mean	251.82	230.48	252.49
	Observations	1,402	2,018	2,939
Medical items	Impact	14.67	14.42*	14.60**
	Standard error	8.13	6.912	5.50
	Non-Pantawid mean	35.34	34.56	34.37
	Observations	1,789	2,100	3,107
Clothing and footwear	Impact	75.28**	73.41**	44.27**
	Standard error	25.63	24.93	17.12
	Non-Pantawid mean	91.52	95.9	107.01
	Observations	1,351	1,453	3,108

* denotes significant at 10% level, ** denotes significant at 5% level, CCT = conditional cash transfer.
Note: Bandwidths refer to optimal bandwidths as proposed in Imbens and Kalyanaraman (2012), termed IK; and Calonico, Cattaneo, and Titiunik (2014a), termed CCT; and the sampling bandwidth as estimated in Grover (2013).
Source: Orbeta et al. (2014).

regressed on the assignment variable, e.g., PMT scores and an intercept dummy. The intercept dummy is a dichotomous variable which takes the value 0 for observations below the threshold and 1 at the threshold and above it. A slope dummy may also be included, that is an interactive term which is the product of the intercept dummy and the assignment variable.

When the threshold is imperfectly applied (a *fuzzy RDD*), a two-stage instrumental variable approach is used (described in section 5.7). The first stage is to regress participation on the assignment variable and calculate the fitted values. In the second stage, the fitted values from the first stage are used in the outcome regression in place of the assignment variable.

What is needed for regression discontinuity design?

Data are required on the assignment variable and the outcome indicator for sufficient numbers of those considered for the program, including those who were accepted and rejected. Data on other variables can be useful for verifying balance across the threshold, and this balance verification can be further strengthened by a baseline survey, which ensures that the covariates are not affected by the program. Many programs do not keep information on those they do not accept, which can make RDD more difficult to apply. Information is needed on how strictly the threshold rule has been applied, but this fact should be apparent from the data. The technique can be implemented in the STATA package "rdrobust" (Calonico et al. 2014b), as described in Appendix 1, section 7.1.

Advantages and disadvantages of regression discontinuity design

RDD more completely controls unobservables than other quasi-experimental matching methods. It can also utilize administrative data to a large extent, thus reducing the need for data collection, though the outcome data for the rejected applicants may need to be collected.

The limits of the technique are that there needs to have been clear assignment criteria and sufficient samples for the analysis. A challenge for RDD is often to have sufficient observations either side of the threshold. The Mongolia Food Stamps Program study collected data from a purposive sample around the PMT threshold to avoid this problem.

A further limitation is that the impact is estimated only for the population close to the threshold. The estimate is called a local average treatment effect (LATE), rather than an average treatment effect for the whole treated population. In principle, this limitation restricts the external validity of the approach. Still, it may be argued that LATE gives information on the effect at the margin of eligibility, and thus is a good proxy for what would be expected if the program were expanded.

5.7 Instrumental Variables

The method in brief

In traditional ordinary least squares (OLS) regression, the outcome may be regressed on either an intervention dummy or a measure of participation in the intervention, such as duration of training attended or distance to a road. Under certain conditions, including that participation is driven by observable measured characteristics, ordinary least squares will be unbiased. However, the presence of selection on unobservables means there will be endogeneity in the estimates from such an approach. To correct this, instrumental variables (IV) are used to obtain consistent estimates by using one or more variables that affect treatment, but not outcomes, as a proxy for the intervention (Reiersol 1945). Natural experiments (discussed in Chapter 3) are the ideal conditions for the application of IV methods, as the exogenous condition determining access to the intervention becomes the instrument.

Description of the method

In the traditional simple OLS approach for dichotomous treatments, the outcome is regressed on a dummy variable for participation W (W=1 for treatment group and W=0 for comparison), along with other variables which affect the outcome. The coefficient on W is the measure of impact.

The problem with this approach is that selection bias can cause the estimate of the impact coefficient to be biased. If selection is entirely on observables, and the regression has included variables on all those observables, then OLS will indeed yield a valid impact estimate. This can rarely be assumed to be the case.

If the unobservables are time invariant, then differencing removes their effect, so estimating the impact equation using differences will be unbiased. However, if there are time-varying unobservables, difference-in-differences will also yield biased impact estimates. Instrumental variable estimation can be a technique to remove the bias.

Instrumental variable estimation is a regression in which the variable which is the source of the endogeneity problem (i.e., W because of selection bias) is replaced by an *instrument* (Z). This instrument has to satisfy two conditions:

1. It is correlated with W (termed "relevance").

2. It is not correlated with the outcome (Y), except through its effect on W; i.e., there is no direct relationship between Z and Y (termed the "exclusion restriction").

A simple example might be an instrument for the effect of smoking on lung cancer. Those who smoke may have other characteristics that differ from those who do not, such as exercise or other risk taking, so that a direct regression on smoking is biased. Yet, taxation of cigarettes affects smoking, but does not affect lung cancer other than through effects on smoking, so that it can be used as an instrument for the effect of smoking. As another example, the impact of electricity access on households was estimated by using the distances from electricity poles as an instrument. Proximity to electricity poles determines the electricity connection fee in Bangladesh, but does not condition outcomes directly, as poorer households tend to be closer to the poles (Box 5.1).

Box 5.1: Using Instrumental Variables to Measure the Impact of Electrification on Rural Households

Electricity generation, transmission, and distribution is one of the largest foci of development expenditures. Yet, there is relatively scant evidence as to the benefits of such interventions for poor rural households. One of the biggest challenges is that only wealthier households can afford electricity connections, so that causal relationships are confounded.

Khandker et al. (2012) explored the pricing arrangements for electricity connections in Bangladesh, and found a large connection cost jump for households more than 100 feet from electric poles, as that distance conditions eligibility for connection subsidies. However, before electrification there is no positive significant relationship between distance from electric poles and outcomes of interest, such as farm and nonfarm income or expenditure. This suggests that distance from electric pole locations is unconfounded but predicts treatment. Household distance of less than 100 feet from electric poles was thus used as an instrument in a village fixed effects regression.

The first stage was to estimate the predicted value of household electricity access (a binary variable) as a function of the instrument, household characteristics, and village attributes. The second stage estimated outcomes, such as income, expenditure, schooling completion, and study time, on the basis of the predicted variable and household and village characteristics. By doing so, the study found significant effects of electrification on nearly all outcomes assessed.

Source: Khandker et al. (2012).

Generally, the challenge is to find a valid instrument that meets both conditions. Two methods already discussed can be seen as examples of IV in which valid instruments were described: RCTs and RDD.

It is common to estimate impact from RCT studies using a regression rather than simply comparing means of treatment and control. In that case, random assignment is being used as an instrument. The random assignment is correlated with participation (but is not the same variable if there are crossovers), and it is not correlated with the outcome by design. Fuzzy RDD is a special case of IV in which the instrument is the assignment variable.

Selection of the instruments is best undertaken by specifying the underlying structural model, which is derived from the theory of change. It will usually be the case that more than one instrument is identified. When there is more than one instrument, instrumental variables is often implemented as two-stage least squares: (i) in stage one, regress the endogenous variable (that measuring program participation) on the instruments and calculate the fitted value; and (ii) in stage two, estimate the outcome equation, replacing the endogenous variable with the fitted values from the first stage. The impact estimate is the coefficient on the fitted values.

What is needed for instrumental variables?

In practice, these two stages are not performed manually: software packages will perform the calculations, which will also give the correct standard errors (which the second stage regression estimates would not if performed manually). For example, in STATA the command for instrumental variables is "ivregress", and "ivreg2" offers useful additional diagnostics (Baum et al. 2010), as described in Appendix 1, section 6.2. IV estimation requires data on treated and untreated observations, including the outcome and the instruments, as well as other confounding variables. If data are being collected for the study, it is important to have determined the instruments beforehand, so the relevant questions are included in the survey instruments.

Advantages and disadvantages of instrumental variables

The advantage of IV is that, given a valid instrument, both observable and unobservable sources of selection bias are controlled. The main disadvantage is that it may be difficult to find a valid instrument, as many factors that affect treatment also affect outcomes in some way. The approach also yields a LATE, which may be difficult for policy audiences to understand.

5.8 Endogenous Treatment and Control Function Approaches

The method in brief

Heckman (1976) applied one of the earliest models in econometrics to deal with selection bias. The model was initially developed to estimate wage equations, the problem being that wages are only observed for those who are employed (analogous to program impact only being observed for those who participate in the program). Wage equations are used to estimate the rate of return to education, with the Heckman model having become standard in such analysis. Control function approaches for endogenous treatment build on the approach. The core concept is that the variation between predicted probabilities of treatment based on observable characteristics and actual treatment can be captured as additional variables used in an outcome regression, which absorb the effects of unobservable determinants of treatment, so that unbiased treatment effects can be estimated.

Description of the method

In this approach, there are two parts. First, a binary variable measuring participation in the intervention of interest is modeled as a function of independent variables. From this regression, predicted values are generated, which are used in a second regression of the outcome of interest on program participation, generalized residuals from the first step, and other factors affecting outcomes.

The approach is a two-element procedure:

1. Estimate a probit equation of program participation (similar to propensity score matching, except that the probit should contain one or more instruments for participation). Calculate the fitted values for the "inverse mills ratio" and "hazard ratio" from the probit.

2. Use the participation variable and fitted values as regressors in OLS estimation of the outcome equation. In the case of treated observations, the inverse mills ratio will be included, and for untreated observations the hazard ratio will be included. The coefficient on the participation variable measures impact, as the additional fitted regressors absorb selection bias.

In practice, econometric software may allow the model to be estimated in a single step.

Identification of the model requires that there is at least one variable in the probit step that affects selection into the program, but not the outcome, which is essentially the same requirement as that for an instrumental variable. However, covariates that affect both selection and the outcome can be used in both stages.

What is needed for endogenous treatment regressions?

Using the Heckman approach requires specification of a participation model which includes at least one instrument. Estimation of the Heckman model requires data on both treatment and comparison groups, with observations on factors affecting participation, as well as factors affecting outcomes for the outcome equation. Statistics packages may include a command for the estimation (e.g. "etregress" in STATA). Appendix 1, section 6.3 provides more information on the technique and its application.

Advantages and disadvantages of endogenous treatment regressions

The advantage of the Heckman selection model is that it is an approach which can often be applied, provided the right data are available. Second, like PSM, the first stage involves estimation of a participation equation, which is a useful part of the analysis for the evaluation. The approach also allows a test of whether selection bias is present, by testing the significance of lambda in the second stage regression. Unlike PSM, the Heckman approach can deal with selection on unobservables under certain assumptions, and unlike traditional IV, it estimates an ATE, rather than a LATE. As a more generalized measure, the ATE may be of greater interest to policy audiences.

For this method there needs to be at least one variable that serves as an instrument, just as in the case of IV. Identification requires some strong assumptions on the normality of error terms and the correlation structure between the unobservable variables that determine treatment assignment and the unobservables that affect outcomes, which if not met means the estimates are not free of bias.

5.9   Endogenous Switching Regressions

The method in brief

Endogenous switching regressions are regression-based methods, which model two outcome equations (two "regimes"), one for treatment and one for comparison, allowing for endogeneity of selection into treatment (Maddala and Nelson 1975). This approach is a special case of the Heckman model, where the second stage (outcome) equation is a switching regression.[4] The major advantages of the approach are that it allows for interaction effects between treatment and the variables affecting outcomes, and that it can estimate distinct estimates for ATT, average treatment effect on the untreated (ATU), and ATE.

Description of the method

Applying endogenous switching regressions starts with the specification of a model:

- As for endogenous treatment models, estimation of the participation equation, which models whether the unit of observation (household, firm, etc.) is in the treatment or comparison group as a function of observable characteristics, from which fitted values are generated.

- Two outcome equations, one for the outcome for those in the treatment group, and another for those in the comparison group. The two equations have the same regressors apart from inverse mills and hazard ratios.

This approach does not yield a single impact estimate. Since the coefficients differ under the two regimes, the expected outcome for two observations—one treatment and one control, which have the same values of independent variables—is different. The expected outcome can be calculated for each potential outcome for treated and untreated populations. Differences between expected values of potential outcomes for participants and nonparticipants with and without treatment allow estimation of ATT, ATE, and ATU. The model has been extended to go beyond these population groupings and estimate marginal treatment effects for custom defined subpopulations (Moffitt 2008).

---

[4]   A switching regression is one in which two separate regression equations are estimated, each equation being called a regime. Each observation is assigned to one of the two "regimes."

What is needed for endogenous switching regressions?

The requirements are generally similar to those of the Heckman selection model. However, the participation equation may need to have greater explanatory power for the regression to solve, given that more parameters need to be estimated. In STATA, the package "movestay" enables automated application of the technique (Lokshin and Sajaia 2004), as described in Appendix 1, section 6.4.

Advantages and disadvantages of endogenous switching regressions

Endogenous switching regressions share many of the same advantages and disadvantages as endogenous treatment models. However, the major additional advantage is that it can estimate distinct ATT, ATU, and ATE values. The disadvantage is that it can be difficult to achieve convergence when estimating the equation, particularly if the selection model is weak, and that poor instruments in the selection equation can lead to biased estimates. The approach also depends on the same strong assumptions as endogenous treatment effects regressions.

5.10 Summary

A range of nonexperimental methods can be used when randomized experiments are not possible. However, all methods require data on both treated and untreated populations, rather than only before and after the intervention (apart from interrupted time series). Even if the counterfactual is implicit, as in regression-based approaches, such as instrumental variables, impact evaluation requires data from a comparison group. All methods apart from difference in differences, fixed effects, and synthetic controls require specification of a model that includes variables determining selection into the program. The selection model also yields additional insights on determinants of participation, which may be independently useful.

The choice of an appropriate method for a particular study will be conditioned by context and data (Table 5.5). This includes the nature of treatment, the number of observations available, the importance of selection on unobservables, and the treatment effect of interest.

Table 5.5: Summary of Nonexperimental Impact Evaluation Methods

Method	Type of treatment evaluated	Minimum data required	Can correct for selection on observables	Can correct for selection on unobservables	Treatment effect estimated
Difference-in-differences/ fixed effects	Dichotomous/ dichotomous, continuous	Panel (2 periods or more)	Yes	Yes, time invariant unobservables	ATT
Synthetic controls	Dichotomous	Panel with several rounds of pretreatment observations	Yes	Approximation of correction	ATT
Propensity score matching	Dichotomous	Cross-sectional	Yes	No	ATT, ATU, ATE
Double robust regression	Dichotomous	Cross-sectional	Yes	No	ATE
Regression discontinuity design	Dichotomous	Cross-sectional around an eligibility threshold	Yes	Yes	LATE
Instrumental variables	Dichotomous, continuous	Cross-sectional, including a valid instrument	Yes	Yes	LATE
Endogenous treatment effects regression	Dichotomous	Cross-sectional, including a valid instrument	Yes	Yes, under specific assumed variance-covariance structure of error terms	ATE
Endogenous switching regression	Dichotomous	Cross-sectional, including a valid instrument	Yes	Yes, under specific assumed variance-covariance structure of error terms	ATT, ATU, ATE

ATE = average treatment effect, ATT = average treatment effect on the treated, ATU= average treatment effect on the untreated, LATE = local average treatment effect.
Source: Authors.

- **Nature of treatment.** Whether the treatment variable is dichotomous (e.g., participating or not in a program) or continuous (e.g., travel time reductions from new infrastructure) affects which models can be used. Methods using a participation equation (endogenous treatment, endogenous switching regressions, propensity score matching) are only applicable for dichotomous treatments, as are difference-in-differences and synthetic control designs. Fixed effects and instrumental variables regressions are applicable when treatment is continuous.

- **Availability of baseline data.** Difference-in-differences, fixed effects models and synthetic controls can only be applied when panel data are available, such that there are observations before and after the intervention, as well as with and without. Synthetic controls additionally requires multiple observations prior to the intervention. Other methods are enhanced if carried out on panel data, but can be applied to cross-sectional data if only one observation period is possible.

- **Presence of instrument.** Instrumental variables, endogenous treatment effects models, and endogenous switching regressions depend on the presence of at least one variable that is appropriate as an instrument. The instrument will need to satisfy the exclusion restriction and have relevance. The assignment variable for a regression discontinuity design also is essentially an instrument.

- **Selection on unobservables.** If there is expected to be selection on unobservables, then propensity score-based techniques cannot be used cross-sectionally (i.e., without a baseline). Moreover, if these unobservables or their effects vary over time, then fixed effects and difference-in-differences will also lead to biased estimates.

- **Impact measure of interest.** Different methods also yield different impact measures. Difference-in-differences/fixed effect models, synthetic controls, propensity score matching, and endogenous switching regressions can estimate ATTs, or the effect on those who choose to participate in the intervention. Double robust and endogenous treatment regressions estimate ATEs, or the effect on the average population (participants and non-participants). Instrumental variables and regression discontinuity design estimate LATEs, or effects on those at the margin of participation, with respect to the instrument. ATTs may be most of interest for accountability about effects to date, whereas ATEs may be more of interest for informing decisions about expanding programs.

References*

Abadie, A., A. Diamond, and J. Hainmueller. 2010. Synthetic Control Methods for Comparative Case Studies: Estimating the Effect of California's Tobacco Control Program. *Journal of the American Statistical Association*. 105 (490). pp. 493–505.

Asian Development Bank. 2014. *Food Stamps and Medicard: Impact Evaluation Report*. Manila.

Baum, C. F., M. E. Schaffer, and S. Stillman. 2010. IVREG2: STATA Module for Extended Instrumental Variables/2SLS and GMM estimation. Statistical Software Components, S425401. Revised 9 February 2016. Boston College Department of Economics. http://ideas.repec.org/c/boc/bocode/s425401.html.

Calonico, S., M. D. Cattaneo, and R. Titiunik. 2014a. Robust Nonparametric Confidence Intervals for Regression-Discontinuity Designs. *Econometrica*. 82. pp. 2295–2326.

Calonico, S., M. D. Cattaneo, and R. Titiunik. 2014b. Robust data-driven inference in the regression-discontinuity design. *The Stata Journal*. 14 (4). pp. 909–946. https://sites.google.com/site/rdpackages/rdrobust/Calonico-Cattaneo-Titiunik_2014_Stata.pdf.

Grover, D. 2013. Sampling Recommendations for Second Wave Impact Evaluation of the Pantawid Pamilya Program Applying Regression Discontinuity Design. Project Document.

Heckman, J. 1976. The common structure of statistical models of truncation, sample selection and limited dependent variables and a simple estimator for such models. Annals of Economic and Social Measurement. 5: 475–492.

Imai, K. and M. Ratkovic. 2014. Covariate Balancing Propensity Score. *Journal of the Royal Statistical Society: Series B*. 76 (1). pp. 243–263.

Imbens, G. and K. Kalyanaraman. 2012. Optimal Bandwidth Choice for the Regression Discontinuity Estimator. *Review of Economic Studies*. 79. pp. 933–959.

Jalan, J. and M. Ravallion. 2001. Does Piped Water Reduce Diarrhea for Children in Rural India? World Bank Policy Research Working Paper. WPS 2664. Washington, DC: World Bank.

Khandker, S. R., D. F. Barnes, and H. A. Samad. 2012. The Welfare Impacts of Rural Electrification in Bangladesh. *The Energy Journal*. 33 (1). pp. 187–206.

King, G. and R. Nielsen. 2016. Why Propensity Scores Should Not Be Used for Matching. Working Paper. http://j.mp/2ovYGsW.

---

*   ADB recognizes "Vietnam" as Viet Nam.

Lokshin, M. and Z. Sajaia. 2004. Maximum likelihood estimation of endogenous switching regression models. *The STATA Journal.* 4 (3). pp. 282–289.

Lunceford, J. K. and M. Davidian. 2004. Stratification and Weighting via the Propensity Score in Estimation of Causal Treatment Effects: A Comparative Study. *Statistics in Medicine.* 23. pp. 2937–2960.

Maddala, G. S. and F. D. Nelson. 1975. Switching Regression Models with Exogenous and Endogenous Switching. Proceedings of the Business and Economics Statistics Section. American Statistical Association. pp. 423–426.

Moffitt, R. 2008. Estimating Marginal Treatment Effects in Heterogeneous Populations. *Annales D'Économie Et De Statistique.* (91/92). pp. 239–261.

Mu, R. and D. Van de Walle. 2011. Rural Roads and Local Market Development in Vietnam. *Journal of Development Studies.* 47 (5). pp. 709–734.

Orbeta, A., A. Abdon, M. del Mundo, M. Tutor, M. Theresia Valera, and D. Yarcia. 2014. Keeping Children Healthy and in School: Evaluating the Pantawid Pamilya Using Regression Discontinuity Design Second Wave Impact Evaluation Results. Unpublished draft.

Quistorff, B. and S. Galiani. 2017. The synth_runner package: Utilities to Automate Synthetic Control Estimation Using Synth. Version 1.6.0. August 2017. https://github.com/bquistorff/synth_runner.

Reiersol, O. 1945. Confluence Analysis by Means of Instrumental Sets of Variables. *Arkiv for Matematik, Astronomi och Fysik.* Band 32A. pp. 1–119.

Rosenbaum, P. R. and D. B. Rubin. 1983. The Central Role of the Propensity Score in Observational Studies for Causal Effects. *Biometrika.* 70. pp. 41–55.

Sween, J. A. and D. Campbell. 1965. The Interrupted Time Series as Quasi-Experiment: Three Tests of Significance. Northwestern University.

Thistlewaite, D. L. and D. T. Campbell. 1960. Regression-Discontinuity Analysis: An Alternative to the Ex-Post Facto Experiment. *Journal of Educational Psychology.* 51. pp. 309–317.

Further Reading

Angrist, J. D. and S. Pischke. 2009. *Mostly Harmless Econometrics: An Empiricists' Companion*. Princeton, New Jersey: Princeton University Press.

Caliendo, M. and S. Kopeinig. 2005. Some Practical Guidance for the Implementation of Propensity Score Matching. IZA Discussion Paper. No. 1588. http://ftp.iza.org/dp1588.pdf.

Funk, M. J., D. Westreich, C. Wiesen, T. Stürmer, M. A. Brookhart, and M. Davidian. 2011. Doubly Robust Estimation of Causal Effects. *American Journal of Epidemiology*. 173 (7). pp. 761–767. https://doi.org/10.1093/aje/kwq439.

Imbens, G. and T. Lemieux. 2008. Regression Discontinuity Designs: A Guide to Practice. *Journal of Econometrics*. 142. pp. 615–635. https://doi.org/10.1016/j.jeconom.2007.05.001.

O'Neill, S., N. Kreif, R. Grieve, M. Sutton, and J. S. Sekhon. 2016. Estimating Causal Effects: Considering Three Alternatives to Difference-in-Differences Estimation. *Health Services & Outcomes Research Methodology*. 16. pp. 1–21. http://doi.org/10.1007/s10742-016-0146-8.

Pokropek, A. 2016. Introduction to Instrumental Variables and Their Application to Large-Scale Assessment Data. *Large-Scale Assessments in Education*. 4 (4). https://link.springer.com/content/pdf/10.1186%2Fs40536-016-0018-2.pdf.

Ryan, A. M., J. F. Burgess, Jr., and J. B. Dimick. 2015. Why We Should Not Be Indifferent to Specification Choices for Difference-in-Differences. Health Services Research. 50 (4). pp. 1211–1235. https://www.ncbi.nlm.nih.gov/pmc/articles/PMC4545355/pdf/hesr0050-1211.pdf.

Wooldridge, J. M. 2012. *Introductory Econometrics: A Modern Approach*. Fifth Edition. Mason, Ohio: South-Western, Cengage Learning.

Chapter 6
What and How to Measure: Data Collection for Impact Evaluation

Key Messages

- Data are key to impact evaluation. It is essential to have sufficient numbers of observations on treatment, program participation, other interventions, variables conditioning participation, variables predicting outcomes, and outcomes for those with and without interventions.

- Data may come from many sources, but often impact evaluation will require new surveys, which often involve multiple levels, such as households, enterprises, facilities, communities, and agencies.

- Reliable survey instrument design requires considerable attention and substantial field testing.

- Sampling should consider spillover effects of the intervention, clustering, and intended subgroup analysis. Several sampling stages are usually needed.

- The data collection process should have careful oversight, with verification, consistency checks, and ample documentation.

6.1   The Importance of High-Quality Data

An impact evaluation is only as good as the data upon which it is based. Poor quality data, insufficient observations, or data without sufficient richness can make determination of an impact estimate impossible or can lead to spurious results. Ensuring the appropriateness of the data collected is at least as important as ensuring that the impact evaluation design is free from potential bias. A flawed design, or when an impact evaluation is not conducted according to plan, can sometimes be rectified by appropriate use of adequate quantities of sufficiently rich high-quality data, whereas data deficiencies often mean that an otherwise well-designed study cannot be rectified at all.

The design of the data collection strategy is oriented toward answering the evaluation questions, which have been derived from the theory of change (discussed in Chapter 2). The strategy should determine the sort of data required, including both quantitative and qualitative factors, to answer the evaluation questions (Box 6.1 provides an overview of survey terminology). An evaluation plan can clearly indicate the data to be used to address each evaluation question.

A key consideration beyond ensuring that the right data are collected is to assure that the data are collected right. This means that bias and error should be minimized. Error consists of sampling and non-sampling error (Banda 2003). *Sampling error* refers to collecting data on units that are not representative of the population of interest. This may be because the sampling protocol introduced bias, sample frames were not representative, or respondents selectively did not respond. *Non-sampling error* can arise because of poor survey design, respondent inaccuracy, enumerator error, or entry problems. It is a key challenge to minimize both types of error.

To avoid redundancy, the evaluation team should carefully assess what data are already available from administrative sources and other data repositories. It is sometimes possible to avoid primary data collection through use of existing data, although this is rare in low- and middle-income countries. It may also be possible to "piggyback" onto an existing survey rather than commissioning a survey specifically for the impact evaluation (discussed in section 6.3).

This Chapter provides an overview of data sources, designing and managing a survey, and sampling. It begins with a brief overview of deciding what data are needed (section 6.2), before discussing data sources (section 6.3), designing a survey (section 6.4), sampling (section 6.5), and managing data collection (section 6.6). Appendix 2 provides a more detailed description of these issues.

6.2 Determining What Data Are Needed

The population to be surveyed and the questions to be asked depend on intervention design, objectives, and the theory of change as to how those objectives will be achieved. The delivery mechanism for the intervention affects sampling design, since the unit of assignment will usually be the first level of sampling. Effects to be evaluated determine the sampling units. For example, if the effect of interest is poverty reduction, household data are required, while if the effect of interest is labor demand, firm-level data may be required.

Evaluation questions from the theory of change provide a first step in deciding what data to collect. Those should identify (i) primary and secondary outcomes of interest, as well as any intermediate outcomes; (ii) important process variables and contextual factors which may mediate intervention effects; (iii) measure of program engagement by intended beneficiaries, which may be either a continuous or "dosage" measure (e.g., loan size or distance from road) or dichotomous (electricity connection or living in project village); and (iv) indicators of program activity, such as construction. In addition, nonexperimental designs need variables to model program participation, which will also serve as control variables in regression-based approaches. If an instrumental variable approach is used, including more than one potential instrument helps to reduce risks that the instrument does not have necessary characteristics.

Once the data are specified, data sources need to be identified. In some cases, existing administrative sources or existing surveys may provide necessary data. If not, the details of a new survey need to be defined. For maximum precision, relevant populations to survey should be identified in as much detail as possible. For example, a firm survey may need to distinguish whether the owner, CEO, manager, or staff is an appropriate informant. The owner may have the best knowledge of the firm's history and its strategic direction, the CEO of how well the business model is functioning and current market conditions, and other staff of more precise information on output, profits, and so on. In a household survey, different modules are often directed at different respondents. For example, for household surveys, questions on children's health and inside household food consumption are asked of a female household member. For community surveys, it is often useful to administer the survey in a group setting of community leaders to obtain a collective response, following ethical procedures on data confidentiality.

6.3 Data Sources

Data may come from the following sources:

- *Census:* data collected from a whole population. Population censuses of all adult residents of a country are typically conducted once every 10 years, although sometimes more frequently. An industrial census of all firms may be carried out more frequently, and are usually restricted to registered enterprises. Agricultural censuses are also carried out in some countries, although sample surveys are more frequent, and increasingly so across Asia and the Pacific. Census data are often useful in providing the sampling frame, or data which can be used to obtain matched comparison groups. However, caution should be exercised if important target groups are missed by the census, such as nomadic populations and those without regular residences.

- *Surveys:* data collected from a sample of the population of interest. A survey is carried out using one or more survey instruments. For an impact evaluation, the population of interest is usually the intended beneficiary population. A sampling strategy is needed to ensure that the sample is representative of this population. The comparison group should also be representative of this population, not the population as a whole.

- *Geographic information systems* and remote sensing can provide data relating to geographic characteristics of an area or characteristics that can be defined based on geography, such as distance measures to facilities, rainfall, or topography. Remote sensing can provide information that helps to monitor events that can condition outcomes, such as flooding, or treatment, such as road extent.

- *Administrative data* include information collected routinely as part of statistical or management systems. Examples include billing data from utilities and data feeding into Education Management Information Systems through an annual school census.

- Other sources of real-time data may be collected from various devices recording traffic flows, pollution levels, and so on. There is also potential for using self-reported data from, say, farmers using mobile phone apps—these same apps can provide farmers customized extension advice.

Piggybacking on an existing survey

Sometimes it will be possible to piggyback onto another survey process, such as a national household income and expenditure survey or a nationwide health and retirement survey, rather than undertaking a separate survey specifically for the impact evaluation. Such an approach can help to improve efficiency and enable large samples if those implementing the other survey are willing to append sufficient modules to collect data for impact evaluation. The data from national surveys undertaken by the national statistical agency are also likely to be of high quality.

However, for these data to be useful, project teams often must allocate time and effort for coordination and additional funding. It will frequently be necessary to request and fund two types of modifications to the survey to be piggybacked. First, it may be necessary to increase the sample size in project areas (what is

Box 6.1: Survey Terminology

Survey instrument: a predesigned form (questionnaire) used to collect primary data during a survey. A survey will typically have more than one survey instrument, e.g., a household survey and a facility survey.

Module: a section of the survey instrument with a specific focus, such as energy use, education, or nutrition. Different modules may require a different respondent within the household or firm. It is not generally good practice to have different respondents within a module, though this may be required within some modules.

Respondent: the individual answering the question. It is often the case that each question should have a single respondent.

Enumerator: the individual who conducts the survey. Well-trained enumerators are essential for the collection of high-quality data.

Baseline: data collected before the intervention starts. In practice the baseline will sometimes take place after the intervention starts. What matters is that data are collected before intended beneficiaries are affected by the intervention in any way. Having baseline data strengthens the possible impact evaluation design.

Midline: data collected midway through the intervention, which may focus on intermediate variables and process, rather than final outcomes.

Endline: data collected at the close of the intervention.

Post-endline: data collected some years after the close of the intervention. Post-endline data allow analysis if intervention benefits have been sustained.

Panel data: data collected from the same units in successive rounds of data collection. Panel data collection is usually necessary for stronger impact evaluation designs involving difference-in-differences or fixed effects models. This approach depends on the ability to relocate respondents.

Source: Authors.

called a "booster sample") in order to get sufficient sample sizes for treated populations. Second, a project-specific module may be added, especially for process aspects of the project. This additional module may only be relevant in project areas.

Piggybacking often will be cheaper than running a new survey. However, it may not be quicker, once the time needed to negotiate and coordinate with the survey organization is considered. This approach is only an option if the timing of the national survey is suitable to the baseline and/or endline periods of the impact evaluation.

6.4 Designing a Survey

Survey design is a key task in the design of the impact evaluation, which requires considerable time investment. It is a task that can benefit from a team approach, with team members including those experienced in survey implementation, experts in the intervention sector, and impact evaluators. This section addresses various issues in survey design.

Linking survey design to the evaluation design

The survey needs to include questions to capture the following variables:

- Participation in intervention activities.

- Outcomes on which effects are being measured, including any outcomes that may not have been foreseen or intended during project design. Some outcomes are not asked directly, but are derived from a range of questions. In some cases, for example household expenditure, many questions may be involved in calculating a single outcome.

- Household or firm characteristics either to conduct matching or to check for balance in the absence of matching.

- Conditioning factors that may affect impact, such as location or gender.

- Instrumental variables (IV) or variables conditioning eligibility in the case of IV or regression discontinuity designs, respectively.

- Intermediate outcomes and process variables along the causal chain, such as awareness of intervention-supported activities; accessibility, cost, and quality of those activities; and availability of complementary products or services. These variables allow for factual and counterfactual analysis along the causal chain. Where the estimation of impact is done through structural modeling, many more variables are necessary than for reduced form methods.

- Details that allow relocating or contacting the respondent for survey validation or follow-up survey rounds.

The identification of each set of variables will come from the evaluation design, which is, in turn, based on the theory of change of how the intervention achieves desired outcomes (discussed in Chapter 2).

The theory of change should also inform plans for subgroup analysis. For example, will the intervention have gender differentiated impacts, or a differential impact between the poor and nonpoor or among minority groups? If so, then the data have to be collected to identify and represent these subgroups.

Multiple survey instruments

The most common survey instrument for impact evaluations is the household survey, as most outcomes of interest relate to household welfare or behavior. Yet, the depth and quality of analysis are often improved by having additional survey instruments. The most common survey instruments are as follows:

- *Household survey:* data are collected by a visit to the household. The target respondent is usually the household head, although different modules may be addressed to different respondents. Common modules are the household roster which includes name, age, sex, education level, and relationship to the household head of all household members, and other modules depending on the focus of the study, for example education, health and anthropometrics, employment, income, and expenditure/consumption.

- *Enterprise survey:* data are collected at the level of the enterprise with the enterprise owner or manager as the target respondent. Modules include employment, sales, expenditures, and credit. A behavioral module may be used to measure variables such as attitudes to risk and the subjective discount rate.

- *Facility survey:* data are collected at the level of the facility such as a school or a health clinic with the head of facility (e.g., principal or head physician) as the target respondent. Modules will cover the quantity and quality of services. Sub-modules may also target regular teachers and doctors.

- *Community survey:* data are collected at the level of the community (which may be a village or administrative district in urban areas such as the *barangay* in the Philippines). Target respondents are community leaders, which may include people such as the *saparnch* (head of a village government) and village secretary in India. Sometimes regular villagers are needed to verify information provided by village heads or to get the opinions of villagers. Enumerations sometimes are carried out with focus groups, rather than one on one. Typical questions cover village facilities (schools, post office, etc.), distances to other facilities not in the community, development projects, and typical livelihoods. It is particularly important to be aware of other development projects in treatment and comparison areas.

- *Agency survey:* data are collected at the level of the agency, such as the nongovernment organization or government district office implementing the intervention with the lead of the agency in the intervention area as the target respondent. Modules may cover the resources, staff (quantity and quality), and procedures of the agency.

- *Worker survey:* data are collected from individual workers, such as teachers or health workers, who are the target respondents. Modules may include qualifications, working environment, job satisfaction, and skills. If the workers have been trained as part of the intervention the survey may test for the knowledge acquired and intended changes in practice.

Multiple data sources may be used for a single study either by implementing several surveys for a study (e.g., community and household) or by linking the evaluation's own survey data with an existing data source, such as rainfall data for an agricultural study. To do so, it is often useful to collect global positioning system coordinates for villages or individual respondents.

When multiple surveys are undertaken as part of the study it is important that ID codes are used which allow the surveys to be linked. For example, the ID code in a teacher survey may be *ccc.ss.ww*, where *ccc* is a three-digit community identification code, *ss* a two-digit school identification code (the school being uniquely identified as *ccc.ss*), and *ww* a two-digit teacher code.

Designing survey questions

Good wording of survey questions is central to an effective survey. A useful acronym is that questions should be BOSS: brief, objective, simple, and specific (Iarossi 2006).

Most questions in an impact evaluation survey will be either quantitative or pre-coded, i.e., there is a limited range of responses. It is important to keep all important quantitative information as continuous, even though it may appear simpler to reduce variables to categories. Where categories are used, responses are expected to be mutually exclusive and fully comprehensive. If that is not the case, then there should be an instruction to "indicate all that apply."

A survey usually contains a *skip pattern*, which directs the enumerator which question to ask next. For example, if a small enterprise owner replies that she or he has not taken a loan in the last year, questions on source and uses of loans taken in the last year are skipped. One important reason for fully testing a survey is that skip patterns can become incorrect during survey revisions.

Each question should require a single response, and questions should not contain implicit assumptions. It is not necessary to start from scratch when designing a survey. There are many surveys available, especially from large global survey programs, which have spent considerable resources developing best practice survey instruments. The most notable examples include the World Bank Living Standards Measurement Surveys and Demographic and Health Surveys. Modules can be copied and adapted from these surveys, having obtained consent where necessary. Adaptation includes adjustments, such as ensuring local inputs, and management practices are included in an agricultural survey, using local measurement units (for which equivalency tables are needed), and relating education questions to the local education system. For purposes of comparability between studies and combining the results of those studies, it may be useful if data are collected using a standardized approach. For more specialized topics, a starting point may be to identify recent relevant large surveys and obtain copies of their survey instruments.

Adopting modules from a proven instrument will avoid errors committed by less experienced survey designers. These errors may include (i) overloading the survey with unnecessary questions; (ii) asking questions the respondent cannot reasonably answer, a particular case of which is asking for aggregates, such as agricultural income, rather than the more accurate disaggregated approach which asks about input costs and production quantities for specific crops, livestock, etc.; (iii) lack of clarity or ambiguity in questions; (iv) capturing continuous characteristics, such as age, as categories, which have much less explanatory power for analysis; and (v) inappropriate skip pattern and an illogical design to the survey sequencing (Appendix 2, section 4 provides more details on survey design).

Test, test, and test again

It is very important that the survey instruments are subject to adequate *pretesting* before the implementation of the survey (Presser and Blair 1994). Testing should be first done within the team, and then with the enumerators, and then pilot testing under field conditions by the enumerators. There often will need to be several weeks of field testing and multiple rounds of revision. Although the process may be time consuming, it is essential to a meaningful impact evaluation. Poorly designed surveys that are not well tested produce poor quality (often useless) data and inconclusive or spurious results.

Supporting documentation

Each survey instrument should be accompanied by a manual which provides the general motivation for the survey, the purpose of each module, and answers any questions enumerators might have. The manuals will also deal with such issues as *community entry* (how to introduce the survey team to community leaders) and the process of respondent selection and replacement if respondents cannot be located.

Translation

In most cases, the native language of the respondent population is not English, and survey translation will be required. In some cases, if enumerators have good English language skills and a good understanding of the questions, then the survey instruments may be left in English. In those cases, the enumerator training should discuss the local language terms for uncommon items or items without an immediately obvious translation. In cases where translation is necessary, translation should occur prior to field testing, so that mistranslation can be identified.

Electronic survey instruments

It is increasingly common to use netbooks or tablets for electronic data collection. Although more time consuming to set up initially than paper questionnaires, there are several advantages to this approach: (i) data collection can often be monitored to ensure that enumerators are spending sufficient time with respondents in the field; (ii) it is usually easier to implement modifications to the survey, even once in the field if necessary, though this is best done if enumerators have internet access so as to update the questionnaire; (iii) the skip pattern, consistency checks, and range limits are built into the software, as can flagging statements, avoiding enumerator error; (iv) invalid responses can be disallowed; (v) data can be transmitted back to study headquarters in real-time for checking, which may flag which respondents need to be revisited or enumeration errors; (vi) there is no need for separate data entry, which not only takes time but is another potential source of error, though ability to edit data may be limited on sponsored platforms such as Survey Monkey; and, finally, (vii) it saves paper! Box 6.2 describes leading software packages for electronic data collection.

Box 6.2: Platforms for Computer-Assisted Personal Interviewing

Several free software platforms have become available for electronic (paperless) data collection, which can make surveys more precise, timely, and lower cost. In addition to the free software listed below, many more commercial products are available, as well.

CSPro is the oldest major computer-assisted personal interviewing (CAPI) platform, and was developed by the United States Census Bureau. It is a closed-source solution, which runs on both Windows and Android. Questionnaires are programmed in a unique language for the platform. Real-time data synchronization can be achieved by use in conjunction with Dropbox or FTP peer-to-peer file sharing. Collected data can be exported directly to major statistical software. https://www.census.gov/population/international/software/cspro/index.html

Open Data Kit (ODK) has been developed jointly by the University of Washington and Google as an open source platform, with data collection via Android tablets or phones. It has several tools to assist in building surveys in a standardized xml format. Use of the platform requires installation of a dedicated Aggregate server. A variety of sensor data, including coordinates from global positioning systems and cameras can be included. Data entry can be monitored in real time via Google Maps or other queries. https://opendatakit.org/

Survey Solutions is the World Bank's CAPI platform. It is closed source, and runs on Android tablets, with a World Bank hosted cloud platform for managing questionnaires and data. Although the software is free, use of the cloud data platform may come at a cost. It uses a simplified C# syntax for questionnaire programming, which may also be done via online designer tools. Like ODK, it can allow various sensor data to be included directly, and data entry can be monitored in real time. This platform also allows direct data export to major statistical software. http://support.mysurvey.solutions/

Source: Authors.

The primary disadvantage is that many—but not all—electronic data collection packages have certain rigidities, as they may restrict question skip order, recording format, or may make it difficult for notes or manual calculations. This rigidity can introduce error if the instrument is not sufficiently pretested, so the onus on pretesting may be increased. The equipment may also have problems, and regular access to power sources, and possibly also Wi-Fi or a strong mobile signal, is needed.

The role of qualitative data

Impact evaluation designs are strengthened by the use of mixed methods, in which quantitative and qualitative data play complementary roles. Qualitative data can play the following roles:

- qualitative data can be used at the formative stage to help inform evaluation and survey design;

- qualitative data can capture sensitive or less well-understood issues relating to intervention implementation, such as barriers to participation, implementation problems, and so on; and

- qualitative data can help to interpret study findings and to generalize conclusions.

A range of qualitative techniques, such as open interviews with project staff and community leaders, oral life histories, focus groups, mapping exercises, and transects may be used to collect these data. It is very useful for the primary study team members to spend some time in the field during some of these exercises. The tools to be used for qualitative data collection need pretesting in precisely the same way as do the structured survey instruments. In some cases, qualitative data collection may be part of an initial diagnostic phase prior to full impact evaluation design.

Proxies for baseline data

Impact evaluation designs are nearly always stronger with baseline data. If baseline data are collected early enough, the evaluators can also use them to check for balance (between treatment and control groups) at baseline, to match on indicators which are necessarily not affected by the intervention, and to calculate a double difference impact estimator, which can reduce sample size requirements.

Yet, baseline data are not always available. In some cases, it may be possible to use proxies for the baseline. In many cases, this may also not be feasible or will not yield data of sufficient quality. Some high-quality impact evaluations have been done when there was no formal baseline but, for example, administrative data were available. The following methods may be used to substitute for the baseline:

- An existing survey from the intervention area conducted close to the start of the intervention, which collected data on the outcomes of interest and characteristics required for matching. Census data should also be considered as they have the clear advantage of universal coverage. However, it may well be that the census date is not close enough to the intervention start, and the breadth of the data is limited.

- Administrative data, such as Education Management Information Systems, have the advantage of national coverage, though often only of public facilities (e.g., private schools may be excluded).

- Satellite data provide information on land use, which may be used for analysis of outcomes, such as cropping patterns and deforestation.

- Recall can be used, but should be restricted to substantial items (such as life events and purchase of large assets), which respondents are likely to recall accurately. Several characteristics that are unaffected by the intervention can be collected *ex post,* such as education of adult household members, religion, sex of household head, and so on.

The analysis plan

An analysis plan can help to target data collection by articulating the mechanics of the identification strategy. The plan can include the specification of all models to be estimated and tables to be reported. To be complete, all variables should be fully defined and linked back to the questions in the questionnaire. Doing a complete analysis plan ensures that there are no gaps later in required data, and can avoid the collection of unnecessary data.

It may be possible to use data collected during piloting the survey, or to generate dummy data for the questionnaires for a test run of the intended analyses. This approach will help to identify unforeseen errors in coding or other problems, which may require revision of the survey instruments.

6.5 Sampling

For a valid impact evaluation, a sampling strategy needs to be designed to ensure that a collected sample (i) is representative of the treatment (beneficiary) population, and (ii) allows identification of a valid control or comparison group. Where spillovers are expected to be present this also has implications for sample design.

Sampling will be based on random selection of survey units from a sampling frame, which lists all eligible units. It is commonly the case that a cluster sample design will be necessary. For example, a firm survey will not randomly select from all firms in the country, but first sample a number of districts or subdistricts and then sample firms within the selected districts or subdistricts. Cluster designs are common as interventions are often delivered at cluster level such as community or district. However, cluster designs require larger sample size than simple random sampling to have equivalent statistical power. The power calculations must allow for clustering (discussed in Chapter 7 and Appendix 2).

Sometimes the sample frame is only available for the first stage of cluster sampling. For example, a list of villages is available but not all households in those villages. In that case, a listing exercise is necessary. Villages are selected from the sampling frame. The team then visits the selected villages to generate a list of eligible households in those villages (i.e., "listing"), from which to take a random sample.

The sample design may also include stratified sampling, which first separates the eligible population into groups (e.g., rural and urban, poor and nonpoor, all households in each county that is part of the survey) and then takes a random sample from each group. Stratification is done when it is planned to conduct subgroup analysis, and so ensures sufficient sample size in each subgroup. Subgroup analysis is possible if stratification has not been done, but will generally require a larger sample. Appendix 2, section 2 provides more details on sampling design.

Random sampling, which is necessary to ensure a representative sample, should not be confused with random assignment of the intervention. Random sampling does not make a study a randomized evaluation, which requires random assignment.

Selecting the comparison group

How to select a valid comparison group is a central theme of this book. The evaluation design should determine the sampling strategy, not vice versa. So if random assignment is being used, it is this random assignment which determines the treatment and comparison populations, as well as survey design. A cluster randomized controlled trial (RCT) requires a cluster sample design. When nonexperimental methods are being used, the sample design should collect data from likely eligible comparison groups to avoid having to discard large amounts of data. For cluster designs, the matched communities may be identified using a different data set, e.g., census or administrative data.

Spillovers

If the intervention is expected to have important spillovers beyond beneficiaries, analysis of spillover effects depends upon non-beneficiaries being included in the sample. These non-beneficiaries are different from the comparison group, which should consist of non-beneficiaries who will not experience spillovers.

Subgroup analysis

Impact heterogeneity means that the impact may vary in different ways: by gender, social group, location, time of year, and so on. For example, computer-assisted learning in the People's Republic of China was found to improve math scores among the bottom, middle, and top thirds of the pretest distribution by 0.43, 0.35, and 0.33 standard deviations, respectively (Linden, Banerjee, and Duflo 2003). The effect was greatest for the weakest students.

The theory of change should give some insights into expected heterogeneity. It is preferable to prespecify the intended subgroup analysis in the protocol for the study design so as to avoid data mining. However, this does not preclude reporting important heterogeneity which may come to light during fieldwork or analysis, if it can be supported with sound reasoning and evidence.

Sampling needs to allow for planned subgroup analysis. An intervention may be found to be effective overall, but may have no significant impact on women. Yet, this may be because the sample size is not sufficient to detect impact on a subsample. The study may find no significant impact on men either!

6.6 Managing Data Collection

To ensure consistency with intended analyses, data collection should be managed by the same team as will undertake the impact evaluation. If this is not the case, then other mechanisms need to ensure adequate coordination between the two teams, so that the data meet the requirements of the impact evaluation.

If the impact evaluation team is responsible for data collection, it may directly hire and train enumerators, and it may hire a local survey company. Appendix 2, section 5 provides more information on how to manage this process. For example, the ADB-supported impact evaluation of the Mongolia Food Stamps Program was undertaken by Oxford Policy Management, which subcontracted the Population Training and Research Centre from the School of Economics, National University of Mongolia to manage the data collection. Impact evaluation organizations with in-country offices, such as the Innovations for Poverty Action in many countries, including India and the Philippines, will usually form their own teams.

In either case, data collection requires careful management by core members of the impact evaluation team. They should be involved in pretesting to ensure that key variables are captured adequately, enumerator training ensures correct understanding of the questionnaire, and independent field supervision is provided during survey implementation.

Enumerator training often requires substantial time to ensure adequate understanding of survey implementation, including testing under field conditions. This training improves the quality of the survey and so reduces non-sampling error. Role play, in which enumerators enumerate each other using the survey instruments, often is an important part of the training. Other participants can observe and discuss the process. The role play may identify additional changes to the instruments to remove ambiguities or errors (e.g., in the skip pattern). Training should also cover the ethical aspects of data collection, such as informed consent.

During data collection, regular checks on data quality by the survey field manager and the impact evaluation team's own independent field supervisor may help to assure adequate enumeration. It is increasingly common to enter data electronically in the field, in which case data consistency checks built into the software help ensure data quality. Electronic data collection can also allow real-time transmission and monitoring.

One way to conduct quality checks is to validate a small sample of the data. This may be done by the field supervisor resurveying selected households. Alternatively, an independent firm or expert may be hired for the resurvey, possibly by telephone where this is feasible. Enumerators who understand the range of typical survey responses may face incentives to shortcut or even fabricate data collection, unless they are aware that measures are in place to catch such practice. For this reason, data should always be validated with respondents, at least for a random subsample, and it may be useful to ensure that geographic coordinates from a global positioning system are recorded, as this can help assure that intended locations were visited.

The survey company is usually responsible for an initial cleaning of the data, although further data cleaning is usually necessary by the team conducting the analysis. The latter process will often result in specific queries to check certain responses. For this reason, the original completed questionnaire forms should be retained until data analysis is complete. A protocol or description of the data cleaning approach should be included and a copy of the uncleaned data should be preserved. This provision should be included in the contract for those conducting the data collection.

Ethical considerations

A large part of the ethics of impact evaluation (discussed in Chapter 8) pertains to data collection.

Key issues pertaining to the ethics of data collection include the following:

1. **Obtaining necessary ethical approvals:** If the research team is from an academic institution, then that institution will likely require review board approval (warning: this can take some time!). The country in which the study is taking place may also have ethical approval requirements.

2. **Informed consent by respondents:** For cluster randomized controlled trials, it may be acceptable to obtain consent at the cluster level, e.g., community leaders for villages, and head teachers for schools. Box 6.3 provides an example of informed consent text.

3. **Remunerating respondents:** For surveys with many questions, compensation for the opportunity cost of time required for informants may be needed to assure a high completion rate. The remuneration should not affect the outcome, which is an issue the study team needs to seriously consider. For households, a small in-kind gift can suffice, such as pen, pencil, and notebook. A donation to a village fund may be appropriate, especially for comparison communities.

Box 6.3: Example of Text for Informed Consent

Hello. My name is _____, and I am undertaking a survey on road usage. The research is conducted by _____ This information will help to determine if road development results in price reductions and benefits for consumers. The survey usually takes up to 30 minutes to complete. Confidentiality of information you provide is assured. We would kindly appreciate your participation.

Participation in this survey is voluntary and you can choose not to answer any individual question or all of the questions. You can choose to stop the survey at any point. However, we hope that you will participate in this survey since your views are important.

At this time, do you want to ask me anything about the survey? Wait for response.

Do you agree to the conduct of this survey? Yes or No.

Source: Authors.

Timing

There are two issues related to survey timing: (i) when to collect data, and (ii) how long the survey process takes. The latter depends on sample size, the geographic distribution of the sample and travel times, the length of the questionnaire, and how many visits are necessary to administer the questionnaire. More than one visit is often necessary, simply because a respondent is not available. Multiple visits may also help to reduce respondent fatigue for long surveys.

There is also the question of how many rounds of data collection to undertake. When surveys are required, an endline is, of course, essential. As stressed throughout this book, a baseline is strongly advised. For longer interventions, a midterm survey may also be advisable, often focused on process aspects or intermediate outcomes. Finally, it can be very useful to have a post-endline survey sometime after the intervention closes to determine if benefits have been sustained or even extended to a broader population.

The timing of surveys is constrained by two sets of factors. First, the timing of the baseline and endline is often linked to the project-specific factors of the start and end of the activities being evaluated and the availability of finance to fund data collection. Second, as for any survey, there are context-specific timing considerations such as not being able to travel easily in the rainy season; major festivals, seasonal migration, and peak seasons affecting respondent availability and the school calendar for education-related surveys.

Many variables are seasonal, so it is important that each round of the survey is conducted at the same time of the year. Of course, data from treatment and comparison areas need to be collected at the same time.

Substantial time is often needed for quality data collection. The time required from starting survey design to enumeration often is several months or more. This time includes developing and testing the survey design and supporting documentation, training enumerators, identifying the sample, and arranging the logistics for data collection.

Survey implementation often takes 2 to 6 weeks depending on the size of the sample and geographic coverage, but it may be longer for large surveys or long survey instruments. A further month or more is required for data entry and preliminary data cleaning for paper surveys.

Permissions

In many countries, the survey team will need official permission to conduct the survey. It can be more problematic conducting surveys in comparison areas, as there is no project presence. In these cases, clear permissions from the relevant authority at the local level are particularly important. The project manager may need to play a role in facilitating those permissions.

Data archiving

To facilitate more use of collected data, it is good practice to archive collected data and supporting documentation, such as questionnaires, in the public domain. It is increasingly common to also archive the files used to conduct the analysis. The data are typically made publicly available 1 to 2 years after the analysis has been completed.

The data should be anonymized before allowing public access. This means that identifiers that allow identification of the household, individuals, or firms should be removed from public versions (although preserved in the non-public archive so that respondents can be revisited). Archiving may need to be included in the contract for the impact evaluation team or survey entity, as it involves some additional effort and resources. There should also be standard labeling of files and storage password encryption for data security. Appendix 2, section 6 provides more information on data management.

References

Banda, J. P. 2003. Nonsampling Errors in Surveys. Paper prepared for Expert Group Meeting to Review the Draft Handbook on Designing of Household Sample Surveys. United Nations Secretariat, New York. 3–5 December 2003.

Iarossi, G. 2006. The Power of Survey Design: A User's Guide for Managing Surveys, Interpreting Results, and Influencing Respondents. Washington, DC: World Bank.

Linden L., A. Banerjee, and E. Duflo. 2003. Computer-Assisted Learning: Evidence from a Randomized Experiment. Poverty Action Lab Paper 5.

Presser, S. and J. Blair. 1994. Survey Pretesting: Do Different Methods Produce Different Results? *Sociological Methodology*. 24. pp. 73–104.

Further Reading

Grosh, M. and P. Glewwe. 2000. Designing Household Survey Questionnaires for Developing Countries: Lessons from 15 Years of the Living Standards Measurement Study. Volumes 1, 2, and 3. Washington, DC: The World Bank. http://go.worldbank.org/NTQLJEEXQ0.

Pollock, H. D., E. Chuang, and S. Wykstra. 2015. *Reproducible Research: Best Practices for Data and Code Management*. New Haven, CT: Innovations for Poverty Action. http://www.poverty-action.org/sites/default/files/publications/IPA%27s%20Best%20Practices%20for%20Data%20and%20Code%20Management_Nov2015.pdf.

Statistical Services Centre, University of Reading. 2009. International Household Survey Network: Survey Quality Assessment Framework. http://www.ihsn.org/sites/default/files/resources/SQAF_Draft.pdf.

Stecklov, G. and A. Weinreb. 2010. Improving the Quality of Data and Impact-Evaluation Studies in Developing Countries. Impact Evaluation Guidelines Technical Notes No. 1. Washington, DC: Inter-American Development Bank. http://www.iadb.org/document.cfm?id=39376032.

United Nations Department of Economic and Social Affairs, Statistics Division. 2005. Household Sample Surveys in Developing and Transition Countries. Studies in Methods Series F No. 96. New York. http://unstats.un.org/unsd/hhsurveys/pdf/Household_surveys.pdf.

Chapter 7
Sample Size Determination for Data Collection

Key Messages

- Statistical power is the probability that the study will find a significant impact when there is one.

- Power calculations have to be done to understand the required sample size to detect impact with the desired probability. The calculations have to be done separately for each outcome variable.

- It is very common for studies to be underpowered for a variety of reasons. This is an important risk to mitigate, as an underpowered study may incorrectly conclude that an intervention is not having a detectable effect.

- Most impact evaluations of development interventions require cluster sampling. The number of clusters matters most for power, rather than the number of sampled units in each cluster.

7.1   Power Calculations: An Introduction

Impact evaluations use a sample from intervention areas and control/comparison areas to estimate effects on outcomes. The larger the sample then the more likely it is to be representative of the population from which the sample is taken.

For example, an agricultural extension program is intended to benefit 10,000 farmers. It would be very costly to survey all these households, as well as an equivalent comparison population. How many farmers should be surveyed? To answer that question, a power calculation should be performed.

Power calculations need to be performed to determine the sample size for a study that is sufficient for finding statistically significant intervention effects. If the sample size is too small then the study is "underpowered," with the risk that the study will not find a significant impact even though there is one. Too large a sample means that the study budget will be larger than it need be. This section explains the intuition behind power calculations and the information required to perform them. Additional considerations are described in Appendix 2.

The most important principles to guide impact evaluation managers are the following: (i) power calculations should be undertaken as part of the study design, (ii) power calculations should be independently checked by someone with the necessary statistical skills, and (iii) sufficient sample size is needed to avoid risk of investment in an inconclusive study.

It may appear that small samples can save time and financial resources, but this comes at the cost of reducing the likelihood of finding significant intervention effects. When an evaluation that is underpowered ends up with a finding that there was no impact, it is impossible to determine if the absence of an impact is due to the fact that the intervention did not work or if the study was underpowered. In such circumstances, the impact evaluation may offer little useful information.

7.2 What Is Power?

The power of the study is the probability that a study will correctly identify the impact of an intervention that actually had impact. There are four scenarios regarding the true impact and study findings (Table 7.1). In two of these four scenarios the study comes to the right conclusion: the intervention works and a significant impact is found, or it does not work and no significant impact is found. In the other two cases, the conclusions are erroneous. When the intervention does not work but the study concludes that it does, this is called a Type I error. When the intervention does work but the study finds no significant impact, then this is a Type II error. The power of a study is 100 minus the probability of a Type II error. To explain why this is so requires some statistics.

Table 7.1: Possible Errors in Estimating Impact

	Find No Significant Impact	Find a Significant Impact
Intervention has no impact	No error (correct conclusion)	Type I error (False positive)
Intervention has an impact	Type II error (False negative)	No error (correct conclusion)

Source: Authors.

In statistical terminology, the null hypothesis (H_0) is that the intervention has no impact. The impact is the difference in the average outcomes (or change in outcomes for a double difference design) in the intervention (treatment) group (μT) and the comparison group (μC). The null hypothesis is that the two are equal, that is, H_0: $\mu T = \mu C$; or, equivalently, H_0: $\mu T - \mu C = 0$. Suppose that the primary outcome variable for the agricultural extension impact evaluation is farm income, then the null hypothesis is that income is the same in intervention and comparison areas. It is assumed here that the parameter of interest is the mean, which is most usually the case. Sometimes it may be another parameter such as variance: microfinance promotes consumption smoothing (less variance in expenditure) or irrigation reduces variability in yield. While the formulas differ, the same basic principles of power calculations apply as discussed in this Chapter.

The average outcome for each group is calculated based on a sample from that group. The sample mean, $\bar{X}$, is used as an estimate for the population mean, μ. When a sample is used, it is unlikely that the sample mean ($\bar{X}$) will be exactly the same as the true (population) mean (μ).

At baseline, that is, before the intervention, the average characteristics should be the same in treatment and comparison areas if possible (i.e., $\mu_T = \mu_C$). This is called the baseline balance test, and it should always be reported where baseline data are available.

Suppose the intervention does not have an effect. That means that at endline the true average outcome in the treatment and comparison populations will be the same ($\mu_T = \mu_C$). However, since the sample means for both treatment and comparison groups are not likely to exactly equal their respective population values, then they will not be equal to each other. Even if the intervention has no impact, the average outcome in treatment and comparison groups is likely to differ to some degree because of sampling error. The statistical significance of the difference, $\bar{X}_T - \bar{X}_C$ is tested to account for this. If it is not significant, then the study concludes that the observed difference may be due to sampling error, and the null hypothesis that the intervention has no impact is accepted. But, if the difference is statistically significant, it means that there is too large a difference to be explained by sampling error, and the alternative hypothesis that the intervention has an impact is accepted, rather than the null hypothesis.

Yet, when the null hypothesis is accepted or rejected, it is not possible to be 100% certain of the determination. There is a risk of error: of either incorrectly rejecting the null as a false positive (Type I error) or incorrectly accepting it as a false negative (Type II error) (Table 7.1). Understanding these errors is key to understanding statistical power.

Figure 7.1 shows the probability distribution of sample means drawn from a population with a true population mean of zero and a normal distribution. The area under the curve between the two vertical lines drawn at $-x_1$ and x_1 is 95%. That means that if a sample is taken there is a 95% probability that the sample mean will fall in the range $-x_1$ to x_1. Similarly, there is 5% chance that the sample mean with be either less than $-x_1$ or greater than x_1.

To test the null hypothesis that the population mean is zero, there needs to be an acceptable range of values into which the sample mean must fall in order to conclude that the difference between the sample mean and the hypothesized population mean of zero is just down to sampling error. This range is determined by the significance level selected, called α. It is most common to select a significance level of 5%. This level is the Type I error: the probability of incorrectly rejecting the null hypothesis.

Once a significance level is selected, the range of sample means within which the null is accepted is defined as $\pm t_{\alpha/2} s_x$, where t_α is the t-statistic and s_x is the standard error of x. The term $t_{\alpha/2}$ is used because the 5% is evenly divided as 2.5% in each tail. The t-statistic depends also on the sample size, but with 5% significance, t is approximately 2. So if the sample mean is within two standard errors of zero, the null hypothesis that the population mean is zero is accepted. If the true population mean is zero, this implies that 5% of the time the sample mean will be outside this range and the null hypothesis will be falsely rejected. That is, there is a 5% chance of a Type I error.

The chance of a Type II error is illustrated in Figure 7.2. In this case, the true population mean, μ_2, is greater than zero. The red line shows the distribution

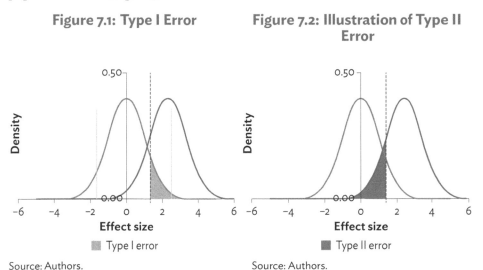

Figure 7.1: Type I Error

Figure 7.2: Illustration of Type II Error

Source: Authors.

Source: Authors.

of sample means given this true population mean. The gray line in the figure shows the distribution from Figure 7.1 under the null hypothesis and the range of sample means within which the null is accepted. It can readily be seen that a substantial proportion of the possible sample means from the distribution of possible means when the true population mean is μ_2 falls within the range for acceptance of the null hypothesis that the true mean is zero. Indeed, around 40% of the distribution falls in this range. That means that 40% of the time a statistical test would accept the null hypothesis that the true mean is zero even though it is in fact greater than zero. This is the Type II error. If these distributions represented treatment effects, nearly half the time the analysis would conclude the intervention has no impact when in fact it does.

One way to reduce Type II error is to reduce the confidence interval. This case is shown in Figure 7.3. By selecting a significance level of 10% rather than 5%, Type II error is reduced from 40% to around 25%. This reduction in Type II error is at the expense of increasing Type I error to 10%. There is a trade-off between Type I and Type II error. The standard in social sciences is to set Type I error at 5%. Natural sciences may require higher levels of confidence.

Type II error is also reduced by increasing the sample size. A larger sample size makes the distribution taller and thinner—with a larger sample, the sample mean is more likely to be close to the true population mean. As shown in Figure 7.4, Type II error falls as sample size rises. This is the essence of power calculations: what sample size does the study need to get an acceptable level of Type II error? That acceptable level is usually set at 20%. Since power is 100 minus Type II error, a probability of Type II error of 20% is the same as a power of 80%. For the power to be higher than that, a larger sample is required.

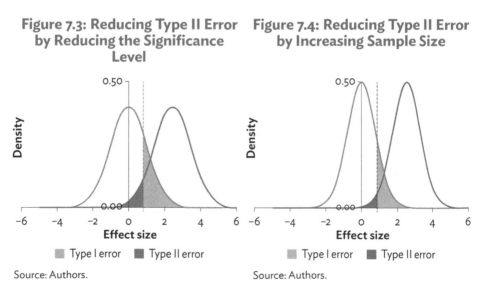

Figure 7.3: Reducing Type II Error by Reducing the Significance Level

Figure 7.4: Reducing Type II Error by Increasing Sample Size

Source: Authors.

Source: Authors.

7.3   Power Calculations for Simple Study Designs

The larger the true population mean effect, the "easier" it is to detect that it is different from zero as a statistically significant difference. This is shown in Figure 7.5. With a larger population mean $\mu_3 > \mu_2$, the Type II error falls from 40% to 20%.

Figure 7.5: A Larger Effect Is Easier to Detect

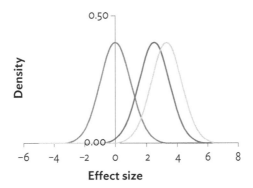

Source: Authors.

Of course, evaluators do not know, and certainly cannot choose the population mean effect—that is what the study estimates. But what can be picked is the minimum effect size (MES), or minimum detectable effect (MDE)—that is, how large (or small) an effect a study can detect. The MES should be based on previous experience of similar interventions and consultation with policy makers. This may be related to the policy objectives of the intervention. Suppose a vocational training program intends to reduce youth unemployment by 10%, and anything less than that will be considered a failure. Then 10% could be the minimum effect size. So, one way to frame the minimum effect size is how large an impact does the program need to have for policy makers to consider the program effective?

As shown below, the minimum effect size depends upon the t–statistic values for the significance level (α) and the chosen level of power ($1-\beta$), as well as the standard error of the outcome variable (σ_y), the proportion of the sample in the treatment group (P), and the sample size (n):

$$MES = \left(t_{\alpha/2} + t_{1-\beta}\right)\sigma_y \sqrt{\frac{1}{P(1 - P)n}} \qquad (7.1)$$

This may be rearranged to give the required sample size as:

$$n = \frac{\left(t_{\alpha/2} + t_{1-\beta}\right)^2 \sigma_y^2}{MES^2 P(1-P)} \tag{7.2}$$

This formula shows the following:

- The larger the sample then the smaller the MES (equation 7.1). To put it another way, the larger the MES is set, then the smaller the required sample (equation 7.2). However, the consequence is to have a low probability of detecting a smaller effect. Hence, setting the MES too large will result in an underpowered study if the intervention does not have such a large impact as expected.

- The MES is minimized with a "balanced sample" (P=0.5), which means that it is usually best to have the same number of observations in treatment and comparison groups.

When applying this formula, the value of σ_y is unknown, since power calculations are done before collecting any data. An estimate of σ_y has to be taken from another data source, preferably from the same country or context. The value of σ_y of course varies by outcome. Power calculations have to be performed separately for each outcome variable. The largest required sample size is the one which has to be chosen. Power calculation software exists to produce the required n based on known parameters.

Returning to the agricultural extension project example introduced at the beginning of the Chapter, suppose that before the project the farmers have an average monthly income of Rs15,000. The project has the target to increase their income by 10%. Data from Andhra Pradesh from a recent income and expenditure survey show a standard deviation of income of Rs12,000. The 10% increase in income is a change of Rs1,500, which is the MES. With α=5% and power of 80% the required sample size is 2,000 (the MES is 1,504).

Examination of equation 7.1 shows it is not linear in n. In other words, to detect a size half as large, the sample size must be more than doubled. Specifically, to detect an effect of a 5% increase in incomes, which is an absolute increase of Rs750, a sample of 8,000 (which gives a MES of 752) is needed. That is, halving the MES quadruples the required sample size. This relationship is shown in Figure 7.6.

**Figure 7.6: Increasing Sample Size Has a Decreasing Effect
on the Minimum Effect Size: Relationship
between Minimum Effect Size and Sample Size**

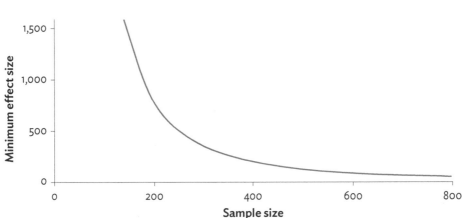

Source: Authors.

This example refers to a simple design, such as a simple randomized controlled trial (RCT). As discussed previously in this book, most impact evaluations use a cluster design. These designs require a modification of the power formula.

7.4 Power Calculations for Cluster Designs

Most impact evaluations of development interventions will require cluster designs in which the unit of assignment contains multiple units for which the data are collected. For example, the agricultural extension program may be assigned by district, village, or farmer group, but outcomes are measured at household level. Education interventions may be assigned to schools, but outcomes are measured for individual students. This has substantial implications for sample sizes, which are often not adequately recognized in impact evaluation studies (Song and Herman 2010).

The intracluster correlation (ICC) coefficient or ρ, is a measure of how similar the units are *within* each cluster. Power is higher the more heterogeneous the units are within a cluster, as reflected in a lower ρ. The ICC is calculated as

$$\rho = \frac{S_b^2}{S_b^2 + S_w^2} \tag{7.3}$$

where S_b^2 is the variance of the outcome variable between clusters, and S_w^2 is the variance of the outcome variable within clusters. The ICC is therefore the fraction of the total variance that is between clusters. When there is no interdependence between individuals within a cluster, the ICC is 0. The ICC would be 1 if there is perfect interdependence between individuals in a cluster. Values of around 0.2 to 0.3 are common.

The best source for the ICC to use in power calculations is from a data set similar to the one that will be used in the evaluation. An ideal data set would be one with the same outcome variable, the same type of cluster, and covering the same population. A second source is from published research articles and reports or publicly available research proposals, registration documents (such as those required for clinical trials), and pre-analysis plans.

Once the sample size has been calculated ignoring statistical dependence within clusters, the sample size needs to be multiplied by the *design effect* to obtain the total sample needed. The design effect is calculated as

$$DE = 1 + (m - 1)\rho \tag{7.4}$$

where m is the number of individuals per cluster and ρ is the ICC. Thus, the true sample size needed, accounting for intracluster correlation, is below.

$$n = \frac{\left(t_{\alpha/2} + t_{1-\beta}\right)^2 \sigma_y^2}{MES^2 P(1 - P)} \left(1 + (m - 1)\rho\right) \tag{7.5}$$

The first point to note is that a cluster design requires more observations than a simple design. Taking again the example from Andhra Pradesh in which it was calculated that with a simple design then, a sample size of 2,000 is required to detect a 10% increase in incomes. With a cluster design if there are 40 observations from 50 clusters, which is 2,000 observations, then the MES is nearly Rs7,000, far in excess of the desired Rs1,500 (ρ=0.2 is used in this example). With a cluster design with 40 observations per cluster and an MES of Rs1,500, 445 clusters are needed or total sample size of 17,800. This is nearly nine times larger than is required for the simple design! Clearly, as this example shows, failure to account for clustering when doing power calculations can result in a seriously underpowered study.

The second important point from equation (7.5) is that the number of clusters is the main factor determining the power of a study for a clustered intervention, rather than the number of observations in each cluster. This fact is clearly illustrated with a numerical example.

In Figure 7.7, the horizontal axis shows the number of clusters (J), and each line corresponds to the number of observations per cluster (n). Consider two samples both with 100 observations: (i) J=10, n=10; and (ii) J=20, n=5. The first of these combinations has a MES of about 820, whereas the second has a MES of around 700. Two samples of the same size do not have the same power, because the number of clusters differs. The sample design with the larger number of clusters is able to detect a smaller effect.

Figure 7.7: Increasing the Number of Clusters Has More Effect on Statistical Power than Increasing the Number of Observations per Cluster

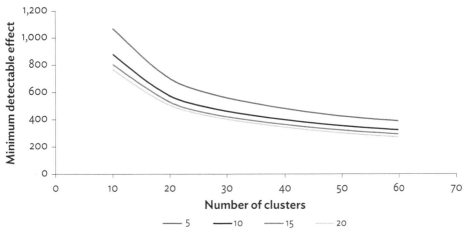

Source: Authors.

These formulas are presented assuming full compliance with an experiment. However, low compliance dilutes the intention to treat effect. Hence, the choice of MES has to take into account compliance rates. Failure to do so will result in an underpowered study.

Actual designs may be more complex still, possibly involving stratified sampling and multiple treatment arms (Appendix 2, section 3 discusses these issues). The approach is also different for regression-based approaches such as regression discontinuity design. It is beyond the scope of this book to present power calculations for such cases. What is important to bear in mind is that power matters, so that power calculations need to be performed and reviewed by someone with the necessary expertise.

7.5 The Danger of Underpowered Studies

Power is the probability of concluding that an intervention has a significant effect when it actually does so. Sample size is usually calculated so that this probability is 80%. If a study is underpowered—that is, the sample is too small—then it has a reduced probability of finding an impact when there is one. It is very common for studies to be underpowered, with a power of only around 50%–60%. Why does this happen?

Studies are commonly underpowered for the following reasons (An-Wen et al. 2008, Noordzij et al. 2010, Rohrer 2010, Fraley and Vazire 2014):

- Project managers or study teams simply select what they think is an appropriate sample size without performing power calculations.

- Clustering of interventions is not considered, and sample power is calculated without considering the ICC. As a result, too few clusters are sampled.

- The ICC is assumed to be lower than is actually the case. Although existing data sources may be consulted, there is considerable variation in ICCs even for the same outcome in the same region. Consideration of the degree of homogeneity (high ICC) or heterogeneity (low ICC) of the population within each cluster can help to lead to more realistic ICC assumptions.

- The MES is set too high. Project targets are often unrealistic. Using these as the basis for the MES will mean that the study will be less likely to detect smaller, but still important, effects. It may also be that the impact evaluation is premature. The effect will reach the expected level, but has not yet done so.

- Overoptimistic assumptions are made regarding compliance/participation.

- The outcome variable may be assumed to have a lower variance than it actually has. This could be the case if the value is taken from a non-comparable population.

- Power calculations are done for one outcome variable, but this may not give sufficient sample size for other outcome variables. Power calculations have to be done for all outcomes of interest and the largest required sample used.

- The study may be powered sufficiently to estimate the average treatment effect, but not for any subgroup analysis. So the study may say there is no heterogeneity in impact between say men and women, or urban and rural areas. But in fact, there was insufficient power for such analysis. The power calculations should allow for any planned subgroup analysis.

- There is attrition in the study design, such that data are actually collected from a smaller sample than originally planned.

7.6 Aids for Considering and Performing Power Calculations

In addition to the potential pitfalls listed above, it is useful to be aware of some general rules of thumb which can serve as an initial guide for assessing the sample requirements for impact evaluation:

- A common rule of thumb is that the required sample size per group is $n = 16/mes^2$ where mes is MES expressed in standard deviations. So if mes=0.5, n=64 per group or a total sample size of 128 if there is just one treatment arm and a comparison arm where there is no clustering. For social and economic interventions the mes is often much smaller, say around 0.1, which gives a required total sample size of 1,600 per arm. The formula is per arm. So for a factorial design with four arms (A, B, A+B, and comparison) the sample size is $4 \times 16/ mes^2$, e.g., 256 with a mes of 0.5, and 4,800 with a mes of 0.1.

- The formulas for rules of thumb for cluster designs are more complex, being dependent on several features of intervention and study design. A crude rule of thumb is that 60 clusters (30 treatment and 30 comparison) can generally be a bare minimum requirement. In some selected cases where the ICC is low and the MES is high, 30 clusters may be sufficient (McNeish and Stapleton 2016). In a subset of those cases, it may be possible to go below 30 clusters with cluster matching (e.g., matched pair randomization).

There are several software options for sample size calculations. The best known software specifically for this purpose is Optimal Design (Raudenbush et al. 2011). Statistics packages such as STATA, SAS, SPSS, and R can also be used to perform power calculations. These are specialized tools which project managers are unlikely to have time to use. A more user-friendly option is the 3ie Excel Power Calculator and associated guide (Djimeu and Houndolo 2016).

Key considerations when planning sample sizes include the following:

- Power calculations should be performed for all outcomes, and the largest required sample size used.

- At least an extra 10% should be added to allow for respondent replacement and partially completed surveys.

- If subgroup analysis is to be carried out, the sample size applies to the subgroup.

- If comparing between treatments (A/B designs), the relevant MES is the difference in effects not the absolute effect. Hence, A/B designs are likely to need larger samples.

- Compliance affects required sample size. If compliance with the program is low, the required sample size increases.

As mentioned above, a power calculation also needs assumptions requiring the ICC and the variance of the outcome variable. Common sources for these are (i) existing impact evaluations on the same topic (a request may need to be sent to the authors of the study for the data), (ii) other quantitative studies in the same country or region, (iii) analysis of public data sets such as income and expenditure surveys, (iv) systematic reviews, and (v) a growing number of papers reporting such data for power calculation purposes.

References

An-Wen, C., A. Hróbjartsson, K. J. Jørgensen, P. C. Gøtzsche, and D. G. Altman. 2008. Discrepancies in Sample Size Calculations and Data Analyses Reported in Randomised Trials: Comparison of Publications with Protocols. *BMJ*. 337. a2299.

Djimeu, E. W. and D. Houndolo. 2016. Power Calculation for Causal Inference in Social Science: Sample Size and Minimum Detectable Effect Determination. 3ie Impact Evaluation Manual. Working Paper 26. Delhi: 3IE. www.3ieimpact.org/media/filer_public/2016/07/08/wp26-power-calculation.pdf and http://www.3ieimpact.org/media/filer_public/2016/03/22/3ie-sample-size-minimum-detectable-effect-calculator.xlsx.

Fraley, R. C. and S. Vazire. 2014. The N-Pact Factor: Evaluating the Quality of Empirical Journals with Respect to Sample Size and Statistical Power. *PLoS ONE*. 9 (10). doi:10.1371/journal.pone.0109019

McNeish, D. M. and L. M. Stapleton. 2016. The Effect of Small Sample Size on Two-Level Model Estimates: A Review and Illustration. *L. M. Educational Psychology Review*. 28 (2). pp. 295–314. https://doi.org/10.1007/s10648-014-9287-x.

Noordzij, M., G. Tripepi, F. W. Dekker, C. Zoccali, M. W. Tanck, and K. J. Jager. 2010. Sample Size Calculations: Basic Principles and Common Pitfalls. *Nephrology Dialysis Transplantation*. 25 (5). pp. 1388–1393.

Raudenbush, S. W., H. Bloom, J. Spybrook, and A. Martinez. 2011. Optimal Design Software for Multi-Level and Longitudinal Research (Version 3.01) [Software]. http://hlmsoft.net/od/.

Rohrer, J. E. 2010. Nonrandomized Impact Evaluation Studies: Errors and Tips. *Journal of Primary Care & Community Health*. 1 (2). pp. 70–72.

Song, M. and R. Herman. 2010. Critical Issues and Common Pitfalls in Designing and Conducting Impact Studies in Education: Lessons Learned From the What Works Clearinghouse (Phase I). *Educational Evaluation and Policy Analysis*. 32 (3). pp. 351–371. http://www.jstor.org/stable/40963082.

Further Reading

Batistatou, E., C. Roberts, and S. Roberts. 2014. Sample Size and Power Calculations for Trials and Quasi-Experimental Studies with Clustering. *The Stata Journal.* 14 (1). pp. 159–175. www.stata-journal.com/article.html?article=st0329.

Bell, B. A., G. B. Morgan, J. A. Schoeneberger, J. D. Kromrey, and J. M. Ferron. 2014. How Low Can You Go? An Investigation of the Influence of Sample Size and Model Complexity on Point and Interval Estimates in Two-Level Linear Models. *Methodology: European Journal of Research Methods for the Behavioral and Social Sciences.* 10. pp. 1–11. http://econtent.hogrefe.com/doi/abs/10.1027/1614-2241/a000062.

Reich, N. G., J. A. Myers, D. Obeng, A. M. Milstone, and T. M. Perl. 2012. Empirical Power and Sample Size Calculations for Cluster-Randomized and Cluster-Randomized Crossover Studies. *PLoS ONE.* 7 (4). e35564. http://doi.org/10.1371/journal.pone.0035564.

Schulz, K. F. and D. A. Grimes. 2005. Sample Size Calculations in Randomised Trials: Mandatory and Mystical. *The Lancet.* 365 (9467). pp. 1348–1353. https://www.ncbi.nlm.nih.gov/pubmed/15823387.

Chapter 8
Managing the Impact Evaluation Process

Key Messages

- Impact evaluation planning should consider the contribution that can be made beyond existing evidence, demands for the evidence, and evaluability of the intervention.

- Stakeholder engagement is critical, not only to ensure relevance, but also to ensure integrity of the design.

- Some impact evaluations may take several years to conduct, and appropriate mechanisms need to be created to ensure stewardship over the period, which may not correspond exactly with the project cycle.

- Careful review and engagement by project staff and experienced impact evaluators are necessary to ensure fidelity of study design, implementation, data collection, and the validity of analysis.

8.1 Introduction to Managing Impact Evaluations

Generating a meaningful impact evaluation depends as much on getting the process right as on having a rigorous methodology. This Chapter addresses issues that those who manage impact evaluations may face. This includes (i) planning impact evaluations, (ii) selecting an impact evaluation design, (iii) budgeting and managing an impact evaluation, (iv) impact evaluation resources, and (v) interpreting impact evaluation findings.

8.2 Planning Impact Evaluations

For which interventions should impact evaluation be performed?

Impact evaluations only have value if the evidence generated is used. They should be oriented toward generating evidence that can help to improve development programming, in terms of "proof of concept" that can support continuing, replicating, or upscaling an intervention, or more specific insights on how interventions can be made more effective. To do so, there should be a clear conceptualization of how impact evaluation of a particular intervention contributes to the body of evidence already generated. This means that impact evaluation priorities should be based on gaps that exist between information needs of key audiences and existing evidence.

A starting point can be discussions with development policy makers (from governments, donor agencies, academia, and other organizations) in a particular sector and/or geographic region, so as to understand information needs regarding intervention effects and opportunities for influence. These needs will often include much that goes beyond the remit of impact evaluation, but it still is essential to understand how impact evaluation can meet such needs, so that use is enhanced (IEG 2012). To determine whether the information demands can be informed by impact evaluation, they may be screened against the following questions: (i) does the information need pertain to the theory of change of an existing, planned, or pilotable intervention?; (ii) does it concern outcomes/effects conditioned by (human) behavioral responses to interventions?; (iii) is it possible to do field implementation of the intervention of interest in the time frame of the information need?

The next step can be to compare demands with existing information supply. There is a rapidly growing body of *systematic reviews*, which are based on comprehensive literature inventories for particular topics and meta-analyses to identify associations between intervention attributes and effect estimates. These reviews serve as good starting point for understanding evidence available. To go beyond this, original queries may be conducted in the impact evaluation repository and scholarly databases of the International Initiative for Impact Evaluation (3ie), and web searches may be performed on ongoing studies. Priority may be accorded to studies that evaluate interventions with scant evidence, outcomes that have not been investigated, or broader theories that are untested.

Impact evaluation may also be demand-driven and requested by project implementers. In this case, it is good to fully flesh out the possibilities (which may not be an impact evaluation of an entire project) before determining whether, when, and at what scale impact evaluation is appropriate. This will involve detailed discussion to understand information demands to be served, the theory of change, and whether impact evaluation is feasible, or, in other terms, whether the intervention is *evaluable* (Peersman et al. 2015). Evaluability depends on (i) clarity of the theory of change and associated hypotheses to be tested;

(ii) ability to generate sufficient observations for statistical power on outcomes of interest; and (iii) whether there is an impact evaluation design that makes the Stable Unit Treatment Value Assumption appropriate for the intervention.

When does the impact evaluation design need to be prepared?

Although impact is generally measured years after an intervention is initiated, the design of the study is best carried out prior to field implementation of the intervention, via prospective impact evaluation design. Prospective impact evaluation designs are nearly always stronger than those designs prepared once an intervention has been implemented in the field. The main advantages of prospective designs are as follows: (i) baseline data can be captured prior to the intervention having effects in the field, (ii) the possibility of random assignment can be considered, and (iii) key stakeholders can be consulted on and convinced about the importance of evaluation questions early in the process. Baseline data allow a check for balance (whether treatment and comparison groups have the same average characteristics), and estimation of more robust impact estimates.

The key challenge in initiating an impact evaluation prior to field implementation is that intervention rollout may not yet be known, and may be susceptible to changes after baseline initiation, such that control and treatment populations are not stable. This means that impact evaluation is often best considered once expected project implementation plans are sufficiently understood. Possibilities to use impact evaluation for interventions on a trial basis can benefit from very early engagement, so as to embed opportunities for randomization.

Where there are multiple investments in the same or related sectors in the same areas, it may be possible to use a single baseline across several projects. Such an approach could increase up-front coordination costs, but result in substantial cost savings later on.

Ensuring stakeholder buy-in

There is a wide range of stakeholders to include in the early stages of planning an impact evaluation. In the implementing agency, understanding of, and support for, the approach, is necessary from the agency leadership but also from field staff implementing the project/program. Responsible line ministry staff should be engaged, including support at a high level to minimize the risk of political interference that undermines the integrity of the design (most usually by placing the evaluated intervention in comparison areas). The relevant community should be engaged early on, including identification of potential research agencies to undertake the study. Local capacity to implement quality impact evaluations is growing in most countries, and there are also regional research agencies that may be engaged.

Agreement and cooperation of government and project staff will be necessary to understand project rollout, identify participants and nonparticipants, and avoid contamination. Strong buy-in is usually most essential for experimental designs to ensure fidelity, so that the project treats treatment groups and does not treat control groups.

Impact evaluations address the attribution question. But the data collected for the study may address a broader range of evaluation questions such as targeting, reasons for non-participation, and implementation issues. To ensure maximum relevance, stakeholders should be consulted on what other evaluation questions may be of interest to them, possibly via a theory of change workshop. These workshops help the study team's understanding of the project, and to identify relevant evaluation questions in collaboration with the partners. They are also an opportunity for the study team to present the proposed impact evaluation design.

8.3 Selecting an Impact Evaluation Design

An identification strategy is the heart of impact evaluation, and all impact evaluations should specify the intended strategy prior to initiation. In many cases, it can be useful to consider which identification strategies may be appropriate before external study teams are involved. The decision guide in Table 8.1 lists the main questions to guide the choice of design, and how they can help to identify an appropriate approach.

Ensuring a rigorous approach

To reduce risk of failure to detect significant effects, it is often useful for proposals to include multiple possible identification strategies. In nonexperimental designs, there may be unexpected associations that affect the validity of certain approaches, such as instrumental variables, program rollout may not be expected, or there may be technical issues in implementing certain regression routines. In experimental designs, there may be failure to adhere to the randomization protocol, improper treatment administration, contamination, or low participation rates. In these cases, it may be necessary to revisit the study design, for example, replacing a randomized controlled trial (RCT) with instrumental variables. In anticipation of such cases, the evaluation design should have a backup identification strategy.

Table 8.1: Selecting an Impact Evaluation Design: A Decision Approach

Q1	Is it a prospective design?	Yes>>Q1.1 No >> Q2
Q1.1	Is random assignment possible?	Yes>>Q1.2 No >> Q2
Q1.2	Is the unit of assignment the same as the unit of treatment and analysis?	Yes>>Q1.3 No: **Cluster RCT**
Q1.3	Are there likely to be important spillover effects?	Yes: **Cluster RCT** No: **Simple RCT**
Q2	Is a natural experiment possible?	Yes: **Natural experiment** No >> Q3
Q3	Is it a universally available intervention which is not universally adopted?	Yes >> Q3.1 No >> Q4
Q3.1	Can a valid encouragement be identified?	Yes: **Encouragement design** No >> Q4
Q4	Are there many treated units of assignment?	Yes: Q5 No: Q4.1
Q4.1	Are there many periods of observations prior to the intervention?	Yes: Q4.2 No: **Consider an alternative to impact evaluation**
Q4.2	Do observations include untreated units that can serve as comparators?	Yes: **Synthetic controls**
Q5	Is there an eligibility threshold rule (including a temporal threshold when the program was introduced)?	Yes >> Q5.1 No >> Q6
Q5.1	Was the rule strictly applied?	Yes: **Regression discontinuity design (RDD) (including ITS)** No: **Fuzzy RDD**
Q6	Is it likely that unobservables affect selection?	Yes >> Q7 No >> Q6.1
Q6.1	Are baseline data available?	Yes: **Difference-in-difference or fixed effects** No: **Propensity score-based approaches**
Q7	Are the unobservables likely to be time invariant?	Yes >> Q7.1 No >> Q8
Q7.1	Are baseline data available?	Yes: **Difference-in-differences or fixed effects** No >> Q8
Q8	Can an identifying restriction or a valid instrument be identified?	Yes: **Instrumental variables, endogenous treatment or switching regression** No: Consider alternatives to impact evaluation

ITS = interrupted time series, RCT = randomized controlled trial.
Source: Authors.

The quality of study design is enhanced by close stakeholder engagement, especially at early stages. This engagement can be through various mechanisms such as theory of change workshops, advisory groups, or involvement in formal peer review.

Many agencies form an advisory group to oversee impact evaluations (as well as other forms of evaluation) (VeLure Roholt and Baizerman 2012). The advisory group should comprise at minimum 3–4 individuals, including at least one with impact evaluation expertise and one with sector knowledge. Local think tanks or other academic institutions should normally be represented on the advisory group. This may be a virtual group, submitting comments by e-mail, or members may participate in workshops at which the proposed design and initial study findings are presented.

Ethical issues

The main ethical issues which arise in conducting an impact evaluation relate to the following:

- Establishing a control group (where the issue is raised most frequently for RCTs, as discussed in Chapter 4)

- Human subject issues in data collection

Very few interventions aim for universal coverage immediately, and even if they do, few attain it. Thus, there is often an untreated population anyway from which to draw a control or comparison group. Impact evaluation does not create the untreated population—it either uses existing variation in treatment, or makes the treatment assignment more systematic. In many cases, RCTs only alter the timing of assignment or provide an additional incentive for participation.

In few cases is there a clear basis for ethical objections to the existence of a comparison or control group. That is not to say that comparison group members may not feel unfairly treated, especially as they are exposed to data collection for an intervention which yields them no direct benefits.

A more complicated array of ethical issues may arise in impact evaluations that include a placebo treatment for the control group, so as to eliminate bias introduced by knowledge of treatment. The ethical issue introduced concerns that respondents may be provided an intervention that is not fully characterized, and where informed consent may be made more challenging. For these situations, the standards applied should be similar to those of medical research, and all efforts should be made to openly present interventions in a non-misleading manner.

Human subject issues mostly regard data collection, as discussed in Chapter 6. As mentioned there, the study design and data collection may well require ethical approval from the research agency or in the country itself. Good practice should be followed in obtaining informed consent. Remuneration for comparison respondents or their communities may need to be considered. The treatment of ethical issues should be described in the impact evaluation report (Box 8.1 provides an example).

Box 8.1: Reporting Treatment of Ethical Issues

A study of handwashing promotion in Karachi reported the following information regarding ethical issues:

"Control households regularly received children's books, notebooks, pens or pencils but no messaging about handwashing or water treatment. An adult in each household provided written informed consent for the household. The protocol was approved by the institutional review boards at the Centers for Disease Control and Prevention and HOPE."

Source: Bowen et al. (2012).

8.4 Timing and Budgeting for Impact Evaluation

Timeline

In traditional project monitoring, the baseline survey is conducted in the first year or two of a project and the endline survey in the last year. Both of these timings may or may not make sense for an impact evaluation. The baseline is a challenge as it may get overlooked during the busy period of project start-up. The endline is a challenge as it may best be done once the project is closed so there is no longer formal donor involvement.

In some cases, a survey is conducted as part of project preparation, and it may seem that this survey could be used for the baseline. Usually this is not feasible because (i) such samples are too small for sufficient sample power (discussed in Chapter 7); (ii) not enough is known about the project to determine either treatment or control sample or survey instrument design; and (iii) such surveys often lack sufficient detail to accurately capture outcomes of interest or conditioning factors.

The baseline should be conducted before services start being delivered to the beneficiary population, but it may still be after project initiation. For example, a project constructing large infrastructure will likely not start to yield benefits until at least 3 to 4 years into the project. Hence, the baseline survey need not be conducted in year 1, but can be conducted up to shortly before the infrastructure is open for use. On the other hand, if services will be available soon after the project starts, such as may be the case for microcredit, the baseline needs to precede the project implementation.

When the endline should be conducted depends on the amount of time required for the desired impact to be observed. The temporal dimension of the theory of change should indicate how long this time is (Chapter 2). The intervention may have an "impact trajectory" by which the observed impact depends on the point at which impact is measured.

The endline survey should only take place once it is expected that there is sufficient impact on a sufficiently large scale to be detectable. The timing difference between baseline and endline may be longer or shorter than the duration of the project or project component being evaluated. In the case of a large infrastructure project, the endline will often need to be at project completion, or even some years later. However, in the case of microcredit, for example, it may be possible to do the endline while project implementation is still ongoing.

Sufficient time has to be allowed for survey design. Survey design, piloting, and enumerator training often take 3–6 months. Survey instruments have to be thoroughly tested. Rushing this process will undermine the quality of the data and therefore the usefulness of the study (Chapter 6 provides more discussion). Once the data have been collected, a further 3–6 months are required for data entry, cleaning, and preliminary data analysis. A similar time needs to be allowed for the analysis of endline data.

While two rounds of data collection are often the minimum for rigorous impact evaluation designs, additional data collection often can further strengthen analysis. For example, if baseline and endline are 3 or more years apart, then a midterm survey may also be considered (Table 8.2). Interventions with effects that vary seasonally or within the year may require seasonal survey implementation. In experimental designs, more frequent data collection may be needed to monitor assignment, treatment, and possible contamination. This may involve short surveys by telephone or in person with a subsample of those surveyed.

Table 8.2: Illustrative Timeline for Impact Evaluation

	1 year before project	3–6 months before project start	Year 0	Year 3	Year 5
Project timeline	Initiate project design	Project approval	Project setup and start	Midterm review	Project close
Impact evaluation timeline	Initiate study design	Finalize study design. Design and test survey instruments	Baseline data collection	Midline data collection: smaller sample, process-oriented	Endline survey and analysis. Report 6 months after survey

Source: Authors.

Managing delays and changes in project design

Delays may occur in both the project interventions and in the impact evaluation. Implementation delays at the start of the project can be an advantage in some cases, as they can give more time to conduct the baseline. A delay in the baseline is, on the other hand, problematic if it means that the survey has taken place after substantial project rollout. A clear and realistic study timeline needs to be agreed up-front, which takes into account any seasonal issues related to the timing of data collection (as discussed in Chapter 6).

Delays in intervention implementation matter if they mean that the project will not have had time or sufficient rollout to deliver the expected impact. The timing and choice to conduct an endline often needs to remain flexible to slower than anticipated project implementation.

Many projects undergo changes to their design as they are implemented. The study team needs to be aware of changes in project design which have implications for the study. Project rollout may continue into control areas, or treatment areas may no longer be targeted by the project. Regular communication with the project team may help to avoid contamination problems.

Impact evaluation stewardship

The length of time between survey rounds can create critical challenges within the organizations that often manage impact evaluations (e.g., donors and the executing agencies in charge of project implementation and funding). Staff turnover can pose significant challenges to ensuring continued attention to impact evaluation. The fact that impact evaluation activities are a noncore segment of each project, with a long period of inactivity between data collection rounds, can easily make attention "fall through the cracks." To ensure continuity, there should be planning for continued long-term impact evaluation oversight even if project staff change.

Budget

The average cost of one survey round of a range of ADB-supported impact evaluations is around $200,000 (Table 8.3), or about $400,000 for an entire study. The average budget for studies supported by 3ie, a well-known organization for impact evaluation, is $450,000. Impact evaluation studies supported by large agencies, such as the United States Agency for International Development and the World Bank, frequently cost in excess of $1 million. These costs can be reduced by using analytical resources from donor and government agencies, rather than costly international consultants.

The main items in the budget for an impact evaluation are the costs of experts and survey costs. Impact evaluations in Asia tend to be somewhat less expensive than the global average due to somewhat lower costs of survey implementation.

Survey costs depend on (i) the number of survey rounds, (ii) sample size, and (iii) the geographic location of data collection. The sample size should be determined by power calculations, and budgeted accordingly. When cost is a constraint, study sites may in some cases be restricted to reduce the survey budget. For example, for a project in 10 districts, only six may be surveyed rather than 10—at the expense of external validity.

Table 8.3: Budgets of Selected ADB-Supported Impact Evaluations, ($)

Item	JobStart (Philippines)	Metro Extension (Georgia)	Medicard and Food Stamp (Mongolia)	Climate Change and Women (Viet Nam)	Labor-Based Road Work (Pacific)	Small and Medium Farmers (Nepal)
Design	Simple RCT	DiD	RDD	DiD	DiD	DiD
International staff	130,000	120,000	121,000	104,000	80,000	102,304
National staff	96,000	70,000	–	–	–	–
Survey	160,000	44,000	87,000	71,000	60,000	110,700
Workshops and travel	10,000	44,000	–	–	35,000	19,000
Other	–	22,000	19,700	–	–	18,560
Total	396,000	300,000	227,700	175,000	175,000	250,564

– = not applicable, ADB = Asian Development Bank, DiD = difference-in-differences, RCT = randomized controlled trial, RDD = regression discontinuity design.
Source: Authors.

Funding source

The fact that projects often need to be financially closed before an endline survey and the ensuing impact evaluation analysis can be completed may preclude funding by the assessed project. That is a key problem that organizations and project teams need to address whenever planning an impact evaluation effort. For an international financial institution, certain multitranche modalities can better cope with this difficulty, but project modalities are nearly never chosen in function of the needs of the impact evaluation effort. Alternative solutions often need to be devised at the organizational level to pool resources across projects.

Contracting impact evaluations

A high-quality IE depends on engaging a skilled team to conduct the study. However, even with a skilled team, a rigorous peer review process can help ensure relevance and feasibility of the design in the field.

Most impact evaluations are conducted by academic researchers, although private firms are also offering more impact evaluation services. There is a trade-off in the choice of study team. Academic researchers are likely to produce stronger impact evaluation designs, but they are less likely to want to evaluate specific projects or focus on context-specific questions. There is, hence, a danger of "researcher capture" (discussed later in this Chapter). Private consultancies are more likely to "stick to contract" but may be less likely to suggest rigorous or innovative designs. An exception can be the emerging group of private companies that have invested in impact evaluation capacity (Annex 8.1). There are a couple of unique and specific aspects to contracting an impact evaluation:

(i) The skill set for conducting impact evaluations is different to that required for the process evaluations, which are more frequently conducted. Annex 8.1 lists some of the leading agencies conducting impact evaluations. Individual experts may also be found through the 3ie expert roster.

(ii) The team should include prior experience in designing and executing an impact evaluation, preferably in the sector and region of the proposed study. The experience should include fieldwork in a developing country setting if data collection is required for the study. If the latter is not the case, then sector expertise should also be present in the team. Previous impact evaluation reports by the researchers can be used to help understand the skills of proposed teams.

Oversight of impact evaluation conduct

Close and continued engagement between the study team and key stakeholders increases the relevance of the evaluation. This engagement should start at the study design stage, with the theory of change and the evaluation questions. The study team should deliver an inception report with the full study design, sampling strategy, and survey instruments. The actual sample will need to be agreed (at least at cluster level) also once it is determined. The contract should specify a report to be delivered after each survey round and the contents of that report, e.g., balance tests at baseline.

In addition, requirements for data documentation and archiving should be clear from the onset. Data should be shared immediately after cleaning with those managing the impact evaluation. There should be a clear agreement with study teams on minimum data checks to be carried out, including independent verification. These data checks also include checking for balance at baseline.

A particular challenge for impact evaluations is that they are often carried out over a long period of time with a period of inactivity in between. The baseline data need to be properly documented and archived. In the case of panel data, a mechanism for relocating the same primary sampling units is needed, as well as a protocol of what to do when they cannot be relocated. There needs to be comparability between the surveys between rounds; usually the same survey instruments should be used for each round. There may be problems in consistency and incentives if different entities implement different survey rounds.

Quality control of final product

From the onset, it is useful to make publication and dissemination plans clear, along with expected quality control processes. The main study report may be subjected to review by stakeholders and external peer review. This review can come from the advisory group mentioned above, or separately contracted impact evaluation experts. The peer reviewers should include at least one sector specialist and one qualified impact evaluation researcher.

Researcher capture

Most impact evaluations are conducted by academic researchers rather than consultancy firms. Academic researchers are more likely to have the requisite skill set to design and implement impact evaluations, although private firms are also starting to invest in these skills. However, academics are often motivated by the need to publish peer-reviewed articles. "Researcher capture" occurs when the study team designs the study, or conducts analysis to produce papers that may be publishable in academic journals, but which do not directly address the evaluation questions of interest to the evaluation audience. Academic researchers may also have ideas on experiments and data collection that do not correspond with field realities, and thus can take studies in impractical or irrelevant directions (Barrett and Carter 2010).

Research capture can be mitigated in various ways. First, the scope of work should be clearly defined before contracting in a manner that is relevant to the intervention. Second, the evaluation questions should be clearly and unambiguously stated in the terms of reference. Third, use of an advisory group may include an impact evaluation expert who can provide technical scrutiny to the proposal. The impact evaluation expert can help confront arguments made by the researchers as to why they can or should not address the evaluation questions of interest to the project. Fourth, the impact evaluation implementation should be closely monitored to ensure that the original evaluation questions will be adequately addressed as the design is finalized and data collection takes place. Fifth, the contract and the review process may be structured so as to allow a final review process, which ensures the final report does answer the agreed evaluation questions.

8.5 Where Help for Impact Evaluation Can Be Obtained

Advice

Noneconomist development practitioners may benefit from discussions with impact evaluators and other economists to obtain feedback on whether an impact evaluation of their project is appropriate to consider. For example, at ADB, there are staff in the Economic Research and Regional Cooperation Department who may be consulted. Relevant academics may also be approached, or impact evaluation-oriented nongovernment organizations may be consulted.

Finding an expert

Impact evaluations require a specific skill set, and the field of practitioners is limited. Competitive bidding for impact evaluation assignments may not attract these practitioners unless the right people and organizations know about the opportunity.

There are four main ways to find experts:

1. A list or roster of experts may be consulted:

   - 3ie maintains a roster of impact evaluation experts which is searchable by county and sector (http://www.3ieimpact.org/en/evaluation/expert-roster/). All those in the roster have agreed to their names being included.

   - Jamal Latif Poverty Action Lab's website lists their affiliates, showing their region of interest (https://www.povertyactionlab.org/affiliated-researchers).

   - The website of Innovations for Poverty Action lists their research affiliates and their broader research network (https://www.poverty-action.org/research).

   - The Bureau for Research and Economic Analysis of Development lists leading economic researchers, mainly in the United States, though not all will work on impact evaluation (http://ibread.org/bread/people).

2. Authors who have conducted impact evaluations on similar interventions to the one to be evaluated or in the same sector in the region may be identified. Existing impact evaluations can be found in the following:

   - The 3ie Evidence Database is a comprehensive listing of impact evaluations in developing countries (http://www.3ieimpact.org/en/evidence/). It is linked to the 3ie expert roster, and is searchable by sector, country, and region.

   - The economics paper database, IDEAS, has a large selection of published and unpublished economics database (https://ideas.repec.org/). It is not impact evaluation specific, but including "impact evaluation" in the search term should yield papers of interest.

   - Google Scholar has the most comprehensive selection of academic papers, but any search is also likely to produce a large number of irrelevant hits (https://scholar.google.com).

3. Those who have experience managing impact evaluations may be asked for their recommendations, based on their experience.

4. Open calls for proposals may be advertised. Impact evaluations are large studies, usually requiring the organization of large-scale data collection. An increasing number of private sector consultancy companies are developing impact evaluation capacity, though some may not have the full skill set required. A list of well-known agencies that produce impact evaluations is included in Annex 8.1.

If the study is put out to competitive tender it is important to ensure that suitably qualified companies are made aware of the opportunity. Some agencies, such as 3ie, can be contacted to feature the announcement on their websites.

8.6 Interpreting and Presenting Impact Evaluation Findings

Threats to validity

Interpretation of impact evaluation findings must consider threats to the validity of the analysis. The first consideration should be internal validity, and whether effects are appropriately identified for the analyzed sample. In general, there are more potential threats to internal validity for a quasi-experimental study than a properly implemented randomized controlled trial.

For a randomized controlled trial, it is imperative to understand that the intended randomization protocol was fully implemented, and that there was no scope for field staff to shortcut the process. Care must be taken also to assure that data collection is comparably conducted for treated and untreated populations. Otherwise, "Hawthorne effects" may mean that differential levels of observation affect behavior, or at least reporting. It is also important to ascertain whether differential knowledge of treatment between treated and controlled groups may bias responses. One form of bias may be a "John Henry effect," such that the control group alters behavior in response to knowing that they are untreated. Conversely, placebo effects may induce changes by the treated based on expectations of treatment.

For quasi-experimental studies, a primary concern will often be omitted variable bias, since not all possible variables can be controlled in regression or matching-based approaches. In these cases, careful scrutiny of the models applied should be performed. For instrumental variables, attention needs to be paid to the instrument selected and whether it is unconfounded with outcomes. For regression discontinuity designs, balance around the eligibility cutoff of the assignment variable should be reviewed.

For all studies, it is essential to ascertain that no other programs than the evaluated intervention are being differentially administered to treated and control populations. In all studies, it is also important to verify that any clustering in intervention administration is appropriately reflected in standard errors reported for treatment effects. After study publication, if possible, data used should be placed in the public domain to enable further analysis.

External validity, or the generalizability of findings that have internal validity, should be the other major area for attention. An impact evaluation reports the impact of a specific design in a specific context. Whether these findings translate to other contexts is known as the external validity of the design. Suppose a study finds that a computer-assisted learning intervention among primary school students in which each student gets 1 hour of computer time a week increases learning outcomes by 10%. This does not mean that the analysis would find the same result in secondary school students. Nor does it imply that doubling the time to 2 hours a week will necessarily give a 20% increase in learning outcomes.

What do the results mean?

The main results of impact evaluation studies consist of treatment effect magnitudes and their statistical significance. When interpreting these findings, it is important not to be "dazzled by the stars." That is, large-n studies often focus on the statistical significance of effects, whereas the effect size is equally important, and is of more interest to many policy makers. With a large sample, very small effect sizes, which may be too small to be relevant for policy, may be statistically significant. So, it is very important to have a metric to interpret the effect size.

The effect size may be reported in units that are readily understandable by policy makers. For example, improvements in learning outcomes are commonly reported as the improvement in test scores in standard deviations. It is known among sector experts that 0.2 standard deviations is a "good improvement." Children typically advance by 0.20–0.25 standard deviations a year. So an intervention achieving a 0.2 improvement is equivalent to the learning from an additional year's schooling. In cases where levels of the outcome variable are well understood, such as crop yields per hectare, effects in levels may be useful. For many interventions, percentage improvements in the outcome variable from untreated to treated may be easy to understand.

Cost-effectiveness analysis can be used to estimate the cost of a standardized improvement in outcomes of interest (Box 8.2 shows an example). Cost-effectiveness analysis is appropriate when there is a single outcome of interest. In other cases, treatment effect estimates may be used as inputs into economic surplus models that can underpin cost–benefit analysis.

Box 8.2: Cost-Effectiveness Analysis of Interventions to Increase School Attendance

Cost-effectiveness analysis requires a common metric for the numerator. In the case shown here, all studies estimate the impact of the respective interventions on years of school attendance.

The first four interventions shown did not have a significant impact.

The other examples illustrate the importance of considering cost. Proving information on the returns to education to parents is by far the most effective intervention—not because it has a notably larger impact but because it is lower cost.

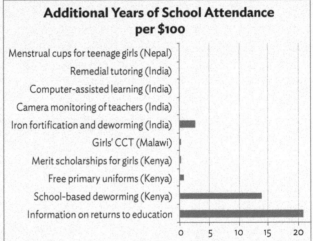

CCT = conditional cash transfer.
Source: Based on Dhaliwal et al. (2012).

8.7 Conclusions: Toward Evidence-Based Directions for Development

The products of impact evaluation will have numerous applications, and can inform decisions at many levels. The impact evaluation process, in and of itself, can become a fulcrum of interaction between applied researchers and development practitioners. It exposes development practitioners to behavioral theories and concepts that they may not have considered, as well as experiences with similar interventions that they may not yet know. Similarly, the process brings researchers into contact with field realities, so that they understand how theoretical considerations actually translate into action. The rigor with which intervention implementation is considered under impact evaluation can also enhance operations, as it can help enforce that field protocols are consistently interpreted and strictly followed.

Generating robust evidence on theories, understanding, and assumptions underpinning development programming can have uses at many levels. It can improve the long-term conceptualization of development, as well designed studies can be published in top tier journals and attract considerable attention in academic communities and the public at large. This can percolate into a range of policy and programmatic improvements across the globe. However, this is only one channel of influence. Impact evaluation findings can also provide more direct evidence to defend and expand interventions that are beneficial, and replicate them elsewhere. They can show how specific types of projects can be done better and offer proof of concept for innovations and enhancements. Impact evaluation can bring attention to things that work in development and help to realign incentives toward organizations and teams that offer new ideas and development results. In short, impact evaluation can allow development practitioners to follow the processes of product testing, learning, and continual improvement that have driven the successes of innovative companies in the private sector.

References

Barrett, C. and M. Carter. 2010. The Power and Pitfalls of Experiments in Development Economics: Some Non-Random Reflections. *Applied Economic Perspectives and Policy*. 32 (4). pp. 515–548.

Bowen A., M. Agboatwalla, S. Luby, T. Tobery, T. Ayers, and R. M. Hoekstra. 2012. Association Between Intensive Handwashing Promotion and Child Development in Karachi, Pakistan: A Cluster Randomized Controlled Trial. *Archives Pediatric Adolescent Medicine*. 166 (11). pp. 1037–1044.

Dhaliwal, I., E. Duflo, R. Glennerster, and C. Tulloch. 2012. Comparative Cost-Effectiveness Analysis to Inform Policy in Developing Countries: A General Framework with Applications for Education. Abdul Latif Jameel Poverty Action Lab (J-PAL). Boston: MIT.

Independent Evaluation Group (IEG). 2012. *World Bank Group Impact Evaluations: Relevance and Effectiveness*. Washington, DC: World Bank. DOI: 10.1596/978-0-82139717-6.

Peersman, G., I. Guijt, and T. Pasanen. 2015. Evaluability Assessment for Impact Evaluation. A Methods Lab Publication. London: Overseas Development Institute.

VeLure Roholt, R. and M. L. Baizerman. 2012. *Evaluation Advisory Groups: New Directions for Evaluation, Number 136*. Hoboken, New Jersey: Wiley.

Further Reading

Bamberger, M. 2006. Conducting Quality Impact Evaluations Under Budget, Time and Data Constraints. *Doing Impact Evaluation No. 2*. Washington, DC: World Bank. http://lnweb18.worldbank.org/oed/oeddoclib.nsf/24cc3bb1f94ae11c85256808006a0046/757a5cc0bae22558852571770059d89c/$FILE/conduct_qual_impact.pdf.

Bedi, T., S. Bhatti, X. Gine, E. Galasso, M. Goldstein, and A. Legovini. 2006. Impact Evaluation and the Project Cycle. *Doing Impact Evaluation No. 1*. Washington, DC: World Bank. http://siteresources.worldbank.org/INTISPMA/Resources/383704-1146752240884/doing_ie_series_01.pdf.

Pritchett, L. and J. Sandefur. 2013. Context Matters for Size: Why External Validity Claims and Development Practice Don't Mix – Working Paper 336. Washington, DC: Center for Global Development. https://www.cgdev.org/sites/default/files/1425010_file_Szekely_Results_Based_Social_Policy_FINAL.pdf.

Székely, M. 2011. Toward Results-Based Social Policy Design and Implementation – Working Paper 249. Washington, DC: Center for Global Development. https://www.cgdev.org/sites/default/files/context-matters-for-size_1.pdf.

Annex 8.1: List of Organizations Engaged in Impact Evaluations

International

Abt Associates: United States (US)-based private research company with large domestic program and growing focus on international development (http://www.abtassociates.com/).

American Institutes for Research (AIR): AIR is a nonprofit, private research agency based in Washington, DC. It has a growing international development research arm which has carried out impact evaluations in many countries (http://www.air.org/).

Centre for the Evaluation of Development Policies (EDePo): Impact evaluation group based at University College London (https://www.ifs.org.uk/centres/EDePo/).

Center for Effective Global Action (CEGA): CEGA is a group based at the University of California, Berkley (http://cega.berkeley.edu/).

Center for Learning on Evaluation and Results (CLEAR): CLEAR is a global partnership backstopped by the World Bank's Independent Evaluation Group, which supports capacity building for impact evaluation, as well as other evaluation approaches. It has regional hubs, including for South Asia and East Asia (https://www.theclearinitiative.org).

Development Impact Evaluation (DIME), World Bank: DIME is the unit that manages impact evaluations within the Development Economics Group of the World Bank (http://www.worldbank.org/en/research/dime).

FHI360: A US-based consultancy with strong focus on research and evaluation, with country offices across Asia (https://www.fhi360.org/).

IDInsight: IDInsight helps agencies develop project designs and the rigorous evaluation of those projects. Based in the US, IDInsight has an office in New Delhi (http://idinsight.org/).

International Food Policy Research Institute (IFPRI): IFPRI focuses on food, agriculture, and rural development, including topics such as market development, infrastructure, and nutrition. IFPRI conducts impact evaluations in all of these areas. IFPRI has country offices in several countries around the world including Bangladesh, the People's Republic of China, India, and Pakistan (http://www.ifpri.org/).

Innovations for Poverty Action (IPA): IPA conducts randomized controlled trials (RCTs) (and only RCTs). Its work has focused on microfinance, but it has also worked in other sectors. IPA has several country offices, and only conducts studies where it has such an office. In the region, IPA has an office in Manila. IPA has research affiliates mostly from US universities. These affiliates are responsible for the design and analysis for the impact evaluations. Data collection is managed by the field office. IPA offers occasional courses and workshops usually on a thematic basis. The have coorganized past events with the Asian Development Bank (ADB). IPA and J-PAL collaborate closely with one another (https://www.poverty-action.org/).

Institute of Development Studies (IDS): A development studies graduate institute that includes the Centre for Development Impact, which is devoted to exploring a range of impact evaluation methods, extending beyond large-n quantitative designs. The center is a joint enterprise with **ITAD**, a private research firm based in the United Kingdom (UK) (http://www.ids.ac.uk/).

International Initiative for Impact Evaluation (3ie): 3ie is a global nongovernmental organization for impact evaluations with offices in New Delhi, Washington, and London. It funds impact evaluations through various grant modalities, and undertakes selected impact evaluations. 3ie will assist in commissioning impact evaluations for other agencies, including external peer review of proposal and deliverables. The organization focuses on supporting study designs which answer policy-relevant questions, using mixed methods involving either experimental (RCT) or nonexperimental designs. 3ie offers occasional workshops. It has co-organized past events with ADB, including the Making Impact Evaluation Matter Conference held at ADB headquarters in September 2014 (http://3ieimpact.org/).

Jamal Latif Poverty Action Lab (J-PAL): J-PAL was the first and best known agency devoted to impact of development programs and to date has been involved in around 300 RCTs. Based out of the Massachusetts Institute of Technology (MIT), J-PAL has a regional network, with South Asian representation in New Delhi. J-PAL has a large network of research affiliates, mostly from US and European universities, which include many of the world's leading figures working on impact evaluation. These affiliates are responsible for study design, which is implemented by program managers who are typically graduate students from the US. Local academics are mostly involved in the management of data collection or increasingly in an advisory role on local context. J-PAL only conducts RCTs. The agency offers the J-PAL Executive Training, a short course on the design and implementation of RCTs. J-PAL and IPA collaborate closely with one another (https://www.povertyactionlab.org/).

Mathematica: Mathematica is a US-based private sector research agency which is engaged in a growing number of impact evaluations in developing countries (https://cipre.mathematica-mpr.com).

NORC: A US-based research company with strong academic connections, NORC undertakes impact evaluations in both the US and overseas (http://www.norc.org).

Oxford Policy Management (OPM): A UK-based private sector company which has been building up impact evaluation capacity. OPM has a regional office in New Delhi (http://www.opml.co.uk).

RTI International: US-based research company with experience focused on impact evaluation (https://www.rti.org/).

Social Impact: Smaller US-based research company focused on impact evaluation (https://socialimpact.com/).

Regional and national

Catalyst Management Services (CMS): Private sector group based in Bangalore with experience in impact evaluation (http://cms.org.in/).

Philippine Institute for Development Studies (PIDS): Government-supported research agency which has developed a strong focus on impact evaluation (https://www.pids.gov.ph).

Sambodhi: Private sector group based in New Delhi with experience in impact evaluation (http://sambodhi.co.in/).

Appendix 1
Application of Estimation Methods for Impact Evaluation

This Appendix provides a more in-depth introduction of how impact evaluation methods can be applied. It starts by introducing the types of notation used in causal analysis and considerations for the selection of methods. Subsequently, the Appendix provides an overview of techniques and STATA routines that are used to estimate the impacts of interventions. Sample applications draw from example data sets held by STATA or publicly released by authors of user-written routines, so that they can be replicated via a simple series of commands.

A brief outline of the sections of this Appendix is as follows:

Section 1: The Potential Outcomes Framework
Section 2: Randomized Controlled Trials
Section 3: Difference-in-Differences and Fixed Effects Models
Section 4: Synthetic Controls
Section 5: Propensity Score-Based Approaches (Matching, Weighting, and Double Robust Estimators)
Section 6: Instrumental Variables Based Approaches (Two-Stage Least Squares, Endogenous Treatment Regressions, and Endogenous Switching Regressions)
Section 7: Regression Discontinuity Design

Section 1: The Potential Outcomes Framework

1.1   The Rubin/Neyman Causal Framework and Associated Notation

Evaluating whether a program has an impact has to do with notions of causality—of cause and effect, which can be represented using standard notation from the Rubin/Neyman Potential Outcomes Framework (Rubin 1974). First, suppose there are data on n treated units (which may be people, households, farm plots, organizations, businesses, etc.), and the intention is to evaluate the impact of an intervention on those units.[1] Second, for the sake of simplicity, assume that whether or not a unit participates in the intervention can be defined using a binary variable that takes one of two values (1 if the individual participates in the intervention and 0 if the individual does not participate). Units that participate in the intervention are termed *treated* and units that do not participate in the intervention are termed *untreated* or *control*.[2] W_i can be a binary (or dummy) variable that denotes whether individual i received the treatment:

$$W_i = 0: \text{Unit i } was \ not \text{ treated}$$
$$W_i = 1: \text{Unit i } was \text{ treated}$$

Variable Y can represent the "outcome" that the intervention (treatment) is supposed to affect. Importantly, for any given unit there are in fact two values of Y: (a) the value that would occur if the unit were *not* treated, which can be denoted as Y_0; and (b) the value that would occur if the unit *were* treated, which can be denoted as Y_1:

$$Y_{0i} = \text{value of Y for unit i if it is } not \text{ treated}$$
$$Y_{1i} = \text{value of Y for unit i if it } is \text{ treated}$$

Here it is important to note that both Y_{0i} and Y_{1i} are defined for *all* units, irrespective of whether in the treatment or control condition. For example, there may be observations of Y_1 for a "treated" unit but *if that unit had not been treated the observations are* Y_0.

Under this notation, the intention of impact evaluation is to estimate $Y_{1i} - Y_{0i}$. This is the *treatment effect* (the impact of the intervention) *for unit i*. The goal is to estimate the treatment effect for each unit in some population of interest (or at least know the average of $Y_{1i} - Y_{0i}$ for the units in the population of interest). The main problem for impact evaluation is that for each unit, there can only be observations of Y_1 or Y_0, but not both, at each point in time.

The last piece of basic notation is the observed value of Y for each unit, which can be denoted as Y_i for unit i. The observed value of Y is the unit's "actual" value of Y based on the actual treatment or control condition that it is in.

There is a very simple relationship between Y_i, Y_{0i}, Y_{1i}, and W_i:

---

[1] It could also be n households, institutions, or any other unit of observation, but to avoid abstract language this text will generally refer to the n units as individuals.

[2] Note that in this case, there is only one treatment condition, and individuals either get that treatment or not. The notation can easily be extended to multiple treatment (and control) conditions.

$$Y_i = Y_{0i} \times (1 - W_i) + Y_{1i} \times W_i$$

In other words, if $W_i = 0$ for unit i, then the Y_i observed for that unit is Y_{0i}. If $W_i = 1$ then the Y_i observed for that unit is Y_{1i}:

$$Y_i = Y_{0i} \text{ if } W_i = 0$$
$$= Y_{1i} \text{ if } W_i = 1$$

1.2 Three Scenarios for How the "W$_i$s" Are Determined

Given the general notation and setup in section 1.1, the ability to estimate the impact of an intervention depends on the process by which W_i is determined for each unit i. From the viewpoint of estimation, there are three possibilities:

Possibility 1 (Random Assignment): W_i is randomly assigned as part of a "randomized experiment."

$$W_i \perp\!\!\!\perp (Y_{0i}, Y_{1i})$$

The basic idea behind randomly assigning individuals to treatment and control groups is, again, that they will be the same (in expectation) on all observable and unobservable characteristics. If participants have been randomly assigned, the impact of an intervention (the treatment effect) can be estimated by comparing the average outcomes across the treatment and control groups.

Possibility 2 (Unconfounded Assignment): W_i is not randomly assigned, but conditional on some observed variables (X_i), it does not depend on (is independent of) Y_{0i} and Y_{1i}. This possibility (or assumption) is alternatively called "unconfounded assignment," "selection on observables" (where the X_i variables are the observables), or "conditional independence" assumption. Formally, this assumption is expressed as the following.

$$W_i \perp\!\!\!\perp (Y_{0i}, Y_{1i}) \mid X_i$$

The basic idea behind the unconfounded assignment assumption is that, once there is control for (condition on) X_i, there is no correlation between W_i and either Y_{0i} or Y_{1i}. That means, in effect, for a given value of X_i, W_i is essentially randomly assigned.

It is important to note that assumption of Possibility 2 is not by any means as strong as Possibility 1 (random assignment). Under random assignment, participants in treatment and control groups should be the same in expectation on both observable and unobservable characteristics. Under the unconfounded assignment assumption, the analyst must assume that if the right X_is are controlled for, then participants in treatment and control groups are the same in expectation on all other observable and unobservable characteristics.

In situations in which one believes that unconfounded assignment assumption is true, the primary impact evaluation method used to estimate treatment effects is matching (most commonly propensity score matching) or regression analysis that controls for the confounding variables. Matching and its relationship to regression analysis with controls are discussed in section 5.

Possibility 3 (Confounded Assignment): W_i depends on Y_{0i} and Y_{1i}, even after conditioning on the observed X_i variables. This is the most difficult to address, but in many cases, also the most plausible possibility. In particular, if unit i is the one making the decision about whether to participate in the program (i.e., whether $W_i = 0$ or 1), then as long as unit i cares about Y_i, it is likely that W_i does depend on Y_{0i} and Y_{1i}.

What can the evaluator do if it is likely that the assignment of W_i is confounded? Methods used in this situation include difference-in-differences estimation (DiD) (section 3), synthetic controls (section 4), and propensity score based approaches (section 5). In addition, analysts may look for subsets of the population or situations in which there is an observable conditioning assignment, and apply instrumental variables (if there is no clear eligibility cutoff) (section 6) or regression discontinuity design (if the variable has a sharp cutoff conditioning participation) (section 7).

1.3 Defining Treatment Effects and Selection Bias

The most common parameter that evaluators try to estimate is the *average treatment effect* (ATE), which is defined as

$$\text{ATE} = E[Y_{1i} - Y_{0i}]$$

In words, this is the treatment effect averaged over all the units in the sample. Different units may have different values of $Y_{1i} - Y_{0i}$, but evaluators are often interested in the average for the whole population. Intuitively, the ATE is the answer to the following question: *How would Y change if the entire sample were "treated" relative to the situation in which no one was treated?*

Probably the second most common parameter that evaluators try to estimate is the *average treatment effect on the treated* (ATT), which is defined as

$$\text{ATT} = E[Y_{1i} - Y_{0i} \mid W_i = 1]$$

In words, this is the average treatment effect (average $Y_{1i} - Y_{0i}$) *for those members of the sample who received the treatment.* Intuitively, the ATT is the answer to the following question: *How does Y change for those units that were actually treated?*

When evaluators would like to understand if a program should be expanded, they may also be interested in the average treatment effect on the untreated (ATU), or the average effect that the intervention could have on those who are not yet participating.

$$\text{ATU} = E[Y_{1i} - Y_{0i} \mid W_i = 0]$$

Selection bias is the effect that evaluators are seeking to eliminate through impact evaluation techniques. This can be represented as the difference between the average outcome of the treated participants and control participants before any treatment is applied to either group of participants. This is defined as

$$E[Y_{0i} \mid W_i = 1] - E[Y_{0i} \mid W_i = 0]$$

Two additional basic econometric concepts should be recognized, which apply in the context of parametric regression methods (where relationships between covariates and outcomes are explicitly modeled as having a functional form). The first is *heteroskedasticity*, which basically means that data have variability that is uneven across the values of variables. To be safe about this possibility, parametric approaches should all use standard errors that are robust to heteroskedasticity and clustering in the data if treatment is correlated within target groups or locations. The second concept is *multicollinearity*—that regression coefficients may not be accurate if correlated independent variables are included. The latter can be checked through tests of variance inflation factors and pairwise correlation coefficients.

Section 2: Randomized Controlled Trials

RCTs, or randomized experiments, have often been called the "gold standard" in impact evaluation (Athey and Imbens 2017). To understand why, it is useful to separately examine the two words "randomized" and "experiment." The key feature common to all experiments is that the evaluator deliberately *manipulates* a cause in order to *discover* its effects. This differentiates experiments from observational studies, which first focus on an effect, and then try to discover causes, a much harder task.

The process of random assignment ensures treatment and control groups (in expectation) are similar on all observed and unobserved average characteristics when a sufficiently large number of units are included. In other words, because of random assignment, every characteristic other than the intervention assignment (the treatment) tends to be the same between units in the treatment and control groups. For people, this includes observable characteristics (X_i) such as age, gender, and wealth as well as unobserved characteristics such as ability and attitudes.

An RCT is an experiment in which, besides the intervention or treatment itself, the treatment and control groups are likely to be equivalent on all other observable and unobservable characteristics. Because of this, differences in the outcome Y_i between the treatment and control groups can be attributed solely to the treatment itself and not to any other cause. This enables the evaluator to obtain an unbiased estimate of the ATE.

Evaluators frequently verify that the random assignment process results in treatment and control groups that look similar (or are "balanced") in expectation. The evaluator does this by conducting statistical tests to see if the treatment and control participants are statistically the same (on average) on observable characteristics. If the treatment and control groups are similar on these characteristics (according to statistical t-tests of differences in means for each of a number of important observable characteristics, for example), then the evaluator can be fairly confident that the treatment effect estimates from the RCT will be unbiased.

When all characteristics are balanced between treatment and control, it is sufficient to estimate the sample averages separately for individuals in the treatment and control groups and to take the difference of those sample averages to get an estimate of the ATE. To improve precision, this is usually applied in a difference in differences framework, where differences between baseline and endline surveys are averaged for treatment and control, and then compared. Standard statistical methods may be applied (e.g., a two-group t-test) to test the null hypothesis of no treatment effect on the population.

Use of a multivariate regression approach can be beneficial, even in the context of a randomized experiment. First, a multivariate regression can help to correct any imbalance that may remain between treatment and control groups. Second, it can help to improve precision of estimates and reduce standard errors. Third, it may help to offer evidence on how treatment effects are conditioned by beneficiary characteristics. Multivariate regression will usually be via fixed effects models.

Section 3: Difference-in-Differences and Fixed Effects Models

3.1 Introduction to Differencing

Outside of a randomized experiment, there is no true "control" population, as treatment is not the only characteristic differing between treated and untreated populations. Thus, the terminology changes to "comparison group" or "untreated." The difference-in-differences (DiD) method relies on data on the treated and untreated groups at two or more points in time: both before the treatment happened and after. In particular, the data need to include values of the outcome variable of interest measured both before and after the treatment and for both the treated and untreated participants.

The DiD method estimates the treatment effect by comparing the pre-post change in the mean outcome of the treatment group with the pre-post change in the mean outcome of the untreated group. The resulting treatment effect estimate can be unbiased if the key "parallel trends assumption" holds. This assumption posits that the pre-post change in the treatment group would have followed the same trend (slope) as the pre-post change in the untreated group *if the treatment group had not been treated.* In other words, the assumption posits that the mean change in the untreated group represents the mean counterfactual change in the treatment group in the absence of treatment. This assumption is violated if only one group (but not the other) changes its trend during the treatment period *because of factors unrelated to the treatment.*[3] Unfortunately, like the assumptions underlying matching and instrumental variables analysis, this assumption often cannot be tested (Ryan et al. 2015).[4]

---

[3] Besides violations in the parallel trends assumption, there are other potential threats to the validity of the difference-in-differences approach. These include differential changes in the composition of the treated and untreated groups (during the treatment period). They also include *Ashenfelter dips* in which program participants experience a sudden dip in their pretreatment outcome variable right before they enter the program and then bounce back to their natural state after the program (but not necessarily because of the program). Finally, the regression specification used to model and estimate the treatment effect also must be chosen carefully.

[4] The evaluator cannot test the plausibility of the parallel trends assumption with two periods of data but can in some cases with more than two periods. If the evaluator has two or more periods of pretreatment data, for example, he or she can examine whether the pretreatment trends of the treated and untreated groups were parallel or not.

3.2   Difference–in–Differences Estimator

The DiD estimator of the ATT can be estimated using the following type of regression specification:

$$Y_{it} = \alpha + \beta_1 W_{it} + \beta_2 T_t + \beta_3(W_{it} \times T_t) + \varepsilon_{it}$$

In the specification, Y_{it} represents the (pre- and post-treatment) outcome variable, W_{it} is a binary variable indicating whether the individual received the treatment or not, T_t is a binary variable indicating pre- and post-treatment periods, α is an intercept, and ε is an error term. The treatment effect is the coefficient β_3, which is equal to $(Y_{11} - Y_{10}) - (Y_{01} - Y_{00})$.

The difference-in-differences estimator is in fact typically estimated using the following regression specification which also controls for other observables, X_i and their coefficients γ, in which the treatment effect is coefficient β_3.

$$Y_{it} = \alpha + \beta_1 W_{it} + \beta_2 T_t + \beta_3(W_{it} \times T_t) + \gamma X_{it} + \varepsilon_{it}$$

Implementing difference-in differences estimator in STATA

The DiD estimator can easily be estimated by creating a time dummy variable for post-treatment observations and a dummy variable for treatment. A linear regression is then simply called using the "regress" command, followed by the dependent variable, the time dummy, the treatment dummy, and an interaction term between the time and treatment dummies. The coefficient on the interaction gives the treatment effect.

The following example uses the United States (US) national longitudinal survey to assess the effect of union membership on the natural log of real wages. It treats 1980 as the pre-intervention period and 1988 as the post-intervention period, with entering a union as the treatment. The effect of union membership is highly significant, with a substantial coefficient on the time#union interaction term.

Commands:
```
webuse nlswork.dta

*Make panel into two periods of observations
keep if year==88 | year==80
gen time=0
replace time=1 if year==88

reg ln_wage time##union, robust
```

Results:

Linear regression

		Number of obs	=	3574
		F(3, 3570)	=	73.67
		Prob > F	=	0.0000
		R-squared	=	0.0534
		Root MSE	=	.47822

ln_wage	Coef.	Robust Std. Err.	t	P>|t|	[95% Conf. Interval]	
1.time	.1377238	.0187794	7.33	0.000	.1009045	.1745432
1.union	.1404369	.0232693	6.04	0.000	.0948145	.1860593
time#union						
1 1	.0885873	.0348885	2.54	0.011	.0201839	.1569906
_cons	1.698597	.0125059	135.82	0.000	1.674078	1.723117

3.3   Fixed Effects Models

An analogous approach to the DiD estimator, which allows application to more than two observation periods, is the two-way fixed effects model. The fixed effects model effectively centers (removes the mean value) the observations for each unit over time, so that the regression is on differences over time for each unit. A functionally equivalent approach is to include dummy variables for each unit in the regression, as well as for time.

$$Y_{it} = \alpha + \beta_1 W_{it} + \gamma X_{it} + \beta_2 T_t + \alpha_i + \varepsilon_{it}$$

In this approach, the outcome regression adds a vector of observed characteristics X and coefficients γ, a time variable T with estimated coefficients, and an addition α_i to the constant α that varies by individual. The individual variable absorbs time-invariant characteristics, while the time variable absorbs the effect of overall trends, so that the coefficient on W gives the same ATT as the coefficient on the WxT interaction term in DiD.

Implementing fixed effects models in STATA

Fixed effects models may be easily implemented in STATA using the command "xtreg", followed by the outcome variable, independent variables, time period, dummy variables, and the option "fe".

The following example uses the US national longitudinal survey to assess the effect of union membership on the natural log of real wages over 1971–1988, controlling for weeks of work, whether the city has substantial population and years of work experience. Individual characteristics, such as education, are time invariant, so they are not included in the model. The effect of union membership is highly significant, with a substantial coefficient.

Commands:

webuse nlswork.dta

xtset idcode year

xtreg ln_wage union wks_work ttl_exp not_smsa i.year, fe robust

Results:

Fixed-effects (within) regression

Group variable: idcode

Number of obs	= 18855
Number of groups	= 4128

R-sq: within   = 0.1601

    between = 0.3129

    overall = 0.2418

Obs per group: min = 1

     avg = 4.6

     max = 12

F(15,4127) = 92.63

corr(u_i, Xb) = 0.1634

Prob > F = 0.0000

(Std. Err. adjusted for 4128 clusters in idcode)

ln_wage	Coef.	Robust Std. Err.	t	P>|t|	[95% Conf. Interval]	
union	.0964293	.0094099	10.25	0.000	.0779808	.1148778
wks_work	.0016111	.0001468	10.98	0.000	.0013233	.0018989
ttl_exp	.0394834	.0024047	16.42	0.000	.0347689	.0441978
not_smsa	-.0954969	.0185183	5.16	0.000	-.1318028	-.0591911
year						
71	.0120917	.0107149	1.13	0.259	-.0089153	.0330988
72	-.0086902	.0125379	-0.69	0.488	-.0332712	.0158908
73	-.0285989	.0138411	-2.07	0.039	-.0557348	-.0014629
77	-.0488101	.0169072	-2.89	0.004	-.0819574	-.0156628
78	-.0396196	.0182474	-2.17	0.030	-.0753944	-.0038449
80	-.1612624	.0204025	-7.90	0.000	-.2012623	-.1212626
82	-.1952173	.0228232	-8.55	0.000	-.2399632	-.1504715
83	-.1404167	.024931	-5.63	0.000	-.1892949	-.0915384
85	-.2274674	.0276147	-8.24	0.000	-.281607	-.1733277
87	-.2650911	.0312928	-8.47	0.000	-.3264419	-.2037404
88	-.2309831	.0343385	-6.73	0.000	-.2983051	-.1636611
_cons	1.488808	.0146594	101.56	0.000	1.460068	1.517549
sigma_u	.3682758					
sigma_e	.25143585					
rho	.68206727	(fraction of variance due to u_i)				

Section 4: Synthetic Controls

4.1 Introduction to Synthetic Controls

The synthetic controls method allows the parallel trends assumption of DiD methods to be relaxed. To do so, it substitutes time-series variation for cross-sectional variation in panel data. The approach works by taking a pool of potential comparison observations and determining a weighting algorithm among the comparison units that maximizes the fit between trends in independent variables and the outcome variable for a synthetic weighted unit (Abadie et al. 2010).

4.2 Synthetic Controls Estimator

The synthetic controls approach assumes that nonintervention outcomes are driven by a factor model composed of shared unobserved common factors (e.g., time fixed effects) with coefficients α, independent observed variables X, independent unobserved variables μ with coefficient ϕ and an error term ε, as follows:

$$Y_{it} = \alpha T_t + \gamma X_{it} + \phi \mu_{it} + \varepsilon_{it}$$

It can be posited that there is a set of weights ω_j applied to the untreated observations that allow both the outcome and independent observed variables to mimic patterns in the treated unit prior to treatment. That is both

$$\sum_{j=2}^{j+1} \omega_j^* Y_{jt} = Y_{1t} \; \forall t \in \{1, \dots T_0\}$$

and

$$\sum_{j=2}^{j+1} \omega_j^* X_{jt} = X_{1t}$$

Under these conditions, it can be assumed that the weights are a reduced form representation of $\phi\mu$. It thus follows that the ATT Δ can be recovered via application of the weights to the untreated observations, summation, and comparison to the treated observations.

$$\Delta = Y_{1t} - \sum_{j=2}^{j+1} \omega_j^* Y_{jt}$$

The approach can be extended to multiple treated units by estimating treated unit vectors independently and averaging the treatment effects across units. Significance is not tested via conventional asymptotic inference. Rather, placebo tests are instead run on the data, and the probability of randomly replicating effects as large as estimated for treatment is estimated.

Implementing synthetic controls in STATA

Synthetic control approaches may be implemented in STATA using the command "synth_runner", followed by the outcome variable, independent variables, and specification of the treatment variable (Quistorff and Galiani 2017). This package allows for multiple treated units. Before doing the run, the panel must be fully balanced, with the panel identifier and time periods declared via "tsset". The treatment must be identified via a binary variable, and treated units must start treatment after the initial period, with no units leaving treatment.

The following example uses the US national longitudinal survey to assess the effect of joining a union on real wages over 1987–1988, following a model 'training period' from 1980 to 1985 from which weights are generated. The model estimates wages as an overall function of race, college graduation, experience, work hours, residing in the south, and residing in a central city. To make the data work for the example, only a subset of the survey data is used. As a result, the treatment effect is much smaller than estimated in the last example, and it is not significant.

Commands:

```
ssc install synth, all
net install synth_runner, from(https://raw.github.com/bquistorff/synth_runner/master/)
replace

webuse nlswork.dta
*Create and declare balanced panel subset of data
drop if year<80
gen wage=exp(ln_wage)
by idcode: egen minunion=min(union)
keep if wage!=. & race!=. & collgrad!=. & c_city!=. & south!=. & ttl_exp!=. & hours!=. & union!=. & minunion==0
drop if union==1 & year<86
by idcode: egen obs=count(year)
keep if obs==6
tsset idcode year

synth_runner wage race wks_work grade collgrad c_city south ttl_exp hours, d(union)
```

Results:

Post-treatment results: Effects, p-values, standardized p-values

```
        |   estimates        pvals       pvals_std
--------------+-----------------------------------------------
    c1|    .5443459      .512112        .182283
```

Section 5: Propensity Score Based Approaches (Matching, Weighting, and Double Robust Estimators)

5.1   Introduction to the Propensity Score

Propensity score-based approaches attempt to model the selection process for an intervention using observable characteristics of program participants and nonparticipants. Specifically, they are premised on the assumption that after controlling for pretreatment characteristics X_i, there is no correlation between W_i and either Y_{0i} or Y_{1i}. That means, in effect, after controlling for X_i, W_i is essentially randomly assigned. If this *unconfounded assignment* or *conditional independence assumption* indeed holds, it is appropriate to use a model of program participation to estimate treatment effects.

The propensity score can be estimated using a logit (or probit) regression of W_i on the X_i vector (giving β coefficients and error term η) and predicting the probability of p_i (p-hat) for each individual (Rosenbaum and Rubin 1983). This p-hat is the propensity score that can be used in various ways to reduce selection bias.

$$logit P(W = 1|X) = \beta X_i + \eta_i, \text{ or } \hat{p}_i = e(X_i, \hat{\beta})$$

There are several ways in which propensity scores can be applied. These include individual case matching, inverse propensity score weighting, and regression estimation in combination with use of the propensity score.

5.2   Propensity Score Matching

The most common application of the propensity score is via "propensity score matching" (Rosenbaum and Rubin 1985). Essentially, for every participant that received the treatment in the observational data, this technique finds one or more matches that did not get the treatment. The match is the untreated person/unit that has the same values on the X_is as the treated participant. After "matching" across the treatment and control groups, the mean of the outcome variable can be compared between treated and untreated to estimate the average impact of the treatment. The propensity score is the probability that a unit will receive a particular treatment given its covariate vector X_i.

The major problem with using matching to conduct an impact evaluation, however, is that *unconfounded assignment* is a fairly strong assumption. Even if the evaluator can control for a large number of observable characteristics (X_is), it could still be the case that there are important unobservable factors (in η_i) that may affect both W_i and Y_i. Thus, at the very least, for matching to produce relatively unbiased estimates, the evaluator must find and control for every important observable factor that is simultaneously correlated with both W_i and Y_i.

There are numerous ways to match treated to untreated individuals. Among the different choices the evaluator has to make when conducting matching is to choose the number of matches that should be made per treated or untreated individual, whether matching will be made with or without replacing individuals that have already been matched, whether to impose "exact" matching on the propensity score value or to allow matching within a range of scores, and the type of algorithm that matches all the treated individuals with all of the untreated individuals.

It may be tempting to think of matching as having little difference from traditional multivariate linear regression. Both methods rely on the assumption of unconfounded assignment (discussed in section 1.2). In fact, regression that statistically controls for covariates is a form of pseudo-matching. However, a difference is that whereas matching does not rely on statistical modeling or functional form assumptions, regression does. Whether regression analysis can estimate unbiased treatment effects therefore hinges not only on the assumption of unconfounded assignment but also on the assumption that the model underlying the regression was chosen correctly. At the same time, when the number of individuals in the observational data set is small, matching and other nonparametric methods are less efficient (have less statistical power) than parametric methods such as regression analysis. In addition, when there is correlation between covariates and treatment of interest, traditional linear regression techniques may be affected by multicollinearity, whereas matching techniques are not.

Implementing propensity score matching in STATA

Propensity score matching may be implemented in STATA 13 and 14 using the command "teffects psmatch", followed by the outcome variable, the treatment variable, and independent variables that determine or differ between treated and untreated groups prior to treatment.

A simple example of the technique can be applied using one of STATA's example data sets. The following evaluates the impact of prenatal care in the first trimester of pregnancy on subsequent birth weight in grams, with matching on several other determinants of weight. It finds a positive effect that is not statistically significant.

Commands:

webuse cattaneo2.dta

teffects psmatch (bweight) (prenatal1 mbsmoke mmarried mage fbaby medu alcohol)

Results:

Treatment-effects estimation

Number of obs   =   4642

Estimator   : propensity-score matching

Matches: requested   =   1

Outcome model   : matching

min   =   1

Treatment model : logit

max   =   68

		Al Robust					
bweight		Coef.	Std. Err.	z	P>|z|	[95% Conf. Interval]	
ATE							
prenatal1							
(Yes vs No)		43.97727	30.37611	1.45	0.148	-15.5588	103.5133

5.3   Inverse Probability Weighting

Matching is not the only technique that makes use of the propensity score. Inverse probability weighting approaches may also be used. Under this approach, each observation in the regression is weighted by the inverse of the probability of participation, so as to create a pseudo-population in which characteristics are similar in treated and untreated populations.

$$\widehat{\Delta}_{IPW} = n^{-1} \sum_{i=1}^{n} \left[\frac{W_i Y_i}{\hat{p}_i} \right] - n^{-1} \sum_{i=1}^{n} \left[\frac{(1 - W_i) Y_i}{1 - \hat{p}_i} \right]$$

The inverse probability weighted estimator, $\widehat{\Delta}_{IPW}$, represents the ATE.

Implementing inverse probability weighting in STATA

Inverse probability weighting may be implemented in STATA 13 and 14 using the command "teffects ipw", followed by the outcome variable, the treatment variable, and independent variables that determine or differ between treated and untreated groups prior to treatment.

A similar example to propensity score matching can be applied to the same STATA example data sets. As in the above, it evaluates the impact of prenatal care in the first trimester of pregnancy on subsequent birth weight in grams, with control for several other determinants of weight. Unlike for propensity score matching, here the effect is significant at the 5% level.

Commands:
webuse cattaneo2.dta
teffects ipw (bweight) (prenatal1 mbsmoke mmarried mage fbaby medu alcohol)

Results:

Treatment-effects estimation   Number of obs   =   4642
Estimator   : inverse-probability weights
Outcome model   : weighted mean
Treatment model : logit

bweight		Coef.	Robust Std. Err.	z	P>|z|	[95% Conf. Interval]	
ATE							
prenatal1							
(Yes vs No)		53.51234	26.99469	1.98	0.047	.6037186	106.421
POmean							
prenatal1							
No		3317.837	25.29863	131.15	0.000	3268.252	3367.421

5.4   Double Robust Estimators

Double robust (DR) estimators may also be used. These techniques blend the precision of parametric approaches with the ability of propensity score techniques to isolate participation from other covariates. The concept of DR estimators was introduced by Robins et al. (1994) and expounded by Lunceford and Davidian (2004). The unique feature of DR estimators is that they only require that either of the propensity score model or the regression model is correctly specified to correctly estimate the effect of participation on the outcome.

As a second step after propensity score estimation, models are fitted for the outcome on the covariates for the treated group ($W_i = 1$) and the untreated group ($W_i = 0$) separately. Predicted values of Y are then obtained using both sets of coefficients with observed covariates, denoted as $m_1(X_i, \hat{\beta}_1)$ and $m_0(X_i, \hat{\beta}_0)$.

$$\text{postulated } E(Y_i \mid W_i = 1, X_i, \hat{\beta}_i) = \hat{Y}_1 = m_1(X_i, \hat{\beta}_1) = \alpha_1 + \beta_1 X_1 \text{ , and}$$
$$\text{postulated } E(Y_i \mid W_i = 0, X_i, \hat{\beta}_0) = \hat{Y}_0 = m_0(X_i, \hat{\beta}_0) = \alpha_0 + \beta_0 X_0$$

The estimator controls for confounding by taking the inverse of $\hat{p}_i$ or the predicted probability that a unit participates in treatment, i.e., $1/\hat{p}_i$ for the treated and $1/(1 - \hat{p}_i)$ for the untreated to weight the observed data and predicted values from the switching regression. Weighting by this quantity creates a pseudo-population in which the distributions of confounders among the treated and untreated are the same as the overall distribution of those confounders in the original total population.

The resulting predicted and actual values of Y_1, Y_0, p are then applied in the DR estimator given in the following equation:

$$\hat{\Delta}_{DR} = n^{-1} \sum_{i=1}^{n} \left[\frac{W_i Y_i}{\hat{p}_i} - \frac{\{W_i - \hat{p}_i\}}{\hat{p}_i} m_1(X_i, \beta_1) \right] - n^{-1} \sum_{i=1}^{n} \left[\frac{(1 - W_i)Y_i}{1 - \hat{p}_i} + \frac{\{W_i - \hat{p}_i\}}{1 - \hat{p}_i} m_0(X_i, \beta_0) \right]$$
$$= \hat{\mu}_1, DR - \hat{\mu}_0, DR$$

The double robust estimator, $\hat{\Delta}_{DR}$, represents the ATE.

When implementing the technique, all observed variables affecting outcomes that differ in levels prior to treatment (but are not affected in levels by treatment) are usually included in the selection equation. Additional variables affecting selection may be included to improve precision.

Implementing double robust estimators in STATA

Augmented inverse probability weighting may be implemented in STATA using the command "teffects aipw", followed by the outcome variable, independent variables conditioning outcomes, the treatment variable, and independent variables that determine treatment.

A similar example to propensity score matching and inverse probability weighting can be applied to the same STATA example data sets. As in the above, it evaluates the impact of prenatal care in the first trimester of pregnancy on subsequent birth weight in grams, with control for several other determinants of weight. Note that here the effect is significant at the 10% level.

Commands:

webuse cattaneo2.dta

teffects aipw (bweight mbsmoke mmarried mage fbaby alcohol) (prenatal1 mbsmoke mmarried mage fbaby alcohol medu), aequations vce(robust)

Results:

Iteration 0   : EE criterion = 4.898e-20
Iteration 1   : EE criterion = 5.930e-26

Treatment-effects estimation   Number of obs   =   4642
Estimator   : augmented IPW
Outcome model   : linear by ML
Treatment model : logit

bweight	Coef.	Robust Std. Err.	z	P>|z|	[95% Conf. Interval]	
ATE						
prenatal1 (Yes vs No)	51.17366	26.54113	1.93	0.054	−.8460014	103.1933
POmean						
prenatal1 No	3321.505	24.7926	133.97	0.000	3272.912	3370.097
OME0						
mbsmoke	−169.8073	39.23131	−4.33	0.000	−246.6993	−92.91539
mmarried	156.5209	43.76734	3.58	0.000	70.73846	242.3033
mage	.6265175	4.466949	0.14	0.888	−8.128541	9.381576
fbaby	−61.49277	42.76311	−1.44	0.150	−145.3069	22.32138
alcohol	−143.5852	80.82422	−1.78	0.076	−301.9978	14.82732
_cons	3249.977	108.006	30.09	0.000	3038.289	3461.665
OME1						
mbsmoke	−242.8674	27.31882	−8.89	0.000	−296.4113	−189.3236
mmarried	150.3321	26.14595	5.75	0.000	99.08699	201.5772
mage	1.205585	2.052459	0.59	0.557	−2.817161	5.22833
fbaby	−49.61927	19.38907	−2.56	0.010	−87.62115	−11.61739
alcohol	−14.2429	55.9502	−0.25	0.799	−123.9033	95.41748
_cons	3303.01	57.82122	57.12	0.000	3189.683	3416.338

bweight	Coef.	Robust Std. Err.	z	P>|z|	[95% Conf. Interval]	
TME1						
mbsmoke	-.1866845	.0965382	-1.93	0.053	-.3758958	.0025269
mmarried	1.099739	.0956205	11.50	0.000	.9123265	1.287152
mage	.0697882	.0096489	7.23	0.000	.0508767	.0886998
fbaby	.6101609	.0901322	6.77	0.000	.433505	.7868168
alcohol	-.6779378	.1912115	-3.55	0.000	-1.052705	-.3031703
medu	.1493282	.020514	7.28	0.000	.1091215	.189535
_cons	-3.043925	.2875023	-10.59	0.000	-3.607419	-2.480431

Section 6: Instrumental Variables Based Approaches (Two-Stage Least Squares, Endogenous Treatment Regressions, and Endogenous Switching Regressions)

6.1 Concepts and Assumptions Underlying Instrumental Variables Analysis

Another way to estimate program impacts when the assumption of unconfounded assignment does not hold is by using instrumental variables (IV) analysis. IV analysis is best illustrated using the framework of linear regression. Suppose that there is the following linear regression equation:

$$Y_i = \alpha + \beta_1 W_i + \gamma X_i + \varepsilon_i$$

in which treatment assignment W_i is correlated with a characteristic unobservable to the researcher ε_i, such that $cov(W, \varepsilon) \neq 0$. Another way of stating this is that there is something in the error term (ε_i) of the equation that affects not only Y_i but W_i as well. Furthermore, since ε_i is unobservable, one cannot simply control for it through inclusion of a variable and then examine the unbiased impact of W_i on Y_i.[5]

The idea behind instrumental variables analysis is to locate and "carve out" the part of W_i that is not correlated with ε_i and further use only that exogenous part to estimate the treatment effect. To be able to do this, there needs to be a special kind of variable called an *instrumental variable* (or *instrument* for short).

---

[5] This is another formulation of the problem of "selection bias" (discussed in section 1.1) or "endogeneity" or "omitted variable bias."

A viable instrumental variable (Z_i) must, however, satisfy two conditions. First, it must be partially and sufficiently correlated with the treatment (W_i), after controlling for Z_i.[6] Second, the instrument must only affect the outcome (Y_i) through the treatment (W_i) and not through any other channel, such that the error term of the outcome is not correlated with the instrument. In other words, outside of working through W_i, Z_i should not have an independent impact on Y_i. In situations in which the evaluator only finds one instrument variable for a treatment variable, the assumption that the instrument is uncorrelated with the error term is a matter of faith—it cannot be tested and verified using the data. In situations in which the evaluator is able to find two or more instruments for a single treatment variable, the evaluator may be able to conduct additional statistical tests to justify whether the instruments are valid (these are called tests of "overidentifying restrictions").

When an evaluator finds potentially viable instrument(s), however, he or she must be able to provide rational arguments for why the instrument(s) is uncorrelated with the error term. Essentially, the evaluator must defend his or her belief in the idea that the instrument affects the outcome only through the treatment variable and not through any other channel. It is necessary to conduct tests associated with instrumental variables analysis (including, for example, tests for whether the instrument is partially and sufficiently correlated with the treatment) to support these hypotheses, as well.

6.2 Two-Stage Least Squares Regression

The most popular way to estimate impacts using instrumental variables is to run a *two-stage least squares* (2SLS) regression. It is represented in the following linear regression models:

$$\widehat{W}_i = \beta_0 + \beta_3 Z_i + \beta_2 X_i + \eta_i$$
$$Y_i = \alpha + \beta_1 \widehat{W}_i + \gamma X_i + \varepsilon_i$$

As the name suggests, 2SLS regressions are conducted in two stages. In the first stage, the evaluator regresses the treatment variable on the instrument Z_i while controlling for the X_is. After running this regression, the evaluator calculates the predicted value of W_i (often called W_i-hat). In the second stage, the evaluator runs a regression of the outcome variable Y_i on W-hat, while still controlling for the X_is. The coefficient associated with W-hat from this second stage regression is the instrumental variables estimate of the impact of the treatment W_i on Y_i.

---

[6] The evaluator can verify this by regressing W_i on the instrument(s) and X_i, and determining whether the estimated F-statistic associated with the instrument(s) is large (typically, greater than 10).

It is important to note that the instrumental variables estimator does not represent an ATE or an ATT, but rather estimates what is called a *local average treatment effect* (LATE). This is the average treatment effect on those participants that were *caused by the instrument* to get treatment or not.

Implementing two-stage least squares regression in STATA

STATA contains "ivregress", which allows a range of instrumental variables regressions. There is also a user-written routine, which provides automatic diagnostics of regression results, which can be helpful to ascertain instrument validity (Baum et al. 2010). The syntax for the latter is "ivreg2", followed by the outcome variable, independent variables conditioning outcomes, and (instrumented variable = instruments).

The following example uses data on female employment characteristics and evaluates the impact of unions on wages in 1972 in the US. In this example, union membership is instrumented by whether a woman identifies as being of "black" race, lives in the south, and her age. The finding is a significant positive effect of union membership on wages. Diagnostics of the instruments suggest that the instruments are valid, as the p-value of the over- and under-identification tests indicate significance, and the weak identification test statistic is acceptable.

Commands:
```
ssc install ranktest
ssc install ivreg2
webuse union3
ivreg2 wage wks_work ttl_exp not_smsa grade (union= black south age), robust
```

Results:
IV (2SLS) estimation

Estimates efficient for homoskedasticity only
Statistics robust to heteroskedasticity

		Number of obs	=	1203
		F(5, 1197)	=	91.92
		Prob > F	=	0.0000
Total (centered) SS	= 6529.780859	Centered R2	=	0.2639
Total (uncentered) SS	= 45121.78109	Uncentered R2	=	0.8935
Residual SS	= 4806.687808	Root MSE	=	1.999

wage	Coef.	Robust Std. Err.	z	P>|z|	[95% Conf. Interval]	
union	2.228736	.7924016	2.81	0.005	.675657	3.781814
wks_work	.017831	.0048998	3.64	0.000	.0082275	.0274344
ttl_exp	.222175	.0452564	4.91	0.000	.1334742	.3108759
not_smsa	-.8238825	.1372525	-6.00	0.000	-1.092892	-.5548726
grade	.499475	.0456322	10.95	0.000	.4100376	.5889125
_cons	-2.298186	.5495487	-4.18	0.000	-3.375282	-1.221091

Underidentification test (Kleibergen-Paap rk LM statistic):		34.401
	Chi-sq(3) P-val =	0.0000
Weak identification test (Cragg-Donald Wald F statistic):		12.826
	(Kleibergen-Paap rk Wald F statistic):	12.721
Stock-Yogo weak ID test critical values:	5% maximal IV relative bias	13.91
	10% maximal IV relative bias	9.08
	20% maximal IV relative bias	6.46
	30% maximal IV relative bias	5.39
	10% maximal IV size	22.30
	15% maximal IV size	12.83
	20% maximal IV size	9.54
	25% maximal IV size	7.80

Source: Stock-Yogo (2005). Reproduced by permission.
NB: Critical values are for Cragg-Donald F statistic and i.i.d. errors.

Hansen J statistic (overidentification test of all instruments):		61.165
	Chi-sq(2) P-val =	0.0000

Instrumented	:	union
Included instruments	:	wks_work ttl_exp not_smsa grade
Excluded instruments	:	black south age

6.3 Control Function Approaches for Endogenous Selection into Treatment

A variant of the instrumental variables approach pioneered by Heckman (1979) is to model the selection process for treatment as involving components explained by observable variables and components involving elements of the residual term that are treated as an additional variable. This is done as a probit regression from which additional terms are predicted for treated and untreated populations, which are used as regressors in a second stage regression.

The probit must include some independent variables that are instruments—correlated with treatment but not with outcomes, but also includes outcome variables.

$$probitP(\ W{=}1|Z\ ){=}\ \mathcal{B}_1\ Z_i + \eta_i\ = \hat{p}_i$$

Regimes are classified based on the observed participation status, as follows.

$$Y_i = \begin{cases} Y_{1i} \text{ if } W_i > 0 \\ Y_{0i} \text{ if } W_i = 0 \end{cases}$$

The generalized outcome model is conceptualized, as below, before accounting for selection bias.

$$Y_{1i} = \alpha_1 + \gamma_1 Xi + \varepsilon_{1i}$$
$$Y_{0i} = \alpha_0 + \gamma_0 Xi + \varepsilon_{2i}$$

The control function approach captures the effects of selection bias through an additional regression term. To generate this term, it is assumed that the error term of the probit regression and the error term of the outcome equations are jointly normally distributed with zero means and a variance - covariance structure as follows:

$$\text{cov}(\varepsilon_{1i}, \varepsilon_{2i}, \eta_i) = \begin{bmatrix} \sigma_{\varepsilon0}^2 & . & \sigma_{\varepsilon0\eta} \\ . & \sigma_{\varepsilon1}^2 & \sigma_{\varepsilon1\eta} \\ . & . & \sigma_{\eta}^2 \end{bmatrix}$$

Two ancillary parameters, termed the inverse mills ratio and the selection hazard rate are estimated based on the standard normal density ϕ (.) and the standard normal cumulative distribution Φ (.) for use with the treated (λ_{1i}) and untreated (λ_{0i}) populations, as follows:

$$\lambda_{1i} = \frac{\phi\,(\mathcal{B}Z_i)}{\Phi(\mathcal{B}Z_i)}$$
$$\lambda_{0i} = -\frac{\phi\,(\mathcal{B}Z_i)}{1 - \Phi(\mathcal{B}Z_i)}$$

The simplest application of the ratios to estimate treatment effects is via endogenous treatment effects models, which use the same coefficients for the two outcome regimes. By doing so, the model can estimate an ATE as the coefficient on W after selection bias is absorbed by the inverse mills (for treated) and hazard (for untreated) ratios in the equation.

$$Y_i = \gamma X_i + \beta_1 W_i + \beta_2 W_i \lambda_{1i} + \beta_3 (1 - W_i)\lambda_{0i} + \alpha$$

Implementing endogenous treatment effects regression in STATA

This regression technique can be implemented in STATA 13 and 14 using the command "etregress", followed by the outcome variable and variables conditioning outcomes, "treat" (treatment variable= independent variables conditioning treatment).

The following example uses the same data on female employment characteristics as the 2SLS example and evaluates the impact of unions on wages. In this example, union membership is conditioned by whether a woman identifies as being of 'black' race, lives in the south, and her age. The finding is a significant positive effect of union membership on wages.

Commands:

webuse union3
etregress wage wks_work ttl_exp not_smsa grade, treat(union=black south age) vce(robust)

Results:

Linear regression with endogenous treatment	Number of obs	=	1203
Estimator: maximum likelihood	Wald chi2(5)	=	577.00
Log pseudolikelihood = −3093.8702	Prob > chi2	=	0.0000

	Coef.	Robust Std. Err.	z	P>|z|	[95% Conf. Interval]	
wage						
wks_work	.0189489	.0045733	4.14	0.000	.0099853	.0279125
ttl_exp	.2072293	.044969	4.61	0.000	.1190916	.295367
not_smsa	−.8011546	.1204989	−6.65	0.000	−1.037328	−.5649812
grade	.4607586	.0430331	10.71	0.000	.3764153	.5451018
union	3.330139	.5341358	6.23	0.000	2.283252	4.377025
_cons	−2.061778	.4773057	−4.32	0.000	−2.99728	−1.126276
union						
black	.2237051	.1046224	2.14	0.032	.0186489	.4287613
south	−.5459861	.0878814	−6.21	0.000	−.7182305	−.3737417
age	.045354	.0116589	3.89	0.000	.022503	.068205
_cons	−1.680473	.2687548	−6.25	0.000	−2.207223	−1.153723
/athrho	−.77179	.2231879	−3.46	0.001	−1.20923	−.3343497
/lnsigma	.7684901	.080225	9.58	0.000	.611252	.9257283
rho	−.6479691	.1294794			−.8364484	−.3224237
sigma	2.156508	.1730058			1.842737	2.523705
lambda	−1.39735	.369339			−2.121241	−.6734593

Wald test of indep. eqns. (rho = 0): chi2(1) = 25.47 Prob > chi2 = 0.0000

6.4 Endogenous Switching Regression Approaches

The Heckman approach gives only an ATE, as the γ coefficients for the outcome variables in the outcome equation are held constant across treated and untreated populations. An endogenous switching regression relaxes this assumption by allowing the two regimes to have differentiated coefficients on variables conditioning outcomes. By having differentiated γ coefficients, treatment effects can be differentiated among populations that select into treatment and those that do not (Maddala and Nelson 1975). This means that the ATT may be separately identified from the ATU.

More specifically, the inverse mills and hazard ratios estimated as in the case of the endogenous treatment effects regression, in combination with coefficients from the outcome equations and values of independent variables, give the expectations of outcomes for (1) those treated and participating in treatment; (2) those untreated and not participating in treatment; (3) those participating in treatment if they had not been treated; and (4) those not participating in treatment if they had been treated.

$$1: E(Y_{1i}|W_i = 1) = \gamma_1 X_{1i} + \sigma_{\varepsilon 1 \eta} \lambda_{1i}$$
$$2: E(Y_{0i}|W_i = 0) = \gamma_0 X_{0i} + \sigma_{\varepsilon 0 \eta} \lambda_{0i}$$
$$3: E(Y_{0i}|W_i = 1) = \gamma_0 X_{1i} + \sigma_{\varepsilon 0 \eta} \lambda_{1i}$$
$$4: E(Y_{1i}|W_i = 0) = \gamma_1 X_{0i} + \sigma_{\varepsilon 1 \eta} \lambda_{0i}$$

The differences between conditional expectations define the treatment effects. For example, the average difference between 1 and 3 is the ATT, between 2 and 4 is the ATU, and the weighted average of the ATU and ATT is the ATE.

Implementing endogenous switching regressions in STATA

This regression technique can be implemented in STATA using the user-written package "movestay" (Lokshin and Sajaia 2004). The syntax is given as follows: "movestay" (outcome variable independent variables for the outcome), "select" (treatment variable = independent variables for treatment).

The following example uses the same data on female employment characteristics as the endogenous treatment effects example and evaluates the impact of unions on wages using the same specification. It also finds a large positive effect of union membership on wages as the difference in average conditional expectations for those in unions and those outside of unions.

Commands:

```
ssc install movestay
webuse union3
movestay (wage wks_work ttl_exp not_smsa grade), select(union=black south age) robust
mspredict yc0, yc0
mspredict yc1, yc1
egen ate=mean(yc1-yc0)
display ate
```

Results:

Endogenous switching regression model

Log pseudolikelihood = –3044.2858

Number of obs	=	1203
Wald chi2(4)	=	267.27
Prob > chi2	=	0.0000

	Coef.	Robust Std. Err.	z	P>|z|	[95% Conf. Interval]	
wage0						
wks_work	.0213619	.0046435	4.60	0.000	.0122609	.030463
ttl_exp	.152945	.0465026	3.29	0.001	.0618016	.2440885
not_smsa	.7722602	.1197559	−6.45	0.000	−1.006977	−.537543
grade	.4186368	.0421965	9.92	0.000	.3359331	.5013405
_cons	−1.711028	.5054607	−3.39	0.001	−2.701713	−.7203435
wage1						
wks_work	.0212183	.0111049	1.91	0.056	−.000547	.0429835
ttl_exp	.1937367	.0956872	2.02	0.043	.0061931	.3812802
not_smsa	−.7446781	.2691096	−2.77	0.006	−1.272123	−.217233
grade	.4200887	.0691625	6.07	0.000	.2845327	.5556448
_cons	1.022297	.8620225	1.19	0.236	−.6672363	2.71183
select						
black	.2165804	.0771031	2.81	0.005	.0654612	.3676996
south	−.4740664	.0761678	−6.22	0.000	−.6233525	−.3247803
age	.030676	.0116606	2.63	0.009	.0078217	.0535303
_cons	−1.333329	.269485	−4.95	0.000	−1.86151	−.8051476
/lns0	.8242716	.0690175	11.94	0.000	.6889998	.9595435
/lns1	.8213944	.1002633	8.19	0.000	.624882	1.017907
/r0	−1.659308	.1414636	−11.73	0.000	−1.936572	−1.382044
/r1	−.413224	.1111876	−3.72	0.000	−.6311477	−.1953003
sigma0	2.280219	.1573751			1.991722	2.610504
sigma1	2.273668	.2279654			1.868026	2.767396
rho0	−.9301239	.0190791			−.9592613	−.8814082
rho1	−.3912067	.0941712			−.558842	−.1928546

Wald test of indep. eqns. :   chi2 (2) = 158.64   Prob > chi2 = 0.0000

```
. display ate
2.8555474
```

Section 7: Regression Discontinuity Design

7.1 Basic Concepts of Regression Discontinuity Design

Regression discontinuity design (RDD) is, in fact, a special case of instrumental variables, as it can be applied when a very precise type of instrument is present. This method takes advantage of the fact that in some situations, the likelihood of receiving a treatment changes abruptly or discontinuously at the cutoff point of a particular variable often related to program eligibility (often called the *running, forcing, or assignment variable*—hereafter, this text uses the term *assignment variable* for the sake of readability). That is, there are situations in which a cutoff rule exists such that whenever an individual has a value of the assignment variable greater than "X_0" (the cutoff point), he or she has a greater chance of being treated ($W_i = 1$) than if his or her value is less than X_0. In addition to the existence of the cutoff rule, if the following three other conditions are met, the RDD makes it possible to estimate treatment effects by comparing the outcomes of individuals just above and below the cutoff:

Condition 1: The assignment variable predicts treatment, with a clear discontinuity at an eligibility threshold or cutoff. In other words, the probability of treatment should abruptly change at the cutoff of the assignment variable. Whether or not this is true can be examined by estimating or graphing the trend in the outcome–assignment variable relationship on either side of the cutoff and seeing whether there is a "jump" at the cutoff point. If there is no such discontinuity, RDD is not appropriate.

Condition 2: Among exogenous variables, only the treatment of interest should have a discontinuity at the cutoff. That is, there should be no other reasons for why there is a jump at the cutoff except for differences in assignment to the treatment investigated. This should be manifest in no discontinuity in pretreatment covariates (or potential outcomes) at the cutoff. Whether or not this is true can be examined using the data. Essentially the evaluator can regress the trend in the relationship of other independent variables against the assignment variable just above and below the cutoff to determine if there are "jumps" at the cutoff point. If there are jumps, then this means that RDD may not be appropriate. Such may occur if other programs use the same eligibility criteria as the treatment of interest.

Condition 3: Individuals cannot manipulate the values of the assignment variable to self-select into treatment. It may be the case that individuals have found a way to manipulate the assignment variable to receive or avoid receiving treatment. Although there is no foolproof way of determining whether this has happened, the evaluator can run a "McCrary Test" (McCrary 2008). This is a statistical test which assesses whether there is a jump or discontinuity in the density of observations at the cutoff. If there is such a jump, it likely means that individuals have found a way to manipulate which side of the cutoff they are on. In such cases, RDD also may not be appropriate.

7.2 Sharp Regression Discontinuity Design

In sharp RDD, the probability of receiving the treatment changes discontinuously from 0 (no chance of receiving the treatment) to 1 (100% chance of receiving the treatment) at the cutoff point of the assignment variable X_0. In other words, there is a well-implemented sharp eligibility criterion for the program. Sharp RDD is represented by the following equations:

$$Y_{0i} = \alpha + f(X_0 + \delta_i) + \varepsilon_{0i}$$
$$Y_{1i} = \alpha + \tau_i + f(X_0 - \delta_i) + \varepsilon_{1i}$$

Where Y_0 is the outcome for those above the eligibility threshold, Y_1 is the outcome for those within the eligibility threshold, $f(X_0)$ is a continuous function around the eligibility threshold; τ is the treatment effect; and δ is the distance from the threshold.

The difference in regimes can reveal the treatment effect, as follows:

$$Y_1 - Y_0 = \tau + f(X_0 - \delta) - f(X_0 + \delta) + (\varepsilon_1 - \varepsilon_0)$$

Because there is some random variation in the assignment variable (condition 1) and individuals cannot manipulate whether they are above or below the cutoff point for program eligibility (condition 2), RDD resembles a randomized experiment just around the cutoff point. Individuals just above the cutoff point are similar to individuals just below the cutoff point, except for the fact that individuals to one side of the cutoff point also received the treatment while those to the left did not. Therefore any differences in the average outcomes between those just above and below the cutoff can be solely attributed to the treatment.

It is relatively easy to estimate treatment effects under sharp RDD. In the situation where there are enough observation points around the cutoff, it is possible to estimate the treatment effect by differencing the outcome means just above and below the cutoff. In this situation, it is not necessary for the evaluator to assume any functional forms. If data around the cutoff are sparse, the evaluator can also separately model (a) the trend in Y along the assignment variable, from below the cutoff up to the cutoff point; and (b) the trend in Y along the assignment variable, from above the cutoff up to the cutoff point. The evaluator can then take the difference between the intercepts of the two lines at the cutoff point—this is the treatment effect. Parametric, nonparametric, and semi-parametric regression approaches may be applied for estimating the treatment effect in this situation.

Sharp RDD has an important advantage over other types of quasi-experimental designs such as matching and difference-in-differences. Because the eligibility criterion is known, selection on unobservables becomes a nonissue, and observables can be controlled through selection of populations around the eligibility threshold. At the same time, what RDD estimates is a LATE for populations around the eligibility threshold, not an ATE for the entire population.

7.3   Fuzzy Regression Discontinuity Design

In many cases, eligibility criteria are not implemented with a high degree of precision, or program rollout does not reach 100% of the eligible population. For cases where the probability of receiving the treatment changes discontinuously at the cutoff point but by less than 1 (less than 100%), fuzzy RDD may be used.

To estimate the treatment effect under the fuzzy RDD, the evaluator must separately model (a) the trend of Y along the assignment variable, from below the cutoff up to the cutoff point; (b) the trend of Y along the assignment variable, from above the cutoff to the cutoff point; (c) the trend of W along the assignment variable, from below the cutoff up to the cutoff point; and (d) the trend of W along the assignment variable, from above the cutoff to the cutoff point. The evaluator can then take the difference between the intercepts of the two trends (a) and (b) at the cutoff point (the numerator of the fuzzy RDD estimator) and divide that by the difference between the intercepts of the two trends (c) and (d) at the cutoff point (the denominator of the fuzzy RDD estimator). Parametric, nonparametric, and semi-parametric regression approaches may be applied for estimating the treatment effect in this situation. Although couched in slightly different notation, the estimator for fuzzy RDD is actually the same as the two-stages least squares estimator in instrumental variables analysis.

Implementing regression discontinuity design in STATA

"Rdrobust" can automate RDD in STATA and enables the calculation of standard errors that are robust to heteroskedasticity (Calonico et al. 2014). The syntax is "rdrobust", followed by outcome variable and assignment variable, with an option of "fuzzy" (participation variable) when fuzzy RDD is used.

The following sharp RDD example (from Calonico, Cattaneo, and Titiunik 2014) uses the data included in the "rdrobust" package to illustrate application in STATA. The treatment is whether a member of the Democratic Party wins a US election for a Senate seat representing a State, and the outcome is the margin in the following election. The cutoff value for the assignment variable is 0. The results show that incumbency has a significant positive effect on the margins by which subsequent elections are won.

Commands:

```
net get st0366.pkg
use rdrobust_rdsenate.dta
rdrobust vote margin, all
```

Results:

Sharp RD estimates using local polynomial regression.

Cutoff c = 0	Left of c	Right of c		Number of obs	=	1297
Number of obs	343	310		NN matches	=	3
Order loc. poly. (p)	1	1		BW type	=	CCT
Order bias (q)	2	2		Kernel type	=	Triangular
BW loc. poly. (h)	16.794	16.794				
BW bias (b)	27.437	27.437				
rho (h/b)	0.612	0.612				

Outcome: vote. Running variable: margin.

Method	Coef.	Std. Err.	z	P>|z|	[95% Conf. Interval]	
Conventional	7.4253	1.4954	4.9656	0.000	4.49446	10.3561
Robust	–	–	4.2675	0.000	4.06975	10.9833

All estimates.

Method	Coef.	Std. Err.	z	P>|z|	[95% Conf. Interval]	
Conventional	7.4253	1.4954	4.9656	0.000	4.49446	10.3561
Bias-corrected	7.5265	1.4954	5.0333	0.000	4.59569	10.4574
Robust	7.5265	1.7637	4.2675	0.000	4.06975	10.9833

References

Abadie, A., A. Diamond, and J. Hainmueller. 2010. Synthetic Control Methods for Comparative Case Studies: Estimating the Effect of California's Tobacco Control Program. *Journal of the American Statistical Association.* 105 (490). pp. 493–505.

Athey, S. and G. W. Imbens. 2017. Chapter 3. The Econometrics of Randomized Experiments. In E. Duflo and A. Banerjee, eds. *Handbook of Field Experiments.* Volume 1, 1st Edition. Amsterdam: North Holland.

Baum, C. F., M. E. Schaffer, and S. Stillman. 2010. IVREG2: STATA Module for Extended Instrumental Variables/2SLS and GMM estimation. Statistical Software Components, S425401. Revised 9 February 2016. Boston College Department of Economics. http://ideas.repec.org/c/boc/bocode/s425401.html.

Calonico, S., M. D. Cattaneo, and R. Titiunik. 2014. Robust data-driven inference in the regression-discontinuity design. *The Stata Journal.* 14 (4). pp. 909–946. https://sites.google.com/site/rdpackages/rdrobust/Calonico-Cattaneo-Titiunik_2014_Stata.pdf.

Heckman, J. J. 1979. Selection Bias as a Specification Error. *Econometrica.* 47 (1). pp. 153–161.

Lokshin, M. and Z. Sajaia. 2004. Maximum Likelihood Estimation of Endogenous Switching Regression Models. *The STATA Journal.* 4 (3). pp. 282–289.

Lunceford, J. K. and M. Davidian. 2004. Stratification and Weighting via the Propensity Score in Estimation of Causal Treatment Effects: A Comparative Study. *Statistics in Medicine.* 23. pp. 2937–2960.

Maddala, G. S. and F. D. Nelson. 1975. Switching Regression Models with Exogenous and Endogenous Switching. *Proceedings of the Business and Economics Statistics Section, American Statistical Association.* pp. 423–426.

McCrary, J. 2008. Manipulation of the Running Variable in the Regression Discontinuity Design: A Density Test. *Journal of Econometrics.* 142 (2). pp. 698–714. https://doi.org/10.1016/j.jeconom.2007.05.005.

Quistorff, B. and S. Galiani. 2017. The synth_runner package: Utilities to Automate Synthetic Control Estimation Using Synth. Version 1.6.0. August 2017. https://github.com/bquistorff/synth_runner.

Robins, J. M., A. Rotnitzky, L. P. Zhao. 1994. Estimation of Regression Coefficients When Some Regressors Are Not Always Observed. *Journal of the American Statistical Association.* 89. pp. 846–866.

Rosenbaum, P. R. and D. B. Rubin. 1983. The Central Role of the Propensity Score in Observational Studies for Causal Effects. *Biometrika.* 70. pp. 41–55.

Rosenbaum, P. R. and D. B. Rubin. 1985. Constructing a Control Group Using Multivariate Matched Sampling Methods that Incorporate the Propensity Score. *The American Statistician*. 39 (1).

Rubin, D. 1974. Estimating Causal Effects of Treatments in Randomized and Nonrandomized Studies. *Journal of Educational Psychology*. 66 (5). pp. 688–701. doi:10.1037/h0037350.

Ryan, A. M., J. F. Burgess, and J. B. Dimick. 2015. Why We Should Not Be Indifferent to Specification Choices for Difference-in-Differences. *Health Services Research*. 50 (4). pp. 1211–1235. https://www.ncbi.nlm.nih.gov/pmc/articles/PMC4545355/pdf/hesr0050-1211.pdf.

Appendix 2
Designing Field Surveys

G ood quality data are necessary for credible impact evaluation, and original surveys are often needed to collect these data. This Appendix provides an overview of how field survey instruments can be designed and implemented.

The sections included in this Appendix are as follows:

Section 1: Types of Data Needed for Impact Evaluations
Section 2: Sampling and Representation
Section 3: Additional Considerations for Sample Size and Power Calculations
Section 4: Survey Instrument Design
Section 5: Survey Implementation
Section 6: Data Management

Section 1: Types of Data Needed for Impact Evaluations

The types of data needed for a particular evaluation should be guided by a *theory of change* developed for that evaluation. Specifically, the theory of change of an evaluation can be used to identify

- the primary outcomes/effects of an intervention (i.e., the indicators closely related to the main target of a program or policy) as well as secondary outcomes that may also be affected (outcomes that while not the main target of a particular intervention are also of interest);

- intermediate outcomes or indicators that can be used to evaluate how an intervention worked (or did not work as the case may be); and

- moderating characteristics (indicators that are not affected by a program but may moderate its effect, e.g., gender).

The value of an impact evaluation is greatly increased when data are available on secondary and intermediate outcomes as well as moderating characteristics. These allow one to determine not only if the program worked or not, but also whether any other important outcomes were affected, why or how an intervention worked, and for whom it did and did not work.

When selecting outcomes, particular attention should be paid to whether the evaluation will be powered to detect an effect on those indicators. Indicators that are highly variable, subject to statistical error, are rare, or for which the effects of the program are likely to be small may not be detectable without a large sample size.

In addition to primary outcomes, intermediate outcomes, and moderating characteristics, it is also desirable to collect information on other factors aside from the intervention that could affect the outcomes of interest. Accounting for these factors can increase the statistical power of an evaluation. When quasi-experimental methods are used, information on these other factors may also be necessary for identification or can be used to assess the robustness of a particular identification strategy.

Generally, it is desirable to collect data covering multiple time periods both before and after the program or policy has begun. Baseline data are necessary for many evaluation methods and—even for methods where baseline data are not strictly required (such as randomized controlled trials or regression discontinuity design)—baseline data can be important for checking that assumptions underlying these methods are valid (namely, that baseline characteristics are similar for treatment and control groups). Baseline data can also increase power (often reducing sample size requirements enough to largely offset the costs of collecting baseline data) and allow for analysis of heterogeneous intervention effects.

Multiple stages or rounds of data collection after an intervention has gone into effect can be used to assess short- and long-run impacts. This can allow evaluators to analyze how long it takes for impacts to evolve and how long impacts last.

Section 2: Sampling and Representation

Whether using primary or secondary data, an important consideration is representativeness. It is often necessary to draw conclusions about a large population for which collecting data on every member of that population would not be feasible. In such cases, an appropriate sampling method must be used to collect data that is representative of the population of interest. An appropriate sampling method will be one that (i) avoids bias in the selection procedure, and (ii) achieves maximum precision for a given amount of resources.

What is a representative sample?

When doing an impact evaluation, it is important to select a sample of participants or respondents that are representative of the population of interest. A *population of interest* in the context of an evaluation is a group of people, villages, schools, or other units whose outcomes are to be evaluated. While ideal, it is rarely feasible to conduct a census on the entire population of interest. A sample is a subset of the population for which one can feasibly collect information.

A sample is considered *representative* when it fully reflects the characteristics of the population as a whole. This implies that any effects of an evaluation found in the sample will hold for the overall population. A primary reason a sample may not be representative is if the sample is influenced by some sort of choice-based selection from the population. For instance, individuals who respond to a mail or internet survey will not be representative of the entire population since individuals who respond to these types of surveys are different from those who do not. The representativeness of a sample may also be compromised if the sampling frame—the list of individuals in a population from which the sample is drawn—does not adequately cover the target population.

Choosing a sample

After a population of interest has been appropriately defined, an appropriate sampling strategy will draw a sample that is representative of this population. This is done through *probability sampling*.[1] The basic steps of probability sampling are as follows:

1. Define the population of interest.
2. Choose a sampling frame.
3. Select units from the sampling frame.

A *sampling frame* is the most comprehensive list one can obtain of units in the population of interest. Common sources of sampling frames include population censuses, lists of schools or clinics in a given area, maps showing villages and towns in a given area, etc. In creating a sampling frame, care should be taken

---

[1] Note that nonprobability sampling techniques (such as convenience sampling, snowball sampling, purposive sampling, and quota sampling) will generally not yield representative samples. Nonprobability sampling should only be used when financial or logistical constraints make probability sampling infeasible.

to obtain the most comprehensive list possible of units in the population of interest. Using a sampling frame that excludes units that are in the population of interest (or includes those that are not) can introduce bias into the evaluation. A poor sampling frame, for example, could be something like outdated directory listings that do not list all individuals or businesses.

Once a sampling frame is determined, a sample of units is selected from units listed in the frame. With probability sampling, units are selected with a known probability. This ensures that the selected units are statistically the same as units that are not selected. Thus, any effects found for selected units will be the same among units not selected into the sample.

Although simple random sampling is the most straightforward way to sample, evaluators often deviate from using a simple random sample in order to improve precision, to reduce data collection costs, or because adequate sampling frames covering the entire population of interest are not available. Common deviations include variations on stratified sampling, cluster sampling, and combinations of these two approaches.

Stratified sampling

Sometimes when running an evaluation, an evaluator is interested in outcomes among certain subgroups. For example, there may be interest in how an educational intervention affects girls versus boys or how tax policy affects rich versus poor individuals. In these instances, a *stratified sample* may be appropriate. In stratified sampling, units are first separated into groups (called strata) and a simple random sample is taken within each of these groups. Thus, every unit within a group has the same chance of being drawn. If the sample within each group is large enough, this allows inference about these subgroups— not just the population as a whole. Although inferences can be made about subgroups without stratified sampling, stratified sampling ensures that enough individuals are selected from each subgroup to permit analysis. With simple random sampling, there may not be enough individuals of a subgroup (minority groups, for instance) included in the sample for analysis.

A second advantage of stratified sampling is that a stratified sample can provide greater precision than a simple random sample of the same size. Because of this greater precision, a stratified sample requires a smaller total sample size, reducing the costs of data collection.

Cluster (multistage) sampling

Another common deviation from simple random sampling is to use *cluster sampling* (otherwise known as *multistage* sampling). Often, individual units are grouped into clusters such as villages, schools, or hospitals. In cluster sampling, clusters are sampled first and then individuals within clusters. This creates a sample where sample individuals are not randomly distributed over space, but are grouped geographically.

Cluster sampling has two main advantages over simple random sampling. First, cluster sampling can be an effective way to control the costs of data collection. It is more cost-effective for a survey team to travel from village to village or school to school, spending a longer time in each, than to travel between sampled individuals that are widely dispersed geographically. Second, the absence of adequate sampling frames covering entire populations makes it necessary to first sample clusters and then construct complete lists of individuals within each selected cluster. For these reasons, most surveys in developing countries use cluster sampling.

In impact evaluation, a clustered sample is the natural choice when interventions are clustered, or programs are implemented at a unit higher than the unit of observation. Many programs in education, for example, are implemented school by school, creating clusters of students. For this reason, clustered sampling commonly arises in impact evaluation.

The main disadvantage of cluster sampling is that it provides less precision than simple random sampling or stratified sampling given the same total sample size. Thus, whether cluster sampling should be used will depend on the design of the program to be evaluated, the cost savings from cluster sampling, the availability of sampling frames, and how these compare with the costs associated with the need to draw a larger total sample. Calculating power (precision) given a clustered sample is discussed in detail in Chapter 7.

Although stratified sampling and cluster sampling are similar in that they both first partition the sampling frame into nonoverlapping subsets, they differ in that individuals from all strata will be included in the final sample but individuals from only the selected subset of clusters will be in the sample.

Ultimately, it is most important that the sample chosen be representative of the population of interest. This is achieved by ensuring that the sampling frame accurately and completely covers the population of interest and that an appropriate sampling strategy (whether simple, stratified, or cluster sampling) is used to select units or individuals from that frame.

Section 3: Additional Considerations for Sample Size and Power Calculations

Given a sampling strategy that produces a sample that is representative of the population of interest, the second important consideration is that the sample is large enough to provide adequate statistical power to detect an impact of a program. The sample size required for an impact evaluation is determined through sample power calculations, as explained in Chapter 7. This section covers additional considerations for sample power calculations beyond those covered in the main text.

Baseline data and data waves

A design feature that affects power and sample size requirements is the number of data waves that will be collected. Most notably, the availability of baseline data can significantly increase power. This is because including baseline covariates in the estimation of treatment effects effectively reduces the noise (variance) of the outcome. The largest gains in power are typically from including baseline data on outcomes before the program, particularly if outcomes are highly correlated over time (such as health and education outcomes). The reduction in required sample size resulting from including baseline covariates can (at least partially) offset the costs of additional data collection.

For outcomes that are less correlated over time (such as business profits), controlling for baseline values of the outcome provides less of a gain in power. For such outcomes, if treatment expands over time it may even make sense to forgo baseline data collection and instead devote resources to collecting multiple waves of follow-up data (McKenzie 2012).

Multiple hypotheses

Evaluations often use more than one outcome to assess the impact of an intervention and often aim to compare more than two treatments. These evaluations are simultaneously testing multiple hypotheses (the number of outcomes times the number of comparisons between different treatment groups). The standard approach to hypothesis testing assumes, however, that a single test is being conducted. When multiple hypotheses are being tested, power calculations need to be adjusted to take into account the probability that any one hypothesis test may turn out significant just by random chance. In other words, the probability of finding a significant effect by chance is higher with multiple tests than with a single test because there are more attempts.

Methods of adjusting for multiple hypotheses fall under two main categories: those controlling what is called the false discovery rate (FDR) and those controlling the so-called familywise error rate (FWER). Procedures that control FDR make adjustments by controlling the expected proportion of significant results (rejections of the null hypothesis) that are false discoveries (Type I errors). FWER-controlling procedures control the probability of *at least one* Type I error. FWER-controlling procedures are more often used for calculating power and sample size because they are more conservative than FDR-controlling procedures.

There are many individual FWER-controlling methods available. The simplest is the Bonferroni method further developed by Dunn (1961). With the Bonferroni method, one simply obtains an adjusted significance level (α) by dividing the desired significance level by the total number of hypotheses and uses this new significance level to calculate sample size. For example, if the desired significance level is 0.05 and there are two hypotheses (two outcomes to be tested, for instance) a significance level of 0.025 (0.05÷2) would be used.

The downside of the Bonferroni method is that it assumes hypotheses are independent and may be too conservative as a result. Although there are improvements on this method that are less conservative (e.g., Holm/Hochberg methods), best practice is to use "step-down" approaches that account for the correlation of outcomes being tested (such as those developed by Westfall and Young [1993] and Romano and Wolf [2005]).

Section 4: Survey Instrument Design

In addition to sampling errors (discussed above), so-called *non-sampling errors* can also reduce precision (power) and bias impact evaluation results. Non-sampling errors include errors resulting from issues such as nonresponse (data are missing or incomplete for some individuals), attrition (individuals are lost between survey rounds), and measurement error (there is a difference between the recorded value and the true value of an indicator [Banda 2003]). While sampling errors are determined at the sampling stage, non-sampling errors arise during data collection. How a questionnaire is designed, how questions are phrased, the behavior of the field team, and how data are collected and validated all affect non-sampling error.

In impact evaluation, non-sampling errors can be extremely costly since an evaluation is only as valid as the data used. Although all data analyses are affected by non-sampling error, it poses an arguably larger threat in impact evaluation since errors that are not balanced across treatment and control groups dramatically diminish the interpretability of an evaluation's findings. It is therefore crucial that data collection be planned to reduce non-sampling error as much as possible and to be sure that remaining errors are equally balanced between the treatment and control groups. The best way to accomplish this is by instating uniform standards and embedding repeated quality checks at various stages.

Of course, data collection is almost always subject to important constraints. Taking into account financial constraints (budget available for data collection), operational constraints (the capacity of those implementing the survey), and the ability and willingness of those being interviewed to provide information, the goal is to develop a data collection strategy that will provide data with few errors and cover the important indicators needed for the evaluation. Thus, data collection is a process of prioritization and the weighing of evaluation objectives and constraints.

Questionnaire development

This process of weighing objectives and constraints begins with questionnaire development. When developing questionnaires, there is a strong tendency to collect as much data as possible. However, collecting data that is ultimately unnecessary can be costly. Not only do unnecessarily long questionnaires increase survey costs, they can also affect the quality of all data collected.

It is typical for impact evaluations to contain several levels of surveys and questionnaires, so as to capture variations on program and/or policy implementation and variables conditioning impacts. For example, there may be a facility survey on the facilities delivering the program (such as schools for an educational intervention), a village or community survey to capture the presence of other programs in the location and shared village characteristics, and a household survey to characterize the target population for the program. Relegating questions to the appropriate level can improve survey efficiency.

The process of developing questionnaires and other survey instruments can be specific to the evaluation at hand. At the same time, most surveys attempt to capture variables that have been the object of previous survey efforts. For this reason, it is often useful to consult prior survey modules before initiating new survey design.

Potential sources of survey modules include:

- Living Standards Measurement Survey Forms (which contain many modules for many countries): http://go.worldbank.org/UK1ETMHBN0

- Survey forms from the Demographic and Health Program: http://dhsprogram.com/What-We-Do/Questionnaires.cfm

- Surveys used in the Village Dynamics Studies in South Asia: http://vdsa.icrisat.ac.in/vdsa-questionaires.aspx

- The survey forms included in the World Bank's Impact Evaluation Toolkit: http://siteresources.worldbank.org/EXTIMPEVALTK/Resources/8811875-1346101602804/4.10_Household_Questionnaires.zip

This section gives an overview of a common approach to questionnaire development and provides suggestions for each stage of this process. The underlying theme of these suggestions is to minimize non-sampling error and to ensure uniformity.

Basic steps of questionnaire development

Most questionnaires are developed and arranged in a modular fashion, meaning that similar question types are grouped into different modules—or sections—on a survey form. Modules most often correspond to topics, but they can also correspond to different respondents, for example. Using modules both simplifies the task of creating and organizing the questionnaire and creates breaks in questioning, which can help limit enumerator and interviewee fatigue.

Using a modular approach, questionnaire development can be broken down into seven main steps:

Step 1: Set Modules
Step 2: Design Specific Questions
Step 3: Harmonize
Step 4: Set Order
Step 5: Pretest Questionnaire
Step 6: Revise
Step 7: Repeat Steps 5 and 6

Each step involves important considerations that can have important implications for endline data quality.

Step 1: Set Modules

The choice of particular modules to include will depend on the evaluation. These should be chosen by referring to the list of indicators identified based on the evaluation's theory of change. The process of prioritization should begin at this stage by only including modules on topics most important to the evaluation.

Step 2: Design Specific Questions

Designing specific questions is the most tedious task of questionnaire development. When possible, questions can be taken from existing questionnaires that have been used and validated in a given context. Wherever possible, questions should be posed in a quantitative and continuous manner, even if a categorical characterization may seem easier for enumerators. Continuous variables enable more analytical possibilities later than do categorical variables.

Even seemingly small details of the way questions are phrased can have large effects on the type and amount of error in survey responses. Attention should also be paid to phrasing questions in ways that limit "desirability bias" that arises from respondents telling enumerators "what they want to hear." Desirability bias can be particularly dangerous in impact evaluations that provide some sort of benefit: respondents in the treatment group could feel a need to respond positively if they know that a survey is connected to a particular program or respondents may think that their response may influence subsequent benefits. Given the plethora of issues around question design, it is best to consult some of the many texts that have been written on the subject (e.g., Grimm 2010; Krumpal 2013) and to pretest problematic questions extensively (in Step 5).

It is also important to construct questions in a way that makes the process as easy as possible (for both the enumerator and for the respondent) and leads to uniformity across interviews. Some rules to accomplish this include the following:

- Write questions out fully so that the interviewer can conduct the interview by reading each question from the questionnaire.

- Include precise definitions of all key concepts and/or terms used in the questionnaire.

- Keep questions as short as possible and use common everyday terms.

- Ask questions in units that are natural for the respondent to consider, and which minimize any mental calculations required to answer.

- Design the questionnaire so that most questions have pre-coded answer options.

- Pay attention to local languages and dialects (even if respondents speak a standard national language or dialect, interviews go more smoothly and with less error when done in the local language).

- Include cross-checks in the questionnaire, so that recording of responses is validated.

If forms will be filled by respondents themselves, particular care should be taken to make forms easy to read and easily understood. Forms filled by respondents themselves can contain more measurement error than asked questionnaires, but self-filled forms are sometimes necessary (e.g., in classrooms with large numbers of students).

Step 3: Order Modules

The next step is to order the modules as they will appear in the questionnaire. This order should match the order in which the interview will be conducted.

It is advisable to group conceptually similar modules together. This can smooth questioning since switching topics too often can be tiring for those interviewed. If there is more than one person being interviewed in the questionnaire, grouping questions by respondent (or likely respondent) can allow enumerators to interview individuals one by one. In general, it is best to develop separate questionnaires for different respondents, but it is sometimes difficult to know in advance who will be the most knowledgeable individual on a given topic (when surveying an organization, for example). It is then best to group similar modules to as much as possible avoid the need for enumerators to go back and forth between different respondents.

Other considerations when organizing modules are as follows:

- Modules should be ordered beginning with those easiest to answer.

- More sensitive modules should be asked toward the end of the questionnaire.

- More important modules should be toward the beginning, when interviewees are less fatigued.

Step 4: Harmonize

Once questions for each module have been drafted, edited, and modules placed in order, the questionnaire should be harmonized—meaning that it should be edited for consistency and flow. This includes

- making sure questions are phrased consistently (for example, similar adjacent questions should refer to the same recall period when possible);

- checking that answer codes are consistent across similar questions in the form (also important for reducing the potential for errors at the data analysis stage); and

- including and double-checking "skip codes" in the questionnaire that indicate which questions are not to be asked based on answers to previous questions.

When making questionnaires for an endline survey (after the program has been implemented) questions should also be checked for consistency with questions in previous survey rounds if they were conducted.

Step 5: Pretest

Once the survey is drafted and has been through an iterative process of prioritization, it is necessary to pretest the survey instruments. Pretesting involves trying out the questionnaire on a number of individuals (preferably not in the treatment or control groups of the evaluation) to observe how the questionnaire performs. Pretesting is often best conducted over multiple weeks, using enumerators expected for the survey, under close supervision. This allows real world issues to be revealed, even as enumerator capacity is enhanced.

During pretesting, evaluators should carefully scrutinize the following:

- Timing: How long does the questionnaire take to finish? How long are each of the individual modules (taking into account that a questionnaire in the pilot stage will take longer because of errors in the draft and inexperienced enumerators)? It is also good practice to time individual questions during each pretest, so that that questionnaire can be most efficiently streamlined.

- Fatigue of enumerators and respondents.

- Are any questions difficult for enumerators to explain or for respondents to understand?

- What questions do respondents have trouble answering? Do they have difficulty recalling? Feel uncomfortable?

- Consistency across different enumerators. Can any inconsistencies be addressed with training or should questions be reworded?

If possible, pretesting should happen in several diverse locations. It is also advisable that, in addition to the survey forms, other survey procedures (survey team organization, supervision procedures, quality check procedures, etc.) also be simulated at this stage (generally as part of later pretesting rounds).

Step 6: Revise

Questionnaires should then be revised according to input from pretesting. Good practice is to include the full data collection team in the process of pretesting and revision. Enumerators will often have the best knowledge of what worked and what did not and different people will pick up on different issues.

Step 7: Repeat Steps 5 and 6

The process of pretesting and revision should then be repeated until the questionnaire is satisfactory, meaning that it is as clear and easy to use as possible and reflects the outcome of a careful weighing of the objectives and constraints. At the conclusion of this iterative process, the final version of the questionnaire should be subjected to a final pretest to ensure that all issues are resolved.

Section 5: Survey Implementation

Coordinating fieldwork

Fieldwork for a survey is a complex operation and will depend largely on the context of the survey. In general, however, data quality can best be ensured by (i) making sure enumerators are well trained and supervised, and (ii) incorporating a system for quality control.

Organization of fieldwork

Surveys are most often organized so that individual field teams are responsible for a given subset of locations. Field teams generally include a supervisor, enumerators (often responsible for individual questionnaires or interviewing certain types of survey respondents), and sometimes include a data specialist responsible for entering and checking data in the field.

In terms of how survey teams are matched with different locations, it is a good idea to randomly assign survey teams to locations and to make sure that individual teams are responsible for an equal number of treatment and control units. Ideally, survey teams are not made aware of which units are treatment and which are control, but this is not always feasible.

Enumerator training

The importance of making sure enumerators are well trained cannot be understated. The quality of training can have severe implications for the quality of the data generated.

Enumerator training may emphasize three aspects:

1. *Overall understanding of the structure and objectives of the survey*

Enumerator training should not only teach enumerators how to conduct their own specific responsibilities, but should also provide an understanding of the larger structure and objectives of the survey.

Making sure that enumerators understand larger survey objectives gives them a better sense of how their role fits into the larger process. Most importantly, understanding the structure and others' responsibilities can ease coordination in the field, particularly when unforeseen events (inevitably) happen. Enumeration is hard and often grueling work even in the simplest surveys: a broad understanding of survey objectives can also help maintain motivation throughout the process.

2. *Standardization*

Second, training should be conducted with a goal of standardization. This includes conducting training in a centralized location, which makes it easier to ensure that training is consistent (qualitatively and quantitatively) across all field teams participating in the survey.

3. Practice

Finally, training should entail a large amount of practice. The more practice enumerators have, the more their speed, accuracy, and consistency will improve. Practice can take place in a classroom setting initially with enumerators interviewing each other, taking turns playing the role of the respondent but should also include a fair amount of practice "in the field."

Training manuals

The centerpiece of training should be a detailed and clear set of training manuals. Manuals should be prepared for each member of the survey team that explain

1. the purpose of the survey;

2. overall structure of the survey (where teams are going, all questionnaires that will be asked at each location, etc.);

3. tasks to be performed by each individual on the team;

4. procedures for unusual cases;

5. general principles for unforeseen problems (these are inevitable);

6. details on how to fill out questionnaires (annotated copies of questionnaires are often included in the manuals, although detailed instructions should be included in the questionnaires themselves to the extent possible); and

7. definitions of specific terms, so that there is no variability in their interpretation.

Quality checks

A system of multiple quality checks at different stages and by different individuals should be incorporated into fieldwork. These checks should check for accuracy, consistency, and completeness. Enumerators should check for errors immediately after completing each interview and supervisors should check later, but ideally before leaving a location. Doing these cross-checks in the field allows for errors to be quickly and cheaply corrected. Supervisors should also conduct random spot checks, reinterviewing respondents on a small subset of questions to ensure accuracy of survey implementation while corrections can still be performed.

Almost all respondent sampling methods will result in the selection of respondents who cannot be accessed at the time of survey conduct. A system should be in place for revisiting or replacing respondents not found or respondents of questionnaires with incomplete information.

Section 6: Data Management

The goal of collecting data is to ultimately get it into a form to be used for analysis. The final—but certainly not least—step in this process is collecting and preparing the actual data sets. Carefully collecting, entering, cleaning, and preparing data sets are also important for keeping non-sampling errors to a minimum.

Data collection and entry

Because of familiarity or necessity, many surveys still initially collect data with paper and pencil, but the use of tablet and laptop computers is increasingly common. Using computers to collect data in the field has obvious advantages, including (i) the ability to use programmable software that includes questionnaire skip codes and real-time consistency checks, and (ii) negating the need to separately enter data into the computer as an additional step. Using computers to collect data in the field, however, can also increase the risk of data loss so a system for teams to regularly back up data in the field should be put in place. Electronic survey administration may also require more pretesting as entry forms may have skip logic, units, and formats that have less flexibility than paper forms, which enumerators can modify or annotate.

When survey responses are collected with paper and pencil, it is necessary to have a process to ensure quality during data entry. Data entry software can be used to ease data entry and improve quality with embedded consistency checks. If data entry is also incorporated into survey field operations, errors can also be quickly checked and corrected as with using computers during interviews. The quality of data entry can also be improved using "double entry" where data are independently entered by different individuals. Interview timing and enumerator names associated with each observation should be included in the survey data.

Data cleaning and preparation

Once data are entered, they need to be prepared for analysis. The most important part of this is validating and "cleaning" the data. This refers to the process of checking the raw data for errors and making corrections. During this data-cleaning process, responses should once again be checked for the following:

- Consistency (Are there any contradictory responses to survey items?)

- Validity (Are there any values that are too "extreme" to be true?)

- Completeness (Are any forms missing a large amount of responses? Are certain variables missing more often than acceptable?)

- Distribution (Do data follow the expected distribution, and are there outliers?)

- Integrity (Are data from a given survey team or enumerator suspicious in any way?)

A standardized protocol should be developed covering procedures for identifying and dealing with each of these issues. This involves making a series of important but difficult decisions, including how much "cleaning" should actually be done before analysis (what types of errors should be corrected? how are they defined? how should they be corrected?). Typically, cleaning should be via a documented script file that is shared with the evaluation commissioners, so that it can be replicated, and revised, if necessary.

When problematic observations are identified, they should be coded as outliers, rather than deleted from the data set, so that further analysis is possible and data cleaning is transparent. Causes of outliers should be identified to the degree possible, and correlation with enumerators and other factors should be explored to identify possible errors in survey execution.

It is good practice for a random sample of observations to be independently (of the survey team) validated by resurveying respondents on selected questions. This may be conducted over the phone, at least initially, and in person if a large number of respondent phone numbers do not work. This process provides confidence about the fidelity of survey implementation, and enumerators and survey managers should be informed that it will be conducted independently, so that it incentivizes good survey conduct.

References

Banda, J. P. 2003. Nonsampling Errors in Surveys. Paper prepared for Expert Group Meeting to Review the Draft Handbook on Designing of Household Sample Surveys. United Nations Secretariat, New York. 3–5 December 2003.

Dunn, O. J. 1961. Multiple Comparisons among Means. *Journal of the American Statistical Association.* 56 (293). pp. 52–64.

Grimm, P. 2010. Social Desirability Bias. In J. Sheth and N. Malhotra, eds. *Wiley International Encyclopedia of Marketing.* Part 2. Marketing Research.

Krumpal, I. 2013. Determinants of Social Desirability Bias in Sensitive Surveys: A Literature Review. *Quality and Quantity.* 47 (4). pp. 2025–2047. https://doi.org/10.1007/s11135-011-9640-9.

McKenzie, D. 2012. Beyond Baseline and Follow-Up: The Case for More T in Experiments. *Journal of Development Economics.* 99. pp. 210–221.

Romano, J. P. and M. Wolf. 2005. Exact and Approximate Stepdown Methods for Multiple Hypothesis Testing. *Journal of the American Statistical Association.* 100. pp. 94–108. doi: 10.1198/016214504000000539.

Westfall, P. H. and S. S. Young. 1993. *Resampling-Based Multiple Testing: Examples and Methods for p-Value Adjustment.* John Wiley & Sons.

CPSIA information can be obtained
at www.ICGtesting.com
Printed in the USA
LVHW051957031220
673319LV00027B/3445